THE TRUTHS OF FICTION

The Truths of Fiction

By

ALLAN RODWAY

**Reader in English in the
University of Nottingham**

1970

CHATTO & WINDUS

LONDON

Published by
Chatto & Windus Ltd
40 William IV Street
London W.C.2

*

Clarke, Irwin & Co. Ltd
Toronto

ISBN 0 7011 1638 2

Printed in Great Britain by
Ebenezer Baylis & Son Ltd
The Trinity Press, Worcester, and London

Contents

Acknowledgements

Thanks are due to the following periodicals and publishers for permission to print material deriving, with more or less alteration, from their publications: Chapter 2, from *Contemporary Criticism*, ed. Malcolm Bradbury and David Palmer; Edward Arnold, 1970. Chapter 3, from *Essays in Criticism*, Vol. X, No. 1, January 1960. Chapter 5, from *Comparative Literature Studies*, Vol. 1, No. 3, 1964. Chapter 7, as 'The Truth of Fiction', from *Essays in Criticism*, Vol. VIII, No. 4, October 1958. Chapter 8, from *Essays in Criticism*, Vol. XIV, No. 2, April 1964. Chapter 9, from *Renaissance and Modern Studies*, Vol. VI, 1962. Chapter 10, as 'I Don't Know Why I Don't Know', from *Izraz*, 1965. Chapter 11, as 'Life, Time and the "Art" of Fiction', in *The British Journal of Aesthetics*, Vol. 7, No. 4, October 1967. Chapter 12, from *The Listener*, Vol. LXVIII, No. 1761, December 27, 1962. Chapter 14, from *The Listener*, Vol. LXIX, No. 1762, January 3, 1963. Chapter 15, from *Criticism in Action*, ed. Maurice Hussey, Longmans Green & Co. Ltd, 1969. Chapter 16, from *The London Magazine*, Vol. 4, No. 12, March 1965. Chapter 17, as 'What the Critics Really Need', from *The Twentieth Century*, Winter 1962/3.

Thanks are due to Faber & Faber Ltd., London, for permission to reprint the poems 'Beasts' and 'In The Elegy Season' from Richard Wilbur's *Poems 1943-1956*. Also to Harcourt Brace Jovanovich Inc., New York: 'Beasts' from *Things Of This World* © 1956 by Richard Wilbur; 'In The Elegy Season' Copyright 1950 by Richard Wilbur. Reprinted from his volume *Ceremony Aud Other Poems*. First published in *The New Yorker*.

Special acknowledgement must be made to Professor Mark Roberts who collaborated in writing 'Practical Criticism in Principle and Practice', and to my colleague Mr. Brian Lee who collaborated in writing 'Coming to Terms' (though he is not responsible for the considerable alterations in the version printed here). To Mr. Lee, too, a great debt of gratitude is owed for the stimulation of many long and fascinating discussions on critical theory and critical terminology. To his logical and synoptic mind is owed nearly all *The Tree of Fallacies* (Appendix A) and almost half of the *Table of Terms* (Appendix B). He was also kind enough to read and criticize the final manuscript.

ALLAN RODWAY

Book List

of critical books used or referred to (articles are indexed only)

Abrams, M. L. *The Mirror and the Lamp*, New York 1953.

Auden, W. H. (ed.) *Kierkegaard*, London 1953.

Auden, W. H. *Collected Shorter Poems 1927–57 (Preface)*, London 1966.

Austin, J. L. *Sense and Sensibilia*, Oxford 1962.

Beach, J. W. *The Making of the Auden Canon*, London 1958.

Bodkin, M. *Archetypal Patterns in Poetry*, London 1934.

Booth, W. *The Rhetoric of Fiction*, Chicago 1961.

Bradbrook, M. C. *English Dramatic Form*, London 1965.

Brower, R. A. *The Fields of Light*, New York 1951.

Brown, J. R. *Shakespeare and his Comedies*, London 1957.

Calderwood, J. and Toliver, H. *Forms of Poetry*, New Jersey 1968.

Caudwell, C. *Illusion and Reality*, London 1937.

Clark, A. M. *Studies in Literary Modes*, Edinburgh 1946.

Clements, R. J. *Michelangelo's Theory of Art*, London 1963.

Croce, B. *Aesthetic*, London 1922.

Davie, D. *Articulate Energy*, London 1955.

Davies, H. S. (ed.) *The Poets and Their Critics*, London 1943.

Demetz, P.; Greene, T.; and Nelson, L. (edd.) *The Disciplines of Criticism*, New Haven and London 1968.

Ehrenpreis, I. *The 'Types' Approach to Literature*, New York 1945.

Eliot, T. S. *The Sacred Wood*, London 1920.

Empson, W. *Seven Types of Ambiguity*, London 1930.

—— *Some Versions of Pastoral*, London 1935.

—— *The Structure of Complex Words*, London 1951.

—— *Milton's God*, London 1962.

Enkvist, N. E.; Spencer, J.; and Gregory, M. J. *Linguistics and Style*, London 1964.

Erskine, J. *The Kinds of Poetry*, New York 1920.

Fowler, R. (ed.) *Essays on Style and Language*, London 1966.

Freud, S. *Wit and its Relation to the Unconscious*, translated A. A. Brill, London 1914.

Frye, N. *Anatomy of Criticism*, Princeton 1957.

Gardner, H. *The Business of Literary Criticism*, Oxford 1959.

Graves, R. *The Meaning of Dreams*, London 1924.

—— *Poetic Unreason*, London 1925.

Guerin, W. L.; Labor, E. G.; Morgan, L.; and Willingham, J. R. *A Handbook of Critical Approaches to Literature*, New York and London 1966.

Harding, D. W. *Experience into Words*, London 1963.

Hirsch, E. D. Jr. *Validity in Interpretation*, New Haven and Lon don 1967.

Hoggart, R. *The Uses of Literacy*, London 1957.

BOOK LIST

Hough, G. *Images and Experience*, London 1960.
—— *An Essay on Criticism*, London 1966.
Hyman, S. E. *The Armed Vision*, New York 1955.
Isherwood, C. *Lions and Shadows*, London 1953.
Joyce, J. *A Portrait of the Artist as a Young Man*, London 1916.
Knight, W. *The Wheel of Fire*, London 1930.
Knights, L. C. *Drama and Society in the Age of Jonson*, London 1937.
—— *Poetry, Politics and the English Tradition*, London 1954.
Lewis, C. S. *Rehabilitations*, London 1939.
Livingstone, T. C. *Tristram Shandy* (Introduction), London and Glasgow, 1955.
Lucas, F. L. *Literature and Psychology*, London 1951.
—— *Style*, London 1955.
Macauley, R. and Lanning, G. *Technique in Fiction*, New York 1964.
Nowottny, W. *The Language Poets Use*, London 1962.
Ong, W. J. *The Barbarian Within*, New York 1960.
Potts, J. L. *Comedy*, London 1948.
Pound, E. *Make It New*, London 1934.
Raban, J. *The Technique of Modern Fiction*, London 1968.
Ransom, J. C. *The World's Body*, New York 1938.
Richards, I. A. *Principles of Literary Criticism*, London 1924.
—— *Science and Poetry*, New York 1926.
—— *Practical Criticism*, London 1929.
—— *How to Read a Page*, London 1943.
—— *Speculative Instruments*, London 1955.
—— *The Philosophy of Rhetoric*, New York 1965.
Righter, W. *Logic and Criticism*, London 1963.
Sebeok, T. A. (ed.) *Style in Language*, New York and London 1960.
Sewell, E. *The Field of Nonsense*, London 1952.
Sparshott, F. E. *The Structure of Aesthetics*, Toronto 1963.
Spencer, J. (ed.) *Linguistics and Style*, London 1964.
Tillyard, E. M. W. *The Muse Unchained: An Intimate Account of the Revolution in English Studies at Cambridge*, London 1958.
Watson, G. *The Literary Critics*, London 1962.
Weinberg, B. *History of Literary Criticism in the Italian Renaissance*, Chicago 1961.
Weldon, T. D. *The Vocabulary of Politics*, London 1953.
Wellek, R. and Warren, A. *The Theory of Literature*, New York 1949.
Wellek, R. *Concepts of Criticism*, New Haven and London 1963.
Williams, R. *Culture and Society*, Baltimore 1961.
Wimsatt, W. K. Jr. *The Verbal Icon*, Kentucky 1954.
Wimsatt, W. K. Jr. and Brooks, C. *Literary Criticism: A Short History*, New York 1957.
Woolf, V. *The Common Reader*, London 1948.

Foreword

OF all Arts subjects, 'English' must surely be that most studied and least understood. Sophisticated American theorists seem to have rather neglected elementary problems (though these are by no means the simplest to deal with); while in England 'Theory of Literature' or 'Theory of Criticism' hardly exists as a subject even today; we still prefer to muddle through.

Though a few brilliant critics on both sides of the Atlantic have been able to rear structures of the highest order on rather rapidly laid foundations, it has become apparent that the fledgling critic — that is, the 'common reader' or the average student when seriously engaged with literature — does in fact need to get clear about basic matters if he is to be enriched rather than confused by the variety of activities subsumed under 'English'. Indeed, many published statements suggest that even our best professional critics and teachers would be still better were practice to be underpinned by more consideration of principles. It remains unhappily true that, for all its successes, the modern critical 'revolt against positivism in England is unsystematic, erratic, and frequently quite unclear as to its philosophical implications and affiliations'. (René Wellek, *Concepts of Criticism*, Yale 1963, p. 268).

What this book offers is obviously no more than introductory; almost every chapter could itself be expanded into a book. Whether the chapters *should* be so expanded is a moot point, since too great an elaboration of theory might come to be almost as deleterious to critical practice as the erratic pragmatism so justly censured by Wellek. For the present, at any rate, the risk of oversimplification, in this peculiarly difficult field, has been preferred to that of over-elaboration.

Most of the chapters originated as exploratory forays: at first for the writer's own benefit, and then also for that of undergraduates taking what surely should long ago have been considered essential to any degree in English, a course in the basic theory of what they were doing. Much of the material first appeared as articles in learned journals, but most of the more complex articles have been rewritten and simplified, all the others have been revised, and four less theoretical pieces have been introduced to give some body to the abstraction [Chapters 10, 12, 15 and 16].

The opening chapter, 'English Studies and Theory of Criticism', touches on the main points to be developed later. Indeed, the principle of recurrence operates throughout the book. For going round in circles seems the right means of making headway in this weblike realm where everything is interconnected, so that problems cannot be fully isolated and then definitely dealt with in turn. Progression by spiral staircase may be awkward, but here a straight ladder would get one nowhere.

Nevertheless, there is some rudimentary sequence. *Part I* tends to deal with general principles and current practice; there is more matter of opinion about it. *Part II*, on the other hand, tends to be technical and exemplary. The first section, so to speak is more closely related to the 'Truths' of the title, the second to the 'Fiction' (these terms being taken to cover any rationally supportable propositions about all kinds of creative literature). The first Part, then, is the more general, the second the more particular; and *within* each Part, too, there is a tendency towards increasing particularity, though this has not been adhered to dogmatically – nor, it is hoped, has anything else.

PART I

English Studies and Theory of Criticism

I. AN alarmingly inclusive title for a modest aim: to introduce at an elementary level some crucial points, most of which will turn up later, expanded in different contexts. It may be hoped that this repetitiveness will be sufficiently compensated by a progressive accretion of useful meaning.

Since writers may write about anything, and their works may in principle be considered in relation to almost everything, there is no sharply defined limit to the scope of 'English Studies' ('literature' clearly being the liaison subject *par excellence*). Whatever that scope is, though, it is wider than that of 'criticism'; and any critical theorizing must take account of the fact. The first requirement, indeed, should be to clarify the difference between these terms.[1] Most literary terms, it might be added, could do with clarification,[2] for much critical debate is:

> purely verbal: a further example of the incredible confusion of tongues, the verbal Tower of Babel which seems . . . one of the most ominous features of our civilization.
>
> (René Wellek, *Concepts of Criticism*, New Haven and London, 1963, p. 2)

The term 'criticism' is often used with confusing vagueness, but it is evident that much of English Studies is primarily concerned with something clearly not criticism, something that emphasizes what surrounds the literary work in time or space rather than the work itself.[1] Neither branch of English Studies is preferable, each is necessary to the other, but they cannot be confused with impunity.

> Many eminent men in literary scholarship and particularly in comparative literature are not really interested in literature at all but in the history of public opinion, the reports of travellers, the ideas about national character – in short, in general cultural history. The concept of literary study is broadened by them so radically that it becomes

---

[1] For further discussion, see Chaps 2 and 6.
[2] See Chaps 8 and 9.

identical with the whole history of humanity. But literary scholarship will not make any progress, methodologically, unless it determines to study literature as a subject distinct, from other activities and products of man. Hence we must face the fact of 'literariness', the central issue of aesthetics, the nature of art and literature . . . The work of art, I have argued, can be conceived as a stratified structure of signs and meanings which is totally distinct from the mental processes of the author at the time of composition and hence of the influences which may have formed his mind. There is what has been rightly called an 'ontological gap' between the psychology of the author and a work of art, between life and society on the one hand and the aesthetic object . . . I have called the study of the work of art 'intrinsic' and that of its relations to the mind of the author, to society, etc., 'extrinsic'.

(Wellek, *Concepts*, p. 293/4)

This seems straightforward. It is not universally known by literary practitioners, and where known is not universally accepted. E. D. Hirsch, Jr, for instance grudgingly writes as follows:

Intrinsic criticism is not always useless, and it is certainly an aid to sympathetic understanding, but it is frequently the least interesting form of judgement. Certainly it is not of much use when we want to know whether one text is more valuable in some respect than another . . . . . . if somebody wants to write a vague and unclear essay it is useless to criticise his stylistic competence: it is much more to the point to criticise his attitudes, values, and lack of common sense – all very extrinsic criteria.

(*Validity in Interpretation*, New Haven and London, 1967, p. 153)

This, however, simply exemplifies the crying need in literary studies for an accepted terminology. For Hirsch defines 'intrinsic' much more narrowly than Wellek – and much less profitably, since it *is* almost 'always useless' if limited to 'stylistic competence' divorced from the content of 'attitudes, values' and 'common sense'. This difference is already covered by the terms 'form' and 'content', so it is more sensible to take the difference between intrinsic and extrinsic as one of direction and emphasis, the intrinsic critic focusing on the text itself and using whatever external aids are available to get that focus right, and the extrinsic critic focusing on some external interest and using the text as evidence for whatever case he is making. Wellek again puts it well:

4

Still this distinction cannot mean that genetic relations should be ignored or even despised or that intrinsic study is mere formalism or irrelevant aestheticism. Precisely the carefully worked-out concept of a stratified structure of signs and meanings attempts to overcome the old dichotomy of content and form. What is usually called 'content' or 'idea' in a work of art is incorporated into the structure of the work of art as part of its 'world' of projected meanings. Nothing would be further from my mind than to deny the human relevance of art or to erect a barrier between history and formal study . . . nor would I want to equate literature with language. In my conception these linguistic elements form, so to say, the two bottom strata: the sound stratum and that of the units of meaning. But from them emerges a 'world' of situations, characters, and events which cannot be identified with any single linguistic element, or least of all, with any element of external ornamental form. The only right conception seems to me a resolutely 'holistic' one which sees the work of art as a diversified totality, as a structure of signs which, however, imply and require meanings and values.

(*Concepts*, p. 294)

Bearing in mind these qualifications, then, we may divide English Studies into *extrinsic* and *intrinsic* criticism, in so far as it involves the interpretation of literary texts, and *scholarship*, in so far as it involves the establishing or arranging of facts, the provision of definitive texts or background material—which may be of use for *both* kinds of criticism.

Since extrinsic criticism is not concerned with the literary work for its own sake, to establish its identity, but rather with its significance in relation to something else, it is logically dependent on intrinsic criticism, because the evidence it uses—the text—must have been properly grasped if the argument is to carry any weight. To assert this logical primacy is not to overlook a hermeneutical dilemma similar to those discussed in Chapter 2. Sometimes you cannot grasp the text properly without having understood the background; yet as all metacritical activity is a matter of relating the text to some sort of background, that activity itself implies that grasping the text is necessary for fully understanding the background. The answer is similar to that in Chapter 2. In these cases, it is not the *whole* of the text or the *whole* of the background that is dependent for its interpretation on some knowledge of the other; so you have some leeway and can escape the dilemma by a tacking process: playing off those parts that subtly illuminate the background against those that themselves need 'background' in order to be properly illuminated, so that all bit by bit cast light on each other.

The logical primacy of intrinsic criticism suggests that extrinsic criticism might also be called *metacriticism* (leaving *criticism* for the rest, with the adjective 'intrinsic' in reserve for cases of possible ambiguity.

Scholarship certainly yields *tips*, but this fact has commonly been exaggerated into the idea that it will yield *criteria*, for intrinsic literary assessments; so, like metacriticism, it tends to be associated in critical theory with the Intentional and Affective Fallacies[1] (the notions, that is to say, that works should be judged by their causes or their effects). It is not true, however, that some plain principle of assessment can be derived from within the work either. Literature is multifaceted; there can be *no* single principle of assessment.

If not equated with Stylistics in Hirsch's way, intrinsic studies may be quite general (as in generic criticism)[2] or fairly detailed (as in most Practical Criticism).[3] At the general end of the spectrum there is a shading-off into metacritical study, especially in so far as discussion of content (say, of characters and morality) may insensibly lead to the use of that content as part of an extraliterary topic (ethics). However, even detailed stylistics, at the other end of the spectrum, is not to be *entirely* dissociated from metacriticism, since broad non-stylistic categorizations may nevertheless imply the sharing of some stylistic characteristics in the constituent works. Both interconnections are cogently set out by Calderwood and Toliver:

> History provides us with a 'dictionary' of the past in which we try ot sort out the meanings of a poem's words, concepts, themes, topical allusions and so on: the objective view offers a set of analytic tools by which the structure, statement, and tone of individual poems may be examined closely: and the approach by forms or genres uses both of the other approaches as tools to provide a full 'grammar' of forms . . .
>
> Perhaps the chief advantage of a generic approach as opposed to a strictly historical emphasis is that a 'grammar' of forms may be sought

[1] See Chap. 6 and Appendix A. (p. 95)
[2] See Chap. 2 and Appendix B. (pp. 123/6)
[3] See Chap. 3.

6

primarily within literature itself and can include (quite literally) grammatical elements of language. We shall note in other places, for instance, that recurrent grammatical moods and tenses distinguish certain forms, as pastoral tends to deal in subjunctives of unfulfilled desire (yearnings for a Golden Age) and as satire tends to imply some such imperative as 'alter your ways, transgressor!'

(James Calderwood and Harold Toliver, *Forms of Poetry*, New Jersey, 1968, p. 2)

As the present work happens not to contain anything that more than touches on such matters of large-scale technical criticism a further substantial quotation from *Forms of Poetry* seems excusable as one interesting example of how the detailed approach[1] might impinge upon even a general genre or mode defined non-stylistically:

As we might expect, these recurrent themes, structural methods, and character types are reflected in the narrative manner and language of romance . . . Hence, whereas drama gives us characters like Hamlet standing before us saying 'I am' (first person pronoun, present-tense verb), romance gives us a storyteller using third-person pronouns and either past or 'timeless' present-tense verb ('He was' or 'He is'): 'A gentle knight *was* pricking on the plaine' or 'It is an ancient Mariner, And he stoppeth one of three.' The distance of the past allows for mythic enlargement of the hero, and the 'timeless' present allows dreamlike qualities to permeate the action. In either case the connective links of the narrative are set beyond ordinary causation.

For instance, in the quotation about the ancient mariner, the two lines are held together by the loose conjunction 'and' which is typical of romance as a whole. Tragedy holds its story together by a plot based on probability; it specialises in conjunctions of cause and effect: '*Because* A happens, B happens and *therefore* C and D.' But romance plots are usually episodic.[2] The events are strung out in loose sequence along the line of the quest and connected by means of additive or incremental repetitions indicating sequence rather than cause: 'A happens *and then* B, *then* C.' Since the unity of romance does not arise from tightly-knit plots, it is usually achieved by paralleling actions, balancing and contrasting characters, and playing variations on themes.

[1] See Chaps 4, 14, 15, 16.
[2] And are therefore better distinguished from probability-'plot' by the word 'story'. See Chap. 8 and Appendix B, IIID (p. 126)

This accounts for the high degree of stylization and structural patterning that we mentioned earlier.

Perhaps the most distinctive feature of romance is its use, not necessarily in fact but in imaginative effect, of the subjunctive mood. The subjunctive is an 'if-mood', as befits a world of fantasy and 'illogical' connections of the secret-sharer kind; and though it may appear in all three tenses – 'It might have been,' 'If it now were,' 'It may yet be' – the things and events it refers to are really outside time. Thus although the statement 'A gentle knight was pricking on the plaine' seems to assert a fact, the Redcross Knight did not, does not, and will not take the fabulous allegorical journey depicted by Spenser. Of course, all literature is hypothetical in this sense, but some works, like the realistic novel and satire appear to assert the here-and-now existence of their worlds, to say not 'If this were,' but 'This is or was'.

(Forms of Poetry, pp. 340/1)

Metacritical and critical studies, then, are interrelated in all their branches, nor can any branch be *wholly* independent of fact-finding scholarship. What is important is to be clearminded about relevance, so that interrelationships do not lead to muddleheadedness and that in turn to confused discussion. At the points of intersection, of course, it will be inherently difficult to be clear, for the same material there points impartially towards different tasks. But it may help to bear in mind one further distinction that pinpoints the essential difference between the intrinsic and extrinsic. The distinction is that between meaning and significance.

Obviously, texts must be interpreted before they can be assessed or evaluated, and they must be properly understood before they can be properly interpreted; yet as Hirsch so aptly says:

> Few would deny that the crucial problem in the theory and practice of interpretation is to distinguish between possible implications that do belong to the meaning of a text and those that do not belong.

(Validity, p. 62)

He goes on to say:

> Undoubtedly, the most important preliminary principle of discrimination is that which distinguishes verbal meaning from significance . . . Significance is always 'meaning-to' never 'meaning-in'. Significance always entails a relationship between what is in a man's verbal meaning and what is outside it.

(Validity, pp. 62/3)

'Meaning', therefore, being what is *in* the work is what intrinsic criticism aims to elucidate, as its first and most important task; 'significance', being what the meaning is *related to*, is what meta-criticism is concerned with. The work's *meaning*, is one thing and one only—though perhaps an ambiguous, ambivalent or amorphous one—and once discovered it remains the same, as Hirsch irrefutably argues (in the absence of fresh and valid evidence to the contrary, that is); whereas the work's *significance* is subject to endless change from age to age and area to area:

> Not only can its verbal meaning be related to all conceivable states of affairs—historical, linguistic, psychological, physical, metaphysical, personal, familial, national—but it can also be related at different times to changing conditions in all conceivable states of affairs.
>
> (*Validity*, p. 63)

I I. All theories, all critical approaches, have their limitations; every advantage entails a complementary shortcoming. Concentrate, metacritically, on what the text refers to (life, the world), or the audience it is addressed to, or the writer who composed it, and you lose the specifically literary qualities that are the province of intrinsic criticism. Concentrate on formal qualities—the only *totally* intrinsic criticism[1]—and you may neglect historical and biological material that would illuminate the (intrinsic) meaning; on psychology in the content, and you neglect aesthetic qualities in the form; on symbolism and you miss surface realism.[2] Furthermore, as Hirsch puts it:

> Every interpreter labors under the handicap of an inevitable circularity: all his internal evidence tends to suggest his hypothesis because much of it was constituted by his hypothesis.
>
> (*Validity*, p. 166)

Nor will he find this to be his only dilemma.[3]

Why, then, it is tempting to ask, bother with theory at all? The

---

[1] Study of form is purely critical; of content, either critical or metacritical; of what the work leads to, whether in the way of causes or effects or general topics, purely metacritical.

[2] Guerin, Labor, Morgan and Willingham, in *A Handbook of Critical Approaches to Literature*, New York, 1966, fascinatingly exemplify this point by interpreting a play, a novel, a short story, and poem by each of a number of critical methods in turn. See also Chap. 5.

[3] See Chap. 2.

short answer, of course, is that it is impossible not to have *some* theoretical approach, even if it is hardly conscious enough to get beyond saying, 'I know what I like'; and that being the case, it is better to have thought about what you are up to than to do it thoughtlessly. But the question warrants an answer somewhat less short; and first, three concessions must be made. An accepted clarified terminology and a set of associated concepts will take us only so far. Later degrees of delicacy, in criticizing a particular work, must rely either on subtle formal analysis[1] or on what amounts to ostensive definitions.[2] Quotation and technicality that is to say, become an essential part of refined critical practice. (How else do you show, objectively, that subtle things really *are* there and are not the product of over-ingenuity or the critic's wish that they were there?) The *fairly* precise terms of theory, not being restricted in validity to one literary work, must be for rather general notions; but ostensive definition or technical analysis of the way something works, being more precise, become necessary as one nears the heart of a particular work. That is one concession. Another is that the old intuitive, impressionistic criticism – now entirely discredited – can have a little value; it can put the reader in a receptive mood, tide him over initial resistance. Finally, it has to be conceded that a good deal of critical theory has done as much harm as good, largely owing to the habit of universalizing – a habit that has led to much dispute between rival dogmatic schools.

This last concession, however, also amounts to a powerful argument for further theorizing. People can't help proceeding on some assumption or other, and they can't be forcibly prevented from promoting their assumptions into universal principles, and making them public. The answer then, has to be a better, more eclectic and inclusive theory, or piecemeal theory, clearing up this or that critical crux – at any rate, an approach that opposes absolutism, and inculcates such commonsensical, but not easily applicable, notions as that of knowing just what you are doing at any given time when you are dealing with several intertwined but disparate branches, of

[1] See Chaps 14, 16.

[2] W. Righter, *Logic and Criticism*, London, 1963, p. 88 equates such definition with circular arguments. This is not quite true, at any rate in criticism, for the examples pointed to will illustrate *observable* differences, if they are well chosen, even though they may be too subtle to *formulate* unmistakably in abstract terms.

knowing what standards are appropriate to each job, and what that job is worth *relatively* to various other things.

Theory of literature or theory of criticism,[1] is a sort of philosophy — ultimately inseparable from some wider, extraliterary philosophical position. But there is no reason why it should not be philosophy of a pragmatic sort, the pyramid resting on a broad base in the British manner not Germanically inverted on a metaphysical point. The latter makes for a more logical structure, but the former can be incomplete without collapsing.

The two other greatest traps for the critical theorist, next to the temptation to universalize, are the beliefs that criticism can become a *science* and that it should be an *art* in its own right.

Science is the neutral description of the way things are, whereas criticism cannot avoid values. Science has progressed by successive dehumanizings, shedding first the urge to interpret phenomena in terms of human emotions (the magical view of nature), then the medieval interpretation in terms of the idealizing human will, and finally Newton's vestigial anthropomorphism, the idea of 'force', a relic of human effort abandoned by Einstein; criticism on the other hand, cannot be other than human, since literature is created in one human mind and recreated, when read, in another. Science deals with a given world, material and regular; criticism with an interpreted world, imaginative and (often) unpredictable, Above all, science is ultimately inseparable from experiment, which the nature of creative fiction renders almost entirely inappropriate for criticism.

The idea that criticism could be a science sprang largely from confusing metacriticism and intrinsic criticism, under the inclusive term 'literary criticism'. The views of Darwin, Marx, Frazer and Freud — representatives of less exact sciences, or borderline disciplines — disrupted the traditional world-picture and provided some new assumptions for the modern mind; assumptions obviously relevant to economic, biological, sociological, historical, anthropological and psychological studies of literature. What is perhaps not so obvious is that these studies are all *metacritical* — using the

---

[1] Literature and criticism exist in symbiosis, so both terms are permissible. The latter seems slightly preferable for two reasons: it makes a better pair with 'applied criticism', its proper complementary activity, and the ambiguity in 'of' ('about' and 'for') allows the discussion of practical procedures for writing criticism (the subject of the last chapter here) — something it would be arrogant of the critic to suggest for writers of *literature*.

text as special evidence in some non-literary field—and therefore are studies of *significance* (the meaning of its meaning, its value in relation to something else); they are not studies of the verbal *meaning* and *literary* value of the text itself. Metacriticism can appear to be scientific. Strictly literary interpretation and assessment cannot even appear to be.

Having said that criticism and metacriticism are equally proper and valuable parts of English Studies, why stress now 'verbal *meaning* and *literary* value'? Partly for the reason given: that it is logically primary, since you cannot be a good metacritic without first having grasped the essence of the work you are using as evidence; but more importantly perhaps for this reason: that the only unifying factor to the ramifications of this liaison subject (what makes it 'a subject distinct from other activities and products of man') is that all are based on verbal meaning or literary value or both, that is, on the study of *literary* texts. From various points of view, what the message, morality, psychology, politics or human insights of a work lead to may be its most important contribution to mankind. But from such, metacritical, viewpoints it is a political or philosophical or moral or psychological work. Unless it has something else to offer it is material on which historians, philosophers, moralists or psychologists may be more fitted to pronounce than 'English' specialists. Works of creative literature, it must be inferred (from the fact that they are not written in textbook form even when much concerned with a message) at least *try* to offer something more. They try to use the medium, language, skilfully. If they succeed, they are likely to remain current when their content has been long outmoded. What is *exclusively* important about a historical painting (not shared with, say, history, literature, or music) is not its subject (though the art critic may—sometimes must—go on to consider that) but its painterly qualities. Of two paintings of the same subject, only one may retain interest for the art critic though both will for the historian. The art critic, however, could offer the historian something subtle that comes through his specialized sensitivity, not to the subject, but to the *visualization of the subject*. And so it would be, *mutatis mutandis*, were the same subject to be expressed as music or literature. What alone gives unity and validity to English Studies as a separate—though liaising—subject is that *creative* literature (not necessarily, though usually, fictional) is the significant *verbalization*[1]

[1] See also Chap. 11.

of experience. That is why a man insensitive to language would rightly be considered unsuitable for this subject, as would the tone-deaf or colour-blind for the study of music or painting.

Now it is arguable that the essence of a subject, though *fundamentally* important, may not be what is most important in human terms; it may bear to other, metacritical, matters the same relationship as the foundations of a house bear to the living quarters. This could often be so; in any case there is little point in disputing about it, since no conclusive answer could be given or would be of any use if it could, as one has to start with the foundations anyway. Evidently, though, it is easy to believe that the foundations are important *only* for what is above them; 'mere formalism', 'mere aestheticism', or 'merely stylistic interest' are significantly common phrases. But we should not be misled by analogy. What is fundamental, definitive, to the arts also has a unique sort of importance. Imagine being dumb, deaf or blind, and then ask if the arts which educate the corresponding senses, are not important in their own right—in so far as learning to live in, and partly create, our world may arguably be said to precede all else in importance; speaking, hearing and seeing are vital functions, without which we are crippled for everything else; but are presumably the fitter for everything else the better they are developed (other things being equal, of course). M. C. Bradbrook interestingly applies this general point in the particular field of drama:

> Anything which can be expressed in verbal terms is on the way to integration; the earliest and the terminal stages of schizophrenia are speechless. In ordinary persons the darker and more primitive, the remote and outlying aspects of the self can be expressed only in more primitive forms, in pantomimic gesture or wordless cries. Language is a delicate and complicated tool, and anything which can be handled by this tool must be relatively accessible to reshaping. Hence the importance in any curative process of the patient's ability to recognise a situation by putting it into words (especially the release of emotion from a pre-verbal era of life . . .) . . . The engagement or participation of spectator and actor in drama includes these primitive elements . . . but unites them with the power of speech, of narrative . . . Hence its peculiar potency in reconciling primitive and advanced modes of expression.
>
> (*English Dramatic Form*, London 1965, p. 29)

The vital importance of 'putting it into words', as well as the ultimate inseparability of the verbalization from what is verbalized, the medium from the matter, is well illustrated here. I. A. Richards puts this difficult and crucial point with more philosophic inclusiveness:

> For words cannot and should not attempt to 'hand over sensations bodily'; they have very much more important work to do. So far from verbal language being a 'compromise for a language of intuition'—a thin, but better-than-nothing substitute for real experience,—language, well used, is a *completion* and does what the intuitions of sensation by themselves cannot do. Words are the meeting points at which regions of experience which can never combine in sensation or intuition, come together.
>
> (*Philosophy of Rhetoric*, New York, 1965, pp. 130/1)

Even metacriticism, then, is involved in the peculiar world of literature, a world whose physics are those of a verbal mirror—quite unlike those of the given world open to scientific investigation. In its later stages metacriticism can profitably employ the methods of various sciences as well as those of history or ethics, but it begins where criticism both begins and ends, with material that demands a different approach.

But if neither criticism nor metacriticism can truly be a science, can either be an art?

> ... modern criticism for the most part no longer accepts its traditional status as an adjunct to 'creative' or 'imaginative' literature. If we define art as the creation of meaningful and pleasurable patterns, a definition that would probably get some degree of general acceptance, it is obvious that both imaginative and critical writing are art as defined. Imaginative literature organises its experience out of life at first hand (in most cases); criticism organises its experiences out of imaginative literature, life at second hand, or once-removed. Both are, if you wish, kinds of poetry, and one is precisely as independent as the other, or as dependent . . . The critic requires works of art for his raw material, subject and theme . . .
>
> (S. E. Hyman, *The Armed Vision*, New York; Vintage Books, 1955, p. 8)

Of course, Hyman is here making the common assumption that the extrinsic and intrinsic are one and the same ('modern criticism') rather than two related but different things. To use literature as raw material for work in some other field is metacriticism – which is not art but a specialized form of whatever grows in that field, to be judged by the appropriate standards (and in all such fields the quality of the selection of facts and the inferences drawn from them takes precedence over the quality of their expression; as *subjects*, not imaginative *literature*, their essence lies elsewhere than in the 'verbalization of experience').

Intrinsic criticism, then, should usually *first* concern itself with language, the 'verbalization', (though this is not, as Wellek, Bradbrook and Richards point out, to ignore life, the 'experience'). The only sort of criticism left that could be considered an art is the least valuable: that old impressionistic sort which sometimes creates a 'tone-poem' of the writer's feelings on encountering a primary creative work. This might just as well be called a minor art in order to clear the critical deck – and, of course, is not the sort Hyman means by 'modern criticism'. Other criticism, as distinct from metacriticism, surely, should and must accept 'its traditional status as an adjunct to "creative" or "imaginative" literature'. In that rôle – as interpreter and, where necessary, evaluator – it will take style to be primarily important, if not so important humanly as sense and sensibility. Such criticism is neither art nor science but something betwixt and between. As such it needs a theory that will be objective but not mechanical, flexible rather than dogmatic.

Even bad theories of criticism have at least the merit of making readers pause before leaping to 'instinctive' conclusions, which may well be biased to the point of absurdity (as I. A. Richards's *Practical Criticism* revealed in 1928). Good theory aids objectivity in a more positive way. Why, though, should objectivity be considered a good? Well, what is it to be objective in this field? It is to have an attitude rather than to have achieved a result, to be reasonable but not necessarily rational. The objective critic wants to explore the work, not to exploit it (so, to approach a 'magical' poem like 'Kubla Khan' rationally determined to knit a theme out of those elements that could support one's own metaphysic would be far less objective than a reasonably irrational, emotionally open, approach). Even for the private reader, a critic for himself only, such objectivity brings advantage: read without this attitude literature may be pleasant, like a daydream, but cannot be educative. For it to be both pleasant and educative we must have got out of it as much as possible of what it really says, appreciated the writer's special qualities of expression, and read into it as little as possible. Then we have the writer's work, which extends our being and perception, rather than a work of our own, leaving us just as we were. We also have valid specialized evidence for any metacritical excursions we may wish to undertake, rather than a misinterpretation or misapprehension, which is no evidence at all. For the professional critic, there is also clearly a moral obligation to give a valid account, not a false construction.

The critic then shouldn't avail himself (*pace* Hyman) of the creator's poetic licence. But if he cannot get the advantages of science either surely he cannot be objective? The mistake here is to confuse critical objectivity with accuracy and predictability, to conflate validity and proof. To be objective means to be unbiased, less liable to error but not exempt from it; validity, to go by evidence rather than intuition. In these terms, criticism can be objective in the way of the law court if not the laboratory.[1] The nature of the subject means that the evidence will be circumstantial – but evidence none the less, and the only sort appropriate to the tasks.

These tasks are not easy, for works of creative literature 'exist' in a peculiar way,[2] are peculiarly verbal, and extremely complex in their meanings and significance, yet:

> this does not mean that all interpretations are equally right, that there is no possibility of differentiation between them. There are utterly fantastic interpretations, partial distorted interpretations . . . we know that Hamlet was no woman in disguise. The concept of adequacy of interpretations leads clearly to the concept of the correctness of judgement. Evaluation grows out of correct understanding. There is a hierarchy of viewpoints implied in the very concept of adequacy of interpretation. Just as there is correct interpretation, at least as an ideal, so there is correct judgement, good judgement.
>
> (Wellek, op. cit., p. 18)

After all, if such words as 'relative', 'subjective', 'biased', are meaningful – as they are, and in non-scientific contexts too – then the meaningfulness of their opposites is entailed. To give Wellek the last word:

[1] See Chap. 17.
[2] See Chaps 2 and 6.

There is a difference between the psychology of the investigator, his presumed bias, ideology, perspective and the logical structure of his propositions. The genesis of a theory does not necessarily invalidate its truth, men can correct their biases, criticise their presuppositions, rise above their temporal and local limitations, aim at objectivity, arrive at some knowledge and truth.

(Wellek, op. cit. p. 14)

Even of fictions.

2

The Approach Through Type, Mode and Kind

KINDS go under many aliases (genres, species, forms, types, modes); they have been defined, irrespective of alias, according to the literary works' setting, subject, time, theme, attitude, content, structure, origin, history, purpose, occasion, psychology (correspondence with faculties of the mind), or sociology (correspondence with aspects of society); and the history of genre-criticism is as long as it is complex. To attempt in a preparatory note to summarize the compendious labours of workers in this tangled field would be presumptuous, and also tedious. Even the following drastic selection of general studies and quotations may seem rather a surfeit than an appetizer. However, these are no more than the preliminary minimum the subject demands:

Irvin Ehrenpreis, *The 'Types Approach' to Literature* (New York, 1945):

> Scholars are fairly well agreed today that there is no one definition of a kind of literature. p. 5.

> Irene Behrens has shown that while epic, drama and lyric may have existed from antiquity, none of them has retained the same name for the same kind. p. 6.

> The two millennia of critics from whom these twenty-six examples of lists, names and ranking of kinds have been chosen, show remarkable inconsistency. p. 15.

> Until the end of the eighteenth century the common view of genres was that they were established patterns to which authors conformed. The historical evolutionary view of the nineteenth century changed this. p. 18.

> . . . independent of Herder, the notion of evolution in itself emphasises

genres; theories of literary evolution must by their very nature imply such classifications. p. 19.

The genres to which Europeans and Americans are accustomed have no existence independent of their material and background. They are not implicit in the nature either of literature or of the human mind. p. 50.

René Wellek and Austin Warren, *Theory of Literature* (New York, 1949):

Theory of genres is a principle of order; it classifies literature and literary history not by time and place (period or national language) but by specifically literary types of organisation or structure. Any critical and evaluative—as distinct from historical—study involves, in some form, the appeal to such structures. p. 235.

Anyone interested in genre theory must be careful not to confound the distinctive differences between 'classical' and modern theory. Classical theory is regulative and prescriptive ... Classical theory not only believes that genre differs from genre but also that they must be kept apart, not allowed to mix ... there was a real aesthetic principle ... involved: it was the appeal to a rigid unity of tone, a stylized purity and 'simplicity' ...

Classical theory had, too, its social differentiation of genres. Epic and tragedy dealt with the affairs of kings and nobles, comedy with those of the middle class (the city, the bourgeoisie) and satire and farce with the common people. p. 244.

Modern theory is clearly descriptive. It doesn't limit the number of possible kinds and doesn't prescribe rules to authors. It supposes that traditional kinds may be 'mixed' and produce a new kind (like tragi-comedy). It sees that genres can be built up on the basis of inclusiveness or 'richness' as well as that of 'purity'. p. 245.

William K. Wimsatt, Jr., and Clement Brooks, *Literary Criticism: A Short History* (New York, 1957):

The evolution of criticism has produced four, perhaps five genre conceptions dominant enough in their eras to serve as focuses for the poetic whole. Each of these (with perhaps one exception) seems to have had its advantages, each has enabled a certain understanding not only of one literary genre but of the whole poetic structure and problem. Aristotle's view was dramatic ... and this had the great advantage of opening up the more broadly 'dramatic', the ethically problematic and tensional aspect of poetry as a whole . . . The next basic view is that of Horace, conversational, epistolary, idiomatic, ironic, satiric . . . This view has the advantage of opening up the linguistic, the idiomatic, the metaphoric, and in that sense again the 'dramatic' aspect of all poetry. Next is the high, the grand, the ecstatic view of Longinus – which on the whole opens up more dangers and confusions perhaps than affective advantage, and is not a view according to literary 'species' (but just the opposite) unless we look on it as making a large contribution (via Boileau) to the new genre of the 'heroic' in the third quarter of the seventeenth century . . . Meanwhile, in the same essays of Dryden which defend the heroic, a theory of courtly wit and ridicule is asserted, and by the time of Pope and Swift, this can be considered a second focusing of the Horatian conversational and satiric ideal. And in close liaison, appears the mocking genre of the anti-heroic or burlesque . . . Lastly, the cycle of genres is completed in the era of the romantics with the now affectionately remembered lyric ideal and its attendant opinion that a long poem is a contradiction in terms. This had the advantage of exploiting a new view of 'expression', a view of subjectivity both as cognition and as feeling, and of metaphor as the small-scale model and touchstone of the whole poetic business. pp. 750/751.

Northrop Frye, *Anatomy of Criticism* (Princeton, 1957):

We discover that the critical theory of genres is stuck precisely where Aristotle left it. The very word 'genre' sticks out in an English sentence as the unpronounceable and alien thing it is [*one reason for preferring the words in the title of this essay*]. Most critical efforts to handle such generic terms as 'epic' and 'novel' are chiefly interesting as examples of the psychology of rumour. p. 13.

The strong emotional repugnance felt by many critics towards any form of schematization in poetics is again the result of a failure to distinguish criticism as a body of knowledge from the direct experience of literature, where every act is unique, and classification has no place. p. 29.

See also: John Erskine, *The Kinds of Poetry* (New York, 1920), J. L. Calderwood and M. R. Toliver, *Forms of Poetry* (New Jersey, 1968).

I. Ehrenpreis, then, argues that kinds can be classified, and have been classified, according to any sort of similarity. Wellek and Warren exclude classification by time and place. For them, too, an approach through kinds was necessary for any 'critical and evaluative—as distinct from historical—study'; whereas nineteenth-century evolutionary criticism of this sort was in fact specifically useful in teasing out traditions and influences and relating them to social change—that is to say, it was useful precisely in historical study. Where Ehrenpreis says 'genres . . . are not implicit in the nature either of literature or of the human mind', Frye insists that they are archetypal in both. The long quotation from Wimsatt and Brooks indicates that kind-criticism may have given to the literature of different periods focal concepts as fruitful as 'gravity' or 'relativity' have been to physics. On the other hand, there seems to have been little theorizing on the usefulness of the idea of 'kind' or 'mode' itself to the universe of criticism—save in the cases of Croce (*Aesthetic*, London 1922), who thought it nothing, and Frye, who thinks it everything. And, to come full circle, Frye's enthusiasm for modality leads him not to the 'critical and evaluative' standpoint of Wallek and Warren, but to an appreciation of its indispensability for *un*evaluatively anatomizing the universal body of literature: '. . . criticism has no business to react against things, but should show a steady advance towards undiscriminating catholicity' (*Anatomy*, p. 25). He is concerned with what kinds of literature exist but not with what is worth reading, and on what grounds. Further probing reveals only more differences of opinion or emphasis.

Gregory Smith (quoted by Ehrenpreis, p. 12) very plausibly says that in Elizabethan criticism the practice of dividing literature into kinds was generally a method of carrying on the great project of justifying imaginative literature 'against the attacks of a vigorous Puritanism'. The defenders' aim was to show that poetry is useful and moral; therefore their definitions of kinds were necessarily in terms of content and effect. Turn, however, to detailed studies, and what do we find? In Weinberg's *History of Literary Criticism in the Italian Renaissamce*, II. 13, V. pp. 635–714 (Chicago 1961), nearly a hundred large pages recording thousands of pages of inconclusive wrangling that covered most aspects of the topic, under the umbrella-theme of tradition vs change. Similarly, such comments as this—

though admittedly of the Italian scene – suggest doubts about the full truth of a simple summing up of Elizabethan criticism (apt though it might be as a generalization):

> Yet the rivalry between painting and sculpture forming the argument of so much Renaissance contention, as both Vasari and Michelangelo claimed, had a parallel and precedent in the numerous, often sterile, humanistic debates on the relative values of literary forms: epic vs romance, tragedy vs comedy, rhyme vs prose.
>
> R. J. Clements, *Michelangelo's Theory of Art* (London, 1963), p. 313.

Again, there seems much to be said against the 'biological', evolutionary, kind-criticism of the nineteenth century, and even for Croce's idea of the iniquity of *all* classification. After all, a work is what it is, regardless of how it came to be so. Searching into its antecedents may be supposed to destroy responsiveness to what it uniquely has to offer. Moreover, the supposed antecedents may be merely coincidental analogues. Furthermore, biological analogy may well foster false history as well as superficial responsiveness, by inducing a belief – apparent in a very sophisticated form in Northrop Frye – that literature evolves from more simple forms, getting more varied and complex as it does so but always retaining an archetypal, umbilical link with its origin. Propositions open to question about both their truth and value. On the other hand, a logical point like the following makes it impossible to believe that the analogy with biology is *entirely* mistaken: 'Works of art are not structureless, and their structures must like all structures be mutually comparable,' Sparshott, *The Structure of Aesthetics* (Toronto, 1963), p. 174.

Yet, if nothing is straightforward, it is nevertheless unduly polemical of Frye to assert that two thousand years of discussion have left 'the critical theory of genres stuck precisely where Aristotle left it'. Not only has the discussion led to the 'focusing' concepts already mentioned, and to a procedure for the social and historical study of literature, but it has also led to Frye's own brilliant and stimulating (if fundamentally metacritical) structure of speculation. It has gradually become evident, too, that the grammar of form is more stable, and therefore more useful for classification than the lexis of content. Furthermore the methods of both literature and criticism, have been gradually sorted out and clarified. It has become clear, for instance, that two inclusive classes of kind-criticism exist. Distinguished not by what defining similarities they use but rather by an ultimate philosophic tendency to either universalism or nominalism, idealism or empiricism, they are the *prescriptive* (which urges writers to approximate to some pure Platonic kind) and the *descriptive* (which derives the kinds from existing works, and is likely not to censure the mixing of established kinds but to call the result a new kind or evolved form). It has become clear, too that though the descriptive class is now dominant, it is rather because of the post-Romantic nature of literature, and the consequent multiplication of kinds, in the last century, than because all the philosophic questions have been finally settled. (See pp. 29/30.)

The nominalist-empiricist side have in fact had rather the better of the argument, but we can now see that this is irrelevant; prescriptive kind-criticism clearly derives from, and is relevant to, the 'classical' mode of writing—that which prefers the 'reality' of unmixed feeling (on the grounds that there is something false about a feeling easily infiltrated or supplanted by another), and therefore tends to strict structural form. Since writers who look to authority and the help of given forms will continue to exist alongside those who prefer the perils of freedom, both classes of criticism will continue also. The prescriptive may have been generally discredited in academic circles, but every commercial reader, editor, producer or director who criticizes scripts is of this class, saying, 'If you follow such and such rules, then on the basis of experience we can say you are likely to succeed in this kind'. A much-maligned class of men, but usually helpful and right—for all but original geniuses. Descriptive kind-criticism is innately more useful for the academic pursuits of literary history and for refined discrimination amongst works that might *mistakenly* be thought similar (witness the vague generality of the popular use of 'novel' as against the academic distinction between 'novels' and 'romances', or the preferable 'report-novels' and 'romance-novels'.) Moreover, if it took the less platonic, less authoritarian class of criticism to chart the evolution of literature and its relation to social *change*, it is no less true that the classical sort—with its idea of *decorum* of kind, character and diction—was well aware of the relation of literature to social *order* (especially the order of classes). Even the now universally condemned idea of a hierarchy of kinds can still play a useful part in critical theory. Perhaps there is no point in attempting any longer to adjudicate between tragedy and epic, but there is still some point—and supporting arguments— in asserting the superiority of tragedy as a kind over the thriller as a kind, or comedy over farce.

Above all, long abstruse wrangling has led to a pragmatic assumption that kinds are ideas, not things in themselves. Thus the conception of *usefulness* is gradually superseding that of *truthfulness*. Furthermore, the notion of major and minor kinds, or even of major-major and minor-minor has been clarified out, though not yet an agreed terminology[1] for these useful distinctions.

The most important of the agreed distinctions—going back to Diomedes (fl. *c.* 390 A.D.), repeated in the Middle Ages, rediscovered by French critics in the seventeenth century, and occurring again in Joyce's *Portrait*—is that between those kinds distinguished by what Frye calls 'the radical of presentation' and those based on other criteria. Literature originally to be presented through action (the dramatic) is distinguished from that originally to be sung (lyric) and that to be spoken (narrative), or, in Joyce's version, objective, subjective, and medial expression in relation to the audience, are distinguished.

The distinction is mainly important in a negative way. It marks off something very basic, truly 'radical', but of less importance to a practical criticism than those kinds defined less primitively. Northrop Frye would not agree, but he means by 'criticism' something schematic and reductive: what leads to archetypes within the modes of literature, and indeed finally to 'the archetypal shape of literature as a whole' (*Anatomy*, p. 342).

For those interested in criticism as an aid to the appreciation of particular works of art, these 'kinds' can obviously be given only a minor rôle; and in order to play it without further confounding confusion they may be marked off by the different name, *Types*. This frees '*Modes*' and '*Kinds*' for the larger rôle they can play in aiding such appreciation. This is the one area of genre-criticism so far neglected—an area theoretically remote from that of literary history, though having pragmatic links with it; existing somewhere between the extreme nominalism of Croce and the extreme universalism of Frye, though not as a state of compromise with both so much as a state of lesser abstraction than either.

I I. Croce anathematizes all classification, all concepts of decorum, elevating instead the entirely individual and original (thus tending to appreciate only short poems or pieces of poetry, and to go rapidly

[1] See Chap. 8.

from the poem itself to the 'spirit' of the author). In his view creative works can be classified only at the cost of ignoring everything that makes them works of *art*. This seems to be a reaction, itself excessive, against those excesses of nineteenth-century, evolutionary, species-criticism that brought criticism to the point of being a branch of anthropology; for classification is so much a fact of life that it seems unlikely, *prima facie*, that it must be the death of art, or of the appreciation of art. In life, communication itself would be almost impossible were we unable to refer to classes (men, women, children, houses, furniture) but only to each item as a laboriously described unique entity. Since good literature is the acme of communication it is scarcely surprising to find that artists, audiences and critics have been indebted to literary traditions, conventions, and revolutions, which all necessarily depend on some sort of categorizing. Indeed, both ideas, that art is to be identified with originality and that classification is incompatible with the appreciation of individuality, seem obviously false. Literary works, like the people who create them, are born willy-nilly into a pre-existing society; and far from necessarily preventing individuality, these twin societies, of literature and life are a necessary condition for it, as the laws of the game and the laws of physics are for gifted tennis. Moreover, the appreciation of a literary gift, is in many cases impossible, in most more difficult, if the individual work cannot be seen in relationship to some class or classes. Against what other background would its unique qualities truly manifest themselves?

But if two millennia of critics have bequeathed us little more than 'remarkable inconsistency' (Ehrenpreis), how shall we know *what* classes a work should be seen in relation to? Part of the answer seems to be that it doesn't matter. The long debate has not been a waste of breath; it has made clear, first, that there is no divine truth to be revealed in this stony place; works of literature are multifaceted and they can indeed be categorized in many ways, just like people; second, that it is not *how* you classify that really matters (though some ways return a better yield than others, according to the nature of the particular case) but rather the fact of classifying itself. Take the least promising approach, that through the concept of *Type* — least promising, because most mechanical and simple — and apply it to the least promising sort of material, something very short and very simple, where nothing seems to require critical midwifery:

DOWN HALL

Come here my sweet Landlady, pray how do you do?
Where is *Sisley* so cleanly, and *Prudence* and *Sue*?
And where is the widow that dwelt here below?
And the Hostler that sung about Eight Years ago?

And where is your sister so mild and so dear?
Whose voice to her Maids like a Trumpet was clear.
By my Troth, she replies, you grow younger, I think,
And pray, Sir, what wine does the gentleman drink?

Why now let me die, Sir, or live upon Trust,
If I know to which question to answer you first.
Why things since I saw you, most strangely have vary'd,
And the Hostler is hang'd and the Widow is Marry'd.

(Matthew Prior)

What type of poem is this? Well, *lyric*, of course; if Prior did not write it for music, its 'radical of presentation' is certainly that of song. We might add, moving insensibly towards other categories, that it is in the ballad mode, though it's of the 'popular' not the 'traditional' kind. But on second thought, is it lyric? Going by the radical of presentation alone, perhaps. But is it enough to go by the radical of presentation alone, as we can often make only an informed guess at what it was? The Joycian idea of the rôle of the author, speaking as it were to himself, or to an audience, or entirely through his characters is more determinate. Anyway, if we are asking, Which type? each should be at least considered. Then, *narrative*? On technical grounds, no; since there is no narration (as distinct from dialogue). The main value of the concept of Type—for the criticism that regards itself as a handmaid to literature—is its technicality: it can provide a point of triangulation with the more flexible psychologically-determined concepts of Mode and Kind, and thus minimize the risk of stock response. So, not narrative. In fact, in the light of our definition, it is clearly *dramatic*, nothing but dialogue. But part of our pleasure—most of the aesthetic part—comes from the insolent ease with which 'lyric' structure is fused to dramatic texture. Further there is a pleasure, akin to that of innovation or variation on a theme for those familiar with both kinds, in seeing a method not uncommon in the traditional kind of ballad (witness *Lord Randal*, or *Edward*) skilfully appropriated to the popular kind, where it is rare. Moreover, does not the most fleeting consideration of narrative raise the question of *persona*? Is 'the gentleman' Prior himself? Or is he not a 'character' whom we see — or almost see — being sketched in by a ghostly author who has chosen not to dematerialize entirely? Perhaps not. But at least the question has been raised and our attention directed to character, as well as form and theme. At this point, how we finally categorize the poem becomes irrelevant, for the fact of trying to categorize — even through the crudest approach — has brought us near enough to its individual qualities for genre-criticism to give way to something more subtle.

The concepts of Mode and Kind are themselves more subtle, if only because they are imprecise; and if they are refined (respectively) to the sub-species of Mood and Variety — whether or not we actually name them as such — they probably lead as near to full appreciation as any methodical approach can. Further delicacy must be a matter of personal sensibility and exploration.

All these concepts, can obviously be used both for non-comparative criticism (if they are taken, prescriptively or not, as being of the platonic-idea class), and for comparative criticism or the clarifying of 'traditions and affinities, thereby bringing out a large number of literary relationships that would not be noticed as long as there were no context established for them' — Frye, *Anatomy*, p. 247 — (if they are taken as being of the empirical class). And in all cases there is no reason why they should not be used with all the other basic concepts of a pragmatic criticism: form, structure, texture, tone, subject, theme, and so on.

Northrop Frye, with beautiful economy, tries to define *Mode* solely in terms of character-status, and to reduce all literature to five modes — and what's more he nearly succeeds. These modes run, chronologically as well as logically, from the Mythic (in which the protagonists are superior in kind — gods or demigods — to both men and the environment), through the Romance (protagonists superior in degree — supermen, sometimes aided by magic — to other men and the environment), the High Mimetic (superior to other men but not to the environment — as in most epic and tragedy), the Low Mimetic (superior neither to other men nor to the environment — as in most comedy or realism), and on to the Ironic (protagonists inferior). The last mode might well be dropped, as irony is a formal means or method[1] — even *structural* irony, which is what Frye is

[1] See Chap. 9.

talking about—that could certainly be used in the High Mimetic mode (witness *Lear*) and the Low Mimetic (witness *Emma*), and might conceivably be used in the other two modes. Otherwise the scheme is useful as well as beautiful. Yet its usefulness is like that of *Type*: more evident in metacriticism—to which the study of kinds has always contributed most—less evident in the 'one area' previously mentioned (p. 24) as having been neglected by genre-scholarship: that of intrinsic criticism.

To recapitulate: metacriticism is centrifugal, intrinsic criticism centripetal. The one is concerned with a work's relationships, the other with its identity; the one with its significance, the other with its meaning; in other words, the one moves outwards *from* the work, the other inwards *to* it. Both may use the 'background' material of diligent scholarships; it is how they use it that marks the distinction. Is the material being used to further a process of understanding and appreciating the work itself, inwardly but not oddly? If so, the approach is strictly literary and intrinsic. Is it on the other hand, being used to further a process of understanding and appreciating some other topic *through* literature? Then the approach is metacritical. To study seventeenth-century history and read the Old Testament as a way into Dryden's *Absolom and Achitophel* is perfectly compatible with intrinsic criticism; to use *Absalom and Achitophel* as one way into seventeenth-century history, or as part of a course in Biblical Studies or 'The Social Influence of the Old Testament', is to engage in metacriticism. Both procedures are perfectly proper to English Studies, but the former is logically primary: it is intrinsic criticism that gives *specialized* knowledge, and it is only that specifically literary evidence which justifies critical intrusion into other disciplines. If the metacritic is not also an intrinsic critic he cannot reasonably assume that he has anything to offer the professional historian, theologian, anthropologist, or whatever. It is this primacy that warrants the present attempt to correct the balance of kind-criticism to date—or at any rate to show that it has some part to play in the *literary* appreciation of literature.

For this purpose, Frye's concept of Mode needs to be expanded. He and Croce, though on opposite sides, are in the same game; in as much as they use literature in the service of a metaphysic both are metacritics and need strong, rather than adjustable construction units. Particular books however, unlike most theorics of literature, tend to have a protean nature; and the fact that the critics of two millennia have neither clearly distinguished modes from kinds nor agreed on any one definition of kind is not a reflection on their abilities but on the nature of literature. These students of genre may have been mainly concerned with its use in what were, strictly speaking, metacritical pursuits but since such pursuits depend, as we have seen, on intrinsically literary insights they rightly found themselves, as men of taste, in disagreement, even if they were not conscious of the real basis of it. For the truth is that every way of classifying literature will be right for some books, and for *some purpose* (what *cannot* be found, as the history of genre-criticism shows, is some single demonstrably right principle of classification as a scholarly end in itself). Even similarities as broad as 'period' or 'subject', though they might include such disparates as Shaw's *Getting Married* and Lawrence's *Women in Love*, could conceivably constitute the first means towards some rather general (and probably metacritical) end. The works instanced, perhaps, might form part of the evidence in some socio-literary or literary-historical investigation of the Edwardian revolt against Victorian conventions or the development of wider and freer sexual reference in literature. If the end is one appropriate to intrinsic criticism something less vague than 'period' or 'subject' is likely to be required. But *what*? The proper answer, from a critic who considers it his function to aid potential readers to appreciate particular works, must surely be that the nature of the particular works should dictate that sort of kind — defined by similarity of theme, or content, or structure, or purpose . . . — which he starts from.

At this point, though, we are faced with a variety of the hermeneutical dilemmas, which crop up in so many cruxes of critical theory: a proper conception of 'kind', we are saying, will help to lead us to an appreciation of the nature of the work — but to get that proper conception we seem to need to know the nature of the work already. Why not just read the thing, and hope some aspect will stick out as clearly more prominent than others? In practice, such bulldozing may work well enough in many cases — but not in all; and, in strict theory, it always leads straight into another hermeneutical dilemma: you can't know the proper meaning of any part without knowing what sort of whole it is a part of (for example, absurdities become virtues once you see that the work is a satire and therefore start being sensitive to, say, irony) — but since the whole is the sum of its parts you can't know what sort of whole it is without knowing the proper meaning of the parts. These dilemmas are not inescapable. But their presence is the main reason for evolving a flexible concept of Mode (and indeed also of Kind).

We escape, so to speak, by edging out, tacking from evidence to hypothesis to further evidence to renewed hypothesis. Since the evidence offered by a literary work, however, is of more than one sort, we need to add to Frye's technical definition of Mode a psychological dimension. A work's mode, then, let us say, is whatever it seems to be in its most general aspect—but what *is* most general will depend partly on our current concerns. In certain cases, it might be useful to take as 'mode' what we would more usually style 'fixed form' or even 'minor kind'. Are we concerned first with 'The Sonnet', and only within that framework with the qualities of various sonnets? If so, any particular poem is first scrutinized to see if it has the characteristics that we have decided determine the sonnet-mode. Then we may ask what *kind* of sonnet it is, technically (Petrarchan or Shakespearian), or tonally (denunciatory, melancholic . . .), or thematically (ubi sunt, sorrow of love . . .), and so on. Are we concerned with Satire? Then our most general concern is with whatever constitutes 'the satiric', and this will be the mode. After this, the *kind* of satire: bitter, humorous or whatever. If, however, we were concerned primarily with Humour, the case would be reversed. Thus one critic might quite properly place Pope's *Rape of the Lock* as a humorous mock-heroic kind within the mode of satire, and another, equally properly, as a satiric mock-heroic kind within the mode of the humorous. In general, though— special concerns apart—the mode of a work will be largely a matter of attitude or tone rather than style or form of writing. It will strike the reader as generally tragic, pathetic, comic, farcical, horrific, melancholic. . . We may then further distinguish *moods* within the general mode. Orwell's *1984* is *satirically* horrific, *Twelfth Night*, in its main plot, *wryly* comic. The concept of Kind must be equally flexible—to the point, as we have seen, of being interchangeable with that of Mode—in order to match the variousness of literature and the consequent variety of critical possibilities. But, in general, it will contain a larger element of technicality, being at least as much akin to *Type* as to *Mode*. (*1984* we might style as narrative type, horrific mode—within the Low Mimetic—, satiric mood; for most purposes its major kind would be romance-novel—a technical definition[1]—and minor kinds or varieties would then be distinguished to whatever degree of elaboration was required, 'didactic' being the most obvious.)

A work's mode, mood, type and kind (major and minor), then, eventually add up to what it turns out to be 'in itself', after it has been considered from various aspects; and it is in the fact of providing variables for triangulation that the value of this aspect of the generic approach lies. Not only is the critic prevented from going too far astray in any direction, and the later, subtler, non-generic analysis safeguarded against *irrelevant* ingenuity or *ungoverned* speculation, but also he is given navigational aids in his tacking escape from the landlocking horns of hermeneutical dilemma.

Carefully avoiding the Intentionalist Fallacy, one would normally begin by asking what the work itself *purports* to be or do. Sometimes a kind established by tradition or convention is referred to in the title (*Third Satyre . . . The Lamentable Tragedie of . . .*). This gives a statement of purport, or arouses certain critical expectations, which we check by the further evidence of each succeeding line, revising and re-revising our initial hypothesis of mode or kind if these expectations are not fulfilled. In the absence of such titles, a quick read-through is necessary to obtain a very tentative hypothesis about the mode of the whole (the parts having been taken, so to speak, innocently, at the face value of first impression, to which life, the language and, cumulatively, the context, all contribute). That hypothesis is then checked and refined on second reading into an idea of kind, by the two-way process indicated: successive hypotheses about the whole interacting with the accumulation of evidence as part succeeds part. Finally one is able to say with some confidence: This work purports to be such and such, and *is* in fact of that mode and kind—or, perhaps, is in fact *not* what it purports to be (as Blake and Shelley thought *Paradise Lost* not to be in fact a justification of the ways of God to man). In the latter case, it might be useful to speak of an ostensible purport disguising the real mode and kind. In such instances, concepts of mode and kind are evidently of particular value in helping to ensure that the escape from the hermeneutical dilemma is not bedevilled by authorial misleading (conscious or unconscious) as to the real meaning of certain parts.

[1] Refining on 'Low Mimetic' by indicating the existence of some uncharacteristic quality ('romance')—a not uncommon feature of literary works; Polonius's 'tragical-comical-historical' is not in principle so foolish as it sounds.

Conclusions come to by such a process, of course, can claim neither logical nor empirical *certainty*. But the valid interpretation, as E. D. Hirsch points out, is simply that which is most probable in the light of the available evidence; and when it comes to literature the nature of the most essential evidence can be obtained only by some two-way process, some fluid system of checks and balances, which gradually reduces the likely margin of error (if we make the necessary assumption that what is—or rather what would to the original audience have been—the most coherent interpretation is to be deemed the most probable; it is certainly, anyway, the most preferable). It may seem that traditional or conventional kinds, established by the title or other obvious indication, are an exception. But—leaving aside the possibility of authorial mistake—those kinds themselves, those conventions, must have been the result of some similar dialectic, for until the convention was established the nature of the kind or mode and the nature of the particular works which were to give rise to that category stood to each other in the same dilemmatic relationship as that of whole to the parts in each particular work; and further refinement is always *possible*—witness for example the gradual development of the present-day idea of 'satire', freed first from the influence of false etymology, then from the restriction to verse, to include works that seemed more 'satiric' than anything else though differing from earlier satires.

This dialectical process is not restricted to literature. Induction, and indeed practically all the learning processes of life, are subject to a similar dilemma, and escape it in defiance of logic by a similar spiralling or tacking progress between the particularizing of nominalism and the generalizing of universalism. Few subjects outside mathematics can avoid it; literature least of all.

Accept it, though, and genre-criticism is seen to be progressively useful. Firstly, a kind or mode may focus the literary ideal of a period, (as Wimsatt and Brooks argue). Secondly, once pragmatically accepted by 'tradition' or convention, it contributes metacritically not only to literary history, the sociology of literature, or its anthropology, but also, as we have seen, to intrinsic criticism, by setting up certain expectations (an especially useful function in cases of symbolism, allegory, irony, parody and satire). Thirdly, the act of classifying a work generally by Type and Mode, and specifically by Kind, itself a dialectical process—unless predetermined by a given concern—involves us intimately and inevitably with the subtler dialectic required to establish Purport. The nature of the work should properly guide the choice of mode or kind and, reciprocally, the chosen mode and kind form triangulation points in the progress towards establishing the general purport and thence the inner nature of the work. Where the choice of mode *is* predetermined by an overriding concern (like 'Satire') the process is affected only to this extent: that we are not less, but more aware of the existence of other aspects, other possibilities of approach, since we cannot but know that this one has been as much self-imposed as objectively discovered.

There is, however, a fourth use much more important to intrinsic criticism—or, at any rate, nearer to the heart of the work itself, coming into play only after the stages mentioned have been left behind.

Unfortunately, the idea of 'the work itself', so far taken for granted, faces us with another hermeneutical dilemma, not unrelated to the two already dealt with. Perhaps all three should be regarded as aspects of one problem. But at first sight this one seems to be in a class of its own, as it arises not from the need to establish a work's nature but the need to establish its very existence. Criticism should be objective, but literary works are not objects—or, anyway, in so far as they are, their existence is insignificant; and it is their signifying but non-material existence that the critic wants to be objective about. Merely and literally as 'the words on the page' a literary work exists materially but not meaningfully. The material existence could be altered out of all recognition without affecting the meaning one iota. For instance, the pages might be of different size, shape, quality and colour, the words in Russian script or shorthand signs, but as *literature* 'the words on the page' would remain unaltered. The words, in short, have to be read by somebody in order to come into meaningful existence. In this field, if not in others, Berkeley has some bearing. When a book is replaced on the shelf it ceases to exist (save as an indigestible lump of matter). But if its existence as literature, not lump, is only in the critic's mind, how can he avoid subjectivity? And if he does, how does he know the work he's being objective about will exist in the same way in his reader's mind (especially as any work may be approached—that is, recreated—in various ways)? When another reader digests it, doesn't it turn into *his* reality? How do both of them distinguish between a misreading and a legitimate variant reading?

All these questions can be absorbed into one problem: How to avoid the Affective Fallacy (a combine incorporating as many subsidiaries as the Intentionalist Fallacy).[1] One cannot assume that a work may properly be judged by its effect on the reader's mind and emotions (it might, surely, be a wrong effect due to misreading or emotional bias)—yet it exists only as an effect in the mind and therefore cannot be judged as anything else. This Affective Fallacy is identical with our latest hermeneutical dilemma, which seems theoretically as insoluble as the others. But again there is a pragmatic way out—which will appear less questionable if we alter our terms somewhat; noting that 'objectivity', while admittedly easier in relation to objects, need not be confined to them; it simply combines the ideas of being unbiased and of proceeding from the best available evidence. This means that there is no ruling of principle against being objective about literature. The difficulties are practical; therefore, the solution may be, too. Again, if we speak of a work's 'taking place' when read, rather than its 'existing', we both avoid unnecessary puzzles from the inherent ambiguity of the word 'exist' and also more accurately reflect the facts of reading. Moreover, we reveal the similarity between this and the previous dilemmas—reveal, indeed, that they are in fact only different aspects of one complex problem. For when we said that the nature of a particular work could be 'discovered' by a dialectical tacking between tentative hypotheses about the whole, framed and (if necessary) revised in the light of the cumulative evidence of the parts, starting with the title (the earlier parts of course taking a different colouring by back-reflection from each later, revised hypothesis), we were in fact indicating that the work was being created or, strictly, recreated as we read, though such a form of expression as 'discovered' tended to disguise the fact. In short, it gradually took place. The important thing to note however, is that the very difficulty of the process of recreation far from being a handicap is in fact one of the chief means of ensuring that what does take place corresponds to what should take place.

Attaining this correspondence seems, clearly, to be the chief task of intrinsic criticism—and even of metacriticism, since it must rest on a specifically literary basis—first for the critic himself, and then, simply by his leading his readers or auditors in the same direction, for the public.

[1] See Chap. 8.

The other chief means of attaining it, co-equal with the dialectical tacking and inseparable from it, is assessment by type, mode and kind; for that process both acts as a check on hypotheses about purport and is itself checked during the more detailed process of assessing purport.

If the choice of a defining class-similarity, out of many possibilities, is partly dictated by the nature of works at first only *tentatively* considered for inclusion in that class, a dialectical movement between possible class-parts and the nature of the class-whole is instigated comparable to, and inseparable from, that aiming to establish (or recreate, as we may now say) the nature of each work as a unique, not a class entity. Comparable and inseparable—so it is also the case that the nature of the works is partly dictated by some idea of a class-whole. The common factor, of course, is the concept of 'purport'. Without it, the parts of a particular work cannot be properly assessed. With it, the work is provisionally assigned to a class: a mode, type or kind.

The particular nature of the work reveals itself during a taking place that is a recreation. To be objective, the revelation should be the result of a dialectic. If it is true that during that dialectic the work will seem to assign itself provisionally to a class or classes, it is also true that the dialectic itself requires, as a tentative hypothesis, some idea of a (generic) whole as one of its terms. Thus generic criticism is found, surprisingly, to be also of value in establishing the proper existence of a single work, in ensuring that what does take place is what ought to take place when it is read; that the re-creation is not private and eccentric, that is to say, but as public as possible in the nature of the case. By multiple triangulation, so to speak, we fix what the 'work itself' most validly appears to be when, underpinned if necessary by scholarship, the public, reasonably discussable concepts of Type, Mode, Kind *and Purport*[1] pushing and pulling have done their best to prevent interpretation from flooding amorphously to unjustifiable lengths (or alternatively stagnating in lazy backwaters of the mind). What safeguards the dual process from complete circularity is the presence of various lines to the outside world. In the language itself at least some things are given; regardless of context, some subjects tend to delimit meanings ('spirit' in a religious work is not likely to refer to alcohol); some periods promote certain probabilities; so do some authors, some themes;

[1] See Appendix B, p. 123, for a definition of Purport.

and experience of life often acts as a guide even though times have changed. All these, may themselves depend ultimately on a similar dialectic (of which one paradigm could be the child's progress from known disparate objects, to the idea of sets, and finally to concepts of abstract number that can then be applied back to concrete items at a higher level). But they have justified themselves over a long period as practically useful, and can form a ground for the second-order process. (Hence one's reasonable willingness to accept – at any rate tentatively – certain traditions or conventions as a flying start.)

However, intrinsic criticism should not merely be justifiable, on the most public grounds possible, it should also be sufficiently inward (though still justifiably, not as unsupported assertions of intuition). Then – to return to our main argument – has generic criticism any part to play here? Not so much, it would seem, as 'internal' concepts like structure, texture, syntax, figures, diction, and so forth; yet not so little as one might think. In fact, the part it has to play is that referred to earlier (p. 33) as its fourth and, for intrinsic criticism, most important rôle.

To Croce, this section began by saying, to be generically inward seemed a contradiction in terms; and it is true that generic criticism has traditionally led outward, serving, or itself being metacriticism. It is also true that some works – mostly short lyric poems – do not *demand* any reference beyond their own boundaries. On the other hand, it is equally true, not only that there is no contradiction between generality and particularity, generic classification and the unique inwardness of the individual work, but also that individuality can hardly be seen to be such save when it defines itself by comparison with apparent *semblables*; only against what is common to the class will what is unique to each member stand out. Moreover, if we wish to do more than demonstrate the presence of some characteristic of a work (say mordant wit), wish to go on to its precise quality or degree, how can we possibly succeed save by comparing it with some work of the same kind – and therefore justly comparable – which possesses the same characteristic in a greater or lesser degree? Thus generic criticism turns out to be an instrument for fairly refined and precise intrinsic analysis.

Two important questions remain, perhaps. First, might not such a method still further, and possibly fatally, dehumanize the professional critic? His is already a difficult act of funambulism; he must be at once at home and abroad, feelingly immersed in the work and (in some corner of his being) objectively detached. Might not such a procedure topple him into automatism? Second, will it stifle initiative and encourage longwindedness? One answer, to both questions, is that these lamentable results might follow, but need not. It depends on the person, not the method. The answer could be put more strongly. Theorizing always seems inhuman, being necessarily abstract; but the results of following a reasonable theory should be less lamentable, in any given case, than those of not doing so; for *not* following one simply means muddling through — that is to say, carrying out most of the same operations haphazardly (to be reasonable a theoretical procedure should not bar any useful, necessary or desirable practice). But the best answer is the test of practice.

Take this time, not an apparently simple traditional poem, but an apparently difficult experimental one — about dehumanization, appropriately enough:

PITY THIS BUSY MONSTER, MANUNKIND

Pity this busy monster, manunkind,

not. Progress is a comfortable disease:
your victim (death and life safely beyond)
plays with the bigness of his littleness
— electrons deify one razorblade
into a mountain range; lenses extend
unwish through curving wherewhen till unwish
returns on its unself.

A world of made
is not a world of born — pity poor flesh
and trees, poor stars and stones, but never this
fine specimen of hypermagical
ultraomnipotence. We doctors know

A hopeless case if — listen; there's a hell
of a good universe next door; let's go.

(E. E. Cummings)

Well, let's go. The quick, innocent first reading seems to indicate that the poem does not purport to be entirely serious. But is it serious enough to be satiric though very unlike Pope or Byron, and despite the considerable element of verbal *play*? Some things indicate that it might be: the positionally-emphasized 'not' in the second

37

line, the syntactical placing of 'safely beyond', so that life and death seem beyond the victim's capacities rather than his being beyond their reach as the expected placing would have indicated; and then there's the hyperbole of 'ultraomnipotence', and one or two other things. But let us take a triangulation; first, on Type, as this poem fairly insists on its technicality. Dramatic? No quotation-marks but apparently two voices; the main one being that of the doctor, whose diction—'your victim', 'we doctors know'—suggests that he shares the dehumanization he is diagnosing in the busy monster (and looks at the same advertisements); the other is that of an anti-thetical persona, clearly apparent only in the last line and a half. But there's really no *dialogue* between the voices, and anyway much of the poem seems to be in a medial relationship with the reader, the medical persona materializing and fading like a Cheshire Cat. This is narrative—but subjective, even sentimental enough here and there ('pity poor flesh . . .') to suggest a touch of the lyric type too. This is Polonius poetry. It assigns itself to various categories, and they of course determine its nature.

Perhaps we might call it a work of mixed purport, satiric-didactic? But let us check by Mode. If we are most concerned with Theme, or most struck by it, we shall say *Romantic*, and make Comic Romantic the Kind. But the oversimple, overLawrentian message about man's predicament in a mathematical, mechanized world is less striking than the zing and zest of the verbal texture which is what lends new life to this familiar complaint. So let us reverse the order. Comic (not farcical), then, in mode; and a large part of the comic effect comes as much from the dramatic irony of the doctor's being what he censures as from the bracketing twists at each end, '. . . not' and '—listen . . .' or such figures as paranomasia ('manunkind'—man-kind, man cruel, man unnatural), oxymoron ('comfortable disease'), hyperbole, and substitution ('bigness' significantly used where 'greatness' might have been). Mood? Well, to refine on 'satiric' how about 'ironically didactic'? Didactic on account of what is said, ironic on account of who's saying it. As for Kind—technically a very *un*fixed form of sonnet. Its fourteen lines are surely meant to play against the accepted ideas of sonnet form. No further comparison seems called for. The ruin of a noble form, pretentious in blown-up *experimentalism* (minor kind), well matches the theme of ruined man imagining himself deified.

So far the method of investigation seems to be producing if

anything a naturally disordered, rather than a mechanical progress. On the other hand, it may be a little longwinded. But then, this is not itself a critical account, merely the preliminary jottings for one. The account itself need use none of these generic terms and could be much more compactly organized, for in considering the poem from various angles we have already found some to be angles of intersection – the same points figuring in different categories – and this is where economy could begin. What does seem to be important is that in the process of defining such basic matters as the poem's real nature and mode of existence, by a generic triangulating method designed to minimize tendencies to misreading, bias, and stock-response, we have in fact been led much further into the poem than might have been expected. In this particular case, indeed, little more will need to be done – save by way of polishing and finishing with a finer set of tools the points already touched on – when we have taken the final generic step of comparison.

Comparison with what? Another comic poem? A traditional romantic poem dealing with men and mountains versus machinery? Something anti-Newtonian from Blake (as this seems to be anti-Einsteinian: 'wherewhen', 'returns on its unself')? Or should we take it more technically and use some very modernistic work to bring out by comparison, the individual qualities of its experimentalism? Something from Lawrence's *Nettles* or *Pansies* might feature most of these parallels. Any course is open to us, or all of them. But we already have enough data for commonsense to size up the degree of compulsion to act so – and there seems to be a case for not dissecting to death a clever harmless little poem whose complexities have shown themselves to be all of the surface. There is less in this poem than meets the eye, so to speak.

However, it does offer itself very much as a play of linguistic effects, indeed a play of eccentric usage against the expectations of normal usage (the poem is that *variety* of experimental *kind*). We have noted elements earlier; for instance, in the syntactical placing of 'not' and 'safely beyond', but the characteristic is especially noticeable in the Einsteinian sentence ('lenses . . . unself') which refers us to the inhuman, blown-up quality of a universe made unimaginable by four-dimensional mathematics, made to 'return on its unself' by definition – at the point where observation becomes *in principle* impossible – : an image of magnified self-imprisoned man-monster with no real self to have a real wish. It so happens that this sentence is particularly reminiscent—like much of Cummings—of Orwell's *Newspeak*. And, as we briefly categorized that work earlier but conveniently omitted mention of its essays, we might now use it fleetingly in comparison. Does not *1984*, rightly argue in the essays, and in the narrative exemplify, the dangers and limitations of this sort of language? How *vaguely* clever 'unwish' is!

Once attention is directed to it, this special 'Cummings' quality might come under censure. The traditional poet, by doing something *with* the language we have adds to its resources. Cummings by doing something *against* it (like the dictionary-makers of *1984*) impoverishes it—or rather would be tending to impoverish it if he were trying to substitute the new for the old. Since he is merely playing one against the other, lesser charges are to be preferred: that his are second-order poems (depending for their effect on a first-order of language) and that they are often too playful for their subject. In this case, though, the defects demonstrated by Orwell have become virtues, as such a language perfectly enacts the theme, of dehumanizing 'improvements', and admirably supports the dramatic irony, of the persona whose very detachment marks his involvement with 'manunkind' and whose vocabulary all too well reflects his thesis.

Is it not, though, an outrage to the idea of 'kind' to have compared a poem with an essay or novel? Well, both had in common satire, didacticism, and the theme of dehumanization, as well as linguistic experiment. But the basic answer is that 'kind' is *only* an idea. We began with Ehrenpreis's assertion that kinds 'are not implicit in the nature either of literature or of the human mind', we went on to support pragmatic usefulness against the chimera of absolute, platonic truthfulness, and we may then logically conclude by reiterating that nothing in this particular approach through Type, Mode and Kind need inhibit initiative or commit the critic to automatism. It even permits him, still, a modicum of eccentricity.

3

'Practical Criticism' in Principle and Practice

'Intensive analysis of individual works of literature has more and more become the basis of criticism'

(Arms and Kuntz, *Poetry Explication*, New York, 1950, p. 17)

I. PRINCIPLE (*'It makes us think for ourselves'*)

RECENTLY, two groups of students, one at Nottingham and the other at Sheffield, were asked to give their frank opinions (anonymously) of 'practical criticism' as they had experienced it. The remark quoted at the head of this section was made by a student in one of these groups. To some it may well seem that this is no more than additional, even superfluous, confirmation of something that has been plain for thirty years—ever since I. A. Richards's *Practical Criticism*[1] demonstrated the ludicrous results of an English Tripos which did not provide the training in 'thinking for oneself' about literature that practical criticism tries to give. But the value of practical criticism is, in fact, far from clear to everyone, even today. Indeed, it is surprising how much heat discussion of the subject can still generate.

It is, of course, always possible that certain authoritarians really have no wish for people to think for themselves. On the other hand, one notices that 'intelligence tests' provoke, in some people, a lurking fear of being found unable to do them, and it seems quite likely that hostility to practical criticism sometimes springs from similar

---

[1] Tribute should also be paid, however, to the young M. D. Forbes (d. 1935). See, E. M. W. Tillyard, *The Muse Unchained: An Intimate Account of the Revolution in English Studies at Cambridge* (1958): 'Indeed it is doubtful if without Forbes's support, Chadwick would have carried through the whole of his programme. But there was another side to Forbes's literary tastes, a devoted interest in verbal effects in their subtlest and minutest manifestations' (pp. 47/8) 'By himself Forbes would have achieved nothing tangible. He needed Richards through whom to work' (p. 89) 'Richards used to say that Forbes was his good genius' (p. 133).

roots. Or perhaps archetypal fears of murdering to dissect still haunt the minds of critics subconsciously swayed by the Romantic claim that poetry gives access to a Higher Reality: on this view anything that looks like a questioning of the poet-seer is near-blasphemy. This attitude, clearly, harks back to that cultivation of vague uplift (designed to induce a receptive, hypnoidal state) which commonly passed as the proper approach for criticism until the reaction of Eliot and Murry in the early twenties.

All these suggestions are speculative and may be unjust. Yet most of the objections actually made to practical criticism are so inadequate that it is difficult not to suspect them of being rationalizations. There is not, after all, a choice between this sort of criticism and some other, but only between degrees of practical criticism—at any rate in the wide sense that includes 'close reading'.

In principle, practical criticism amounts to nothing more than reading literature carefully and without bias in order to come to an independent and responsible assessment, instead of reading it in a dependent or careless way. Courses devoted to imparting 'knowledge about' literature often led—and lead—to reading of the latter kind. But to stress, in contrast, the need for the student to have 'experience of' literature is certainly not to imply that one needs to be ignorant in order to be critical: it is simply to urge that 'knowledge about' literature is valuable only as a means, not as an end. The acquiring of facts, indeed, *must* be regarded as an activity subordinate to independent criticism, if literature is accepted as a fit subject for university study. After all, 'knowledge about' a subject has only the value it derives from that subject (one can be deeply learned about railway trains, but no one, presumably, would suggest that railways should be studied as part of the university curriculum). Practical criticism seems, indeed, not merely desirable but essential in a defensible English Course, since it is nothing less than practice in the activity which is fundamental to any literary criticism. To omit it is like omitting the practice of experiment from a Science Course.

There is, however, a view of the undergraduate's university work and of the function of an English school which is based on quite a different attitude. Perhaps its most notable spokesman was the late Professor C. S. Lewis, who derived it from extra-critical principles.

For Professor Lewis, universities existed in order that learning might be pursued, not that young men might be, in the widest sense, 'educated', made full men. Education might be the incidental result of the pursuit for learning, but it was not to be the motive for that pursuit: the pursuit of learning should be undertaken for its own sake by those whose nature compelled them to it.

Now it might have happened that such people were left in civil societies to gratify their taste as best they could without assistance or interference from their fellows. It has not happened. Such societies have usually held a belief – and it is a belief of a quite transcendental nature – that knowledge is the natural food of the human mind: that those who specially pursue it are being specially human; and that their activity is good in itself besides being always honourable and sometimes useful to the whole society. Hence we come to have such associations as universities – institutions for the support and encouragement of men devoted to learning.

You have doubtless been told – but it can hardly be repeated too often – that our colleges at Oxford were founded not in order to teach the young but in order to support masters of arts. In their original institution they are homes not for teaching but for the pursuit of knowledge; and their original nature is witnessed by the brute fact that hardly any college in Oxford is financially dependent on the undergraduates' fees, and that most colleges are content if they do not lose over the undergraduate. A school without pupils would cease to be a school; a college without undergraduates would be as much a college as ever, would perhaps be more a college.

It follows that the university student is essentially a different person from the school pupil. He is not a candidate for humanity; he is, in theory, already human. He is not a patient; nor is his tutor an operator who is doing something to him. The student is, or ought to be, a young man who is already beginning to follow learning for its own sake, and who attaches himself to an older student, not precisely to be taught, but to pick up what he can. From the very beginning the two ought to be fellow students.

(Rehabilitations (1939), pp. 84–85)

Education, as Professor Lewis makes clear elsewhere, is the task of schools: schools mould and knead the young into the shapes society thinks desirable.

On this view, it is never the function of the senior member of the university to offer his fellow student value-judgements: what unites them is their pursuit of knowledge. Of course some value-judgements will—such is the imperfection of all human things—inevitably be transmitted, but that need not disturb our vision of the ideal. We are confronted, in fact, with a view precisely opposed to that advanced earlier in this chapter when it was urged that learning is a means to an end (or ends); here, learning is an end in itself. Of course, education is an end in itself, but this is not Professor Lewis's point.

> Learning is not education; but it can be used educationally by those who do not propose to pursue learning all their lives. There is nothing odd in the existence of such a by-product. Games are essentially for pleasure, but they happen to produce health. They are not likely, however, to produce health if they are played for the sake of it. Play to win and you will find yourself taking violent exercise; play because it is good for you and you will not. In the same way, though you may have come here [*to Oxford*] only to be educated, you will never receive that precise educational gift which a university has to give you unless you can at least *pretend*, so long as you are with us, that you are concerned not with education but with knowledge for its own sake.
>
> (*Rehabilitations*, p. 86)

It may be true that spiritual and intellectual graces come when we court them least, but it is surely a strange notion that a man should go up to Oxford to complete his education and, once there, spend his time fervently pretending that his object is the pursuit of learning. From a writer who has elsewhere had some hard things to say about the 'hypocrisy' of 'pursuing culture' as one's end (v. *The Twentieth Century*, April 1955, p. 340), this comes rather oddly.

> But we have to beware of Education: it is a dangerous thing. I foresee the growth of a new race of readers and critics to whom, from the very outset, good literature will be an accomplishment rather than a delight, and who will always feel, beneath the acquired taste, the backward tug of something else which they feel merit in resisting. Such people will not be content to say that some books are bad or not very good, they will make a special class of 'lowbrow' art which is to be vilified, mocked, quarantined, and sometimes (when they are sick or tired) enjoyed. They will be sure that what is popular must always be bad, thus assuming that human taste is *naturally* wrong, that it needs not only improvement and development but veritable conversion. For

them a good critic will be, as the theologians say, essentially a 'twice-born' critic, one who is regenerate and washed from his Original Taste. They will have no conception, because they have no experience, of spontaneous delight in excellence. Their 'good' taste will have been acquired by the sweat of their brows, its acquisition will often (and legitimately) have coincided with advancement in the social and economic scale, and they will hold it with uneasy intensity.

> (*Rehabilitations*, p. 114)

This is the theme to which Professor Lewis returned after the war in 'Lilies that Fester' (the article in the *Twentieth Century* to which reference was made at the end of the last paragraph). This article was so well rebutted by W. W. Robson in a subsequent number of the *Twentieth Century* that there is no need to consider it in detail here. The picture as Professor Lewis sees it has not changed much since 1939, except that 'culture' is now apparently becoming the royal road to success in the battle of life because it endears a young man to his superiors: now

> we have the adaptable youth to whom poetry has always been something 'set' for 'evaluation'. Success in this exercise has given him pleasure and let him into the ruling class.
>
> ('Lilies', loc. cit.)

This seems, on the evidence, a highly debatable picture. But would it matter so much even if it were true? At least the 'adaptable youth' would have some knowledge of 'the best that has been thought and said in the world' even if there were no real inwardness in his know-ledge. Wasn't knowledge, for Professor Lewis, a good in itself? But that is not the point: the 'uneasy intensity' of cultural *parvenus* makes them

> . . . angry with a true lover of literature who does not take pains to unravel the latest poetical puzzle, and call him a *dilettante*. Having obtained the freedom of Parnassus at a great price, they will be unable to endure the nonchalance of those who were free-born.
>
> (*Rehabilitations*, pp. 114-15)

But doesn't this 'proud Parnassian sneer' give the game away? Ultimately this is snobbery, the same in kind as the snobbery which makes the gentleman born a little reluctant to 'accept' the *nouveau riche* peer. But is it, in fact, so dreadful to acquire one's 'good taste' by the sweat of one's brow?

. . . for an *accurate* taste in poetry, and in all the other arts, as Sir Joshua Reynolds has observed, is an *acquired* talent, which can only be produced by thought and a long continued intercourse with the best models of composition.

(Preface to Lyrical Ballads § 32)

Wordsworth, of course, was a shocking cultural *parvenu*, but one would have thought Sir Joshua Reynolds above reproach.

We must glance, however, at one further paragraph by Professor Lewis:

By making . . . culture a *moyen de parvenir*, you help to drive [it] out of the world. Let our masters leave [this], at least, alone; leave us some region where the spontaneous, the unmarketable, the utterly private, can still exist.

('Lilies that Fester', p. 341)

One might urge that China is one of the supreme examples in history of a nation that made culture a *moyen de parvenir* and that the culture thus officially supported lasted a surprisingly long time. But it is the implications of the second sentence that require examination. Is 'culture' always spontaneous? Or unmarketable? And, in particular, is 'culture' ever 'utterly private'? Isn't it, in fact, precisely the 'public' character of culture that is important? Professor Lewis elsewhere appears to acknowledge that this is so:

. . . the purpose of education is to produce the good man and the good citizen, though it must be remembered that we are not here using the word 'good' in any narrowly ethical sense. The 'good man' here means the man of good taste and good feeling, the interesting and interested man, and almost the happy man. With such an end in view education in most civilised communities has taken much the same path; it has taught civil behaviour by direct and indirect discipline, has awakened the logical faculty by mathematics or dialectic, and has endeavoured to produce right sentiments—which are to the passions what right habits are to the body—by steeping the pupil in the literature both sacred and profane on which the culture of the community is based.

(Rehabilitations, p. 81)

From this it would appear legitimate to infer that a 'culture' which is 'utterly private' is not a culture at all. And this is the starting point of all criticism, 'practical' or 'theoretical'. If criticism is not 'public',

if it does not at least try to be generally valid, if it is merely a statement of personal preferences, it is not criticism. Without the belief
that what one has to say may at least aspire to be valid for other
people, criticism cannot even begin. And for criticism to be 'public',
it is necessary that the thing criticized should be 'public' also.

One of the best ways to find out what general validity one's views
have is, of course, to discuss them with others, and this is what one
does in practical criticism. Professor Lewis, however, does not see
it in this light:

> when we substitute exercises in 'practical criticism' for the old, dry
> papers, a new situation arises. The boy will not get good marks (which
> means in the long run, that he will not get into the Managerial Class)
> unless he produces the kind of responses, and the kind of analytic
> method, which commend themselves to his teacher.
>
> ('Lilies', p. 337)

To Professor Lewis, apparently practical criticism means not discussion, but inculcation. Admittedly in the passage just quoted he
seems to be thinking primarily of the situation in schools, and a
strong case can be made out for thinking that practical criticism,
properly so called, is out of place in schools. People need to be able
to formulate and defend opinions of their own before practical
criticism is of much use to them. At the university level, however,
no competent person should find it unduly difficult to stimulate
discussion, and once started it is surprising how often such discussion leads, of itself, to sensible conclusions which emerge without
prompting as the common opinion of the class. And surely this is
what matters: in criticism there are ultimately no 'right' and 'wrong'
judgements, only better and worse ones. Accordingly there is nothing
to be inculcated, but a very great deal to be examined and discussed. Clearly, some philosophical difficulties have been skated
over—the nature and status of value-judgements, the claims of literary
culture as more than mere self-indulgence and many more. But practical criticism does not stand peculiarly in need of solutions to these
difficulties: all literary studies face the same challenge (and some
attention is given to it in other chapters). Here, it is necessary to
urge only that if works of literature have value, that is, if they offer
similar desirable qualities to different people in different times and
places, if they stand apart to a very great extent from merely personal
'likes' and 'dislikes', practical criticism is the natural, and at present

the best, way to come to grips with these qualities: when full and free discussion terminates in *real* agreement, it is likely that merely personal tastes and preferences will have been transcended. The obtaining of such real agreement is, however, a practical matter.

II. PRACTICE. (*'Analysis and judgment become easier with practice'*)

This remark is confirmed not only by recent psychological work, but by general experience, and it seems to provide a sufficient answer to what is, at first sight, a strong objection to practical criticism work with undergraduates: namely, that no one can be taught to be a critic. It is doubtless true that no one can be taught to be a *good* critic—or a good scholar, presumably—if he hasn't the proper qualities within him, but he can certainly be taught to be better than he is. That this may be of value both to him and to society is indicated by a number of student comments, such as these:

> I think it [*practical criticism*] is invaluable—and I also think there is a definite transfer of this training from literature to life (e.g. in one's reaction to all forms of debased literature, advertisements, newspapers, etc. Also possibly in human relationships).

> There is a definite carry-over from literature to outside life . . . Advertisements become transparent when criticised, revealing their hidden appeals to gregariousness or snobbery . . . Similarly, conversation can often be seen through, after practical criticism has become a normal activity of the mind. The method of practical criticism is thus carried over into life, and is particularly devastating when applied to the speeches of politicians and other dignitaries. I do not think that this extension of practical criticism to events in the outside world should be its main function, but it is inevitable and I believe valuable.

Most students agreed with certain objectors that in practical criticism 'gimmicks' can be used, but almost all added—surely correctly?—that they thought examiners saw through them. One added frankly:

> . . . What is certain is that period papers can be passed without candidates having read texts. Consult and memorise the best criticisms and you are bound to get through.

This comment pairs naturally with another:

It is the only class in which one is required to use one's brain to any great extent, and so is very welcome.

Of course, being trained to use one's sense and sensibility is not the only work which is valuable. The training of the memory, and of the capacity to collect evidence and weigh it without bias according to scholarly principles—these are valuable too. But then, no one suggests that practical criticism should be the only activity of an English Department. The fact that scholarly notes to a text sometimes actually hinder critical assessment by concentrating on irrelevancies, on, for example, what is typical of the age rather than on what is important about the particular work (irrelevance is not the less irrelevant for being scholarly, but it is sometimes more confusing), need not blind us to the fact that, in general, criticism is the better for being informed as well as intelligent. And ultimately, of course, it is impossible to avoid some reliance on memory and information. Another student wrote:

> Practical criticism trains the memory of such things as sentence-structure, language, and the outlook of different ages, but after a greater length of time it does begin to train the sensibility.

It is really a question of emphasis. There are other courses where the primary object is to give the student the information that as a literary critic he will need; the practical criticism course is designed principally to help him acquire the necessary *skill*:

> The student observes subtle details which normally would have escaped him, and this in turn helps him to learn more from the passage. It also has value in illuminating other passages because it sharpens the powers of comparison.

Where background information does turn out to be illuminating—
—and this must happen from time to time, however carefully passages are chosen—the fact can be turned to account and used effectively to link practical criticism to other work.

Nevertheless, the nature of its aim does render the practice of practical criticism liable to certain cogent objections. Firstly, there is the danger of 'interpretation for its own sake'. Where passages are extracted from longer works (something difficult to avoid with prose) this objection cannot easily be rebutted. There *is* a danger of misinterpretation or unnecessarily complex interpretation, simply because the larger context is not known, or of giving the impression

49

that equally close reading of all parts of a long work is desirable (whereas in fact it is not even practicable). These dangers have to be faced if practical criticism is not to be confined to discussion of short lyric poems. Some compromise with the Principle of Unknown Authorship seems inevitable. One might use passages from longer works known to the class only when students have acquired the habit of independent response and are no longer liable to inert acceptance of textbook authority or schoolroom judgments. Or again, one could set an exercise bound to provoke discussion – such as asking members of the group to come prepared to say which passage in a given novel they consider to be the 'key' passage, and why. A further device is the use of some uncharacteristic passage from an established work to see how far the student can resist the pressure of authoritative opinion in assessing that passage, and how far he can resist the pressure of the uncharacteristic passage in forming a judgment of the whole.

Another objection to practical criticism as we know it is that it sometimes leads to abuses: for example, over-ingenious symbol-hunting. But any method can be abused: the proper use of a method is the responsibility of the user. The abuses of practical criticism are the occupational hazard of the critic (although it is worth noting that many extreme symbol-hunters are guiltless of any interest in practical criticism) as pedantry is of the scholar. English studies can never have a 'scientific' method: practical criticism is not a substitute for good sense but merely a means of canalizing it; and in discussion groups one draws upon the good sense of the students as well as of the 'teacher'. Even here, though, good sense can be supplemented by techniques (of a flexible kind). Ockham's Razor should be applied to all symbolic interpretations, tests for coherence within the interpretation and compatibility with all other elements in the work should be made, and finally the interpretation can (and should) be tested for *probability* in the light of the external evidence of literary and historical scholarship – thus keeping the Practical Criticism course in touch with the remainder of the student's work.

The word 'finally' however, is important. For it is necessary to stress once again, as against the 'inculcationist' view of practical criticism, that class-work is designed to encourage students to think for themselves.

But it is sometimes said that practical criticism is too difficult for undergraduates: we overrate the usefulness of his commonsense in this field. Certainly it *is* difficult for him, for his school career has too often accustomed him to 'knowledge about' literature, *rather* than (instead of *as well as*) 'experience of' it. That the difficulty is not insuperable is made clear by several student comments, of which this is typical:

> Practical criticism has changed from an hour which I dreaded to one of enjoyment, which proves that I have more confidence in my ideas and can feel far more than I used to.

The fact is that the path can be smoothed: by graded exercises following some preliminary information about the history, methods and intention of practical criticism; by recommendation of the appropriate books; and by seeing that the groups are small enough to give everyone a chance to speak and large enough to exhibit different viewpoints. Such obvious and humdrum preliminaries can be supplemented in various ways.

If the members of the group already have some literary background, for instance, it may help to begin with dating exercises (choosing, of course, pretty easy and typical pieces). There are a variety of reasons for beginning in this way. In the first place, sensible criticism is hard to achieve without a highly developed feeling for the period to which a work belongs, and dating exercises offer a very good way of helping the student to evolve such a feeling from his own rudimentary knowledge. In the second place, students usually feel at this stage that everything is fluid and uncertain, that they have nothing to hold on to. In dating exercises, one can at least offer them a 'right' answer of sorts: one can say definitely when a given passage was written. At the same time, one need not surrender entirely to the demand for 'right' answers: one can often show that, although a student dated a passage wrongly, he at least dated it more or less sensibly: the piece wasn't written when he thought, but his judgment was not wholly without reason. This is a very useful way of accustoming students to the fundamental purpose of the exercises they are trying to do: later, one can introduce a few examples which are deliberately misleading, in order to drive home the point that, as the Cambridge Tripos papers used to say, 'more credit will be given for sound reasoning than for happy guesses'; it is not the answer that matters but the reasons which support it.

Fairly soon the dating exercises can be varied with 'critical comparisons'; students may compare two (sometimes more) short poems, saying which they prefer and why. In the discussions students usually 'teach' each other: the skill of the 'teacher' is shown as much as anything in his capacity to select passages which will set rival groups at odds and promote vigorous discussion. He also gets many valuable opportunities to show what sorts of critical argument are unsound: he may point out, for example, that it won't do to dismiss a passage simply because it is borrowed, and he may point to the many occasions on which writers have borrowed from others to great effect. But perhaps his principal task at this stage will be to widen his students' tastes. Some people complain that Romanticism is out of fashion nowadays, but experience with students suggests that this is certainly not the case in schools, and much of a lecturer's time is usually taken up with trying to show that the Romantic mode in poetry is not normative, that all poetry is not to be judged according to how closely it approaches or recedes from that mode. Pope is still a great stumbling-block: perhaps Pope is too mature a taste for any but the exceptional undergraduate, although it must be admitted that one sometimes meets surprising departures from the average, as, for example a recent tutorial class of five people, all of whom clearly read Pope with the deepest satisfaction and found Wordsworth, on the other hand a real bore.

Dating exercises and 'critical comparisons' are the standard exercises of practical criticism, but as we have seen, the work is by no means confined to them. These two kinds of exercise are used most often because they are susceptible of so much 'repetition-with-variation'. In the later stages, one can make classes more interesting to the students by having students themselves set dating exercises and run the group in the place of the lecturer. This is an extremely effective way of promoting really free discussion and argument: it helps to make the class feel that the discussion is genuinely 'among themselves'. The lecturer naturally gives his datings and his reasons at the end of the discussion, but before the 'right' answers are announced; when he is right, as most of the time he presumably will be, the class can see the validity of his arguments, and when he is wrong, as he will be from time to time, the class will respect him for not being afraid of 'sticking his neck out' and will also draw the valuable lesson that even in dating no one can be right all the time.

Other work during the year might include the examination of various pieces of critical writing, distinguishing genuine pieces of writing in a given style from deliberate imitation or pastiche, taking two versions of the same poem and asking students to say whether the revisions in the later version constitute improvements or not, and so on. Occasionally it is worth going outside 'literature' altogether, for example to discuss 'popular fiction'. Two or three passages from stories in women's magazines may be examined in the light of the fact that fees as high as £100 for three thousand words have been paid for this kind of thing. Fees of this kind indicate not only that there is a market for such work, but also that the supply is limited: no one would pay such fees if every hack writer could satisfy the demand. But if this kind of writing demands unusual talents, can the literary student afford to say, 'this is not literature', and, without examination, take no further interest in it? If it is 'bad'—from a literary standpoint—he should be able to say why: the fact that it sells or that it is published in women's magazines is nothing to the purpose. At least the resulting discussion is likely to bring out that such stories are often written with great skill, given the ends that the writers propose to themselves. In the second year, some purely technical exercises can be undertaken, to subtilize the perception of syntactical effects, the interplay or rhythm and metre, the management of tone and so on—though one would want eventually to go back to considering works as seamless wholes.

What is the effect of all this on students? Obviously, without further research, only a tentative answer can be given. But their own reports, as well as the experience of teachers, indicate that those not completely unresponsive to literature—one or two usually are—generally find themselves even by the end of a single year, much readier than before to respond to it without wondering what they 'ought' to say about this 'kind' of thing. Instead of simply taking down what lecturers say in lectures and parroting that ever afterwards, they now more readily look at the evidence and decide for themselves whether they agree with what they have been told. Quite often, too, their taste is less narrow. Again, they have usually learnt about at least some of the types of critical argument that will not hold water. In these and in many other ways their outlook is more critical—in the Arnoldian sense that they try to see things as in themselves they really are.

Literature is not a thing totally apart from the rest of life; literature always 'looks at' life in some degree, however apparently fantastic it may be, and this is to say that life enriches literature. Equally, literature enriches life: literature is not ultimately an end in itself, though it may be a temporary and transitional end, and therefore although literature will do nothing for us if we do not enjoy it, it will never be more than a personal indulgence unless it bears fruit beyond the purely literary sphere. On this point one is glad to find Professor Lewis in agreement: 'the real frivolity, the solemn vacuity, is all with those who make literature a self-existent thing to be valued for its own sake' (*Rehabilitations*, p. 196). Of course literature *has* its sphere, its limited autonomy, but this sphere must in the end be transcended. We need not regret this overmuch, however, if it results, through language, in a special sort of awareness of life in all its complexity, in more alert minds, or a greater readiness to think, and think sensibly, for ourselves.

4

Critical Stylistics

I. IF 'practical criticism' is at the heart of intrinsic criticism (in so far as it develops that verbal sensibility without which all the rest is baseless), stylistics is at the heart of practical criticism. This means, however, that the sort of stylistics that is useful for the literary critic tends to have the limitations attendant on practical criticism; while the sort of stylistics that does not have these limitations – of being better for texture than structure, for short pieces than long – tends to be of only peripheral usefulness.

'*Stylistics*', the study of Style. At first, that seems either the narrowest or the widest of subjects. It is sometimes even cut off entirely from *Linguistics*, on the grounds that the one is concerned with the way idiolects differ, the other with what they have in common (though some linguists, on the contrary, would reserve the term 'stylistics' entirely for themselves). On the other hand, the concept of style is sometimes applied, widely, to all the features of a civilization, as in the 'style of an age', and is very often applied to all the works of a single art in a whole period, as when we speak of an eighteenth-century style of writing distinguishable from that of other centuries or periods. Again, it may refer to a very general concept: an Augustan, or a Romantic style. And so on. What is useful to the critic, teacher or student of literature comes somewhere between these extremes. Unless that middle ground is to be fully identified with practical criticism its area is not easy to map out; if it is not to be so identified, but taken as something narrower, it requires careful placing.

Clearly what the non-linguistic critic needs is an idea of style and a version of stylistics which will encourage him to be technical without becoming mechanical, to be centrally concerned with uses of language but not unconcerned with matters of relevance and value. Such a version need not be entirely divorced from grammatical linguistics, but is likely to get more aid from philosophical linguistics, as that is concerned with the richness of semantic meaning

E   55

(the difference, say, between 'love' and 'hate') rather than the thinness of grammatical meaning ('love' and 'loving' or 'loves').

These differences and difficulties are handily illustrated in *Style in Language* (ed. T. A. Sebeok, New York and London, 1960), a formidable record of an American symposium of linguists, psychologists, cultural anthropologists and literary critics. An article by I. A. Richards on 'Variant Readings and Misreading' – one of several brilliant clearings in this jungle of jargon – shows that technical stylistic analysis can be used profitably at one point: 'It is part of the aim of linguistic studies to improve both literary perception and the techniques of describing what is perceived.' Why linguistic studies should at some point be critical and criticism sometimes linguistic, two further passages make clear:

> Perhaps we should not take too seriously those who seem to claim authority from linguistics as a 'science' to tell a rather helpless generation that what is said by enough people thereby becomes what *should* be said (are we to think that what is thought by enough people thereby becomes what should be thought?) (p. 251).

> Similarly with interpretation: what we should seek is not the course that is, or would be, most widely accepted, but what most fully takes into account the situation the utterance is meeting, and the integrity of the language (p. 251).

Most of the contributors to the symposium on *Style in Language* make it abundantly clear that linguistic stylistics can no more provide a foolproof critical method than any of the other 'objective' systems drawn from psychology, history, biography, anthropology, or whatever else in the metacritical armoury. A *critical* linguistic stylistics is obviously necessary – to support and test a sane practical criticism – if the central problem of Schools of Literature is to be satisfactorily faced. That problem is, as Richards puts it, one of:

> improving (if we can) our means of discriminating between variant readings and misreading. This distinction is, I take it, a chief operating assumption in most education . . .: the recognition, on the one hand, of the inevitability and desirability of, diverse understandings and, on the other, their sharp contrast with the mistake, the inadmissible interpretation. (p. 242).

This is indeed, as we have already seen, an aspect of the complex hermeneutical dilemma that constantly confronts the literary critic. To this task of discrimination the improvement of both 'literary perception' and 'the techniques of describing what is perceived' are obviously central. The main point of analytical criticism is not to discover, but firstly to verify that what was intuitively perceived was really there, and secondly to assess it by standards that have themselves been brought to consciousness and assessed as in some way relevant.

Of course, there is no method that can be a substitute for sense in critical stylistics, but in general this collection of papers indicates that the Continental stylistics of linguists, sociologists or psychologists is of much less help than the Anglo-American stylistics of literary critics. It seems evident, for instance, that linguistic data alone cannot confirm or contravert critical judgements – though they may show them to be extra-linguistic. F. W. Bateson puts forward a simple basic explanation of this fact:

> Why is it . . . that so little of critical interest has so far emerged from modern linguistics? One answer, I suggest, stares us all in the face in the movements of *le circuit de la parole*. The linguist must always tend to refer the phenomena of style *back* to their constituents in language . . . rather than *forwards* to the post-linguistic or strictly psychological phase ('Linguistics and Literary Criticism', *The Disciplines of Criticism*, ed. Demetz, Greene and Nelson, New Haven and London, 1968; p. 12)

Bateson also uses Saussure's idea of a continuous circuit from mind-to-sound-to-sign-to-mind in order to establish a definition of 'style' that covers most of what a literary stylistics may profitably be concerned with:

> Saussure's analysis is, of course, incomplete. In the give-and-take of everyday conversation what 'A' has to say to 'B' is counterbalanced by what 'B' has to say to 'A'. Question begets answer, as assertion begets either assent or contradiction. But once the cycle of speech is inflated into what may be called the literary cycle ('the *best* words in the *best* order') and 'A' becomes the author and 'B' the literary audience, the typical situation has changed. The function of the author qua author is to externalize all the time, just as the literary audience . . . is internalizing all the time (Ibid., p. 10)

> 'A' . . . in his role of prophet or entertainer, is always aware, consciously or unconsciously, of the possibility of 'B''s denial of *le circuit de la*

parole; he has therefore developed his own counter-strategy, which is to persuade 'B' to continue silent, interested, and attentive. The eloquence of the orator must now become so irresistible, the story must be told so amusingly or so excitingly, that 'B' cannot choose but hear. In other words, rhetoric is now added to speech. Unless rhetoric in its most general sense, *is* added to speech, the prolongation of 'A''s role in the speech cycle will tend sooner or later to be resisted or refused by 'B'. A club bore cannot hold his audience, because his rhetoric is inferior or non-existent, because he is innocent of the *ars dicendi*.

Literature is committed by the nature of its audience relationship to the superimposition upon speech of the specially heightened rhetoric that we call 'style'. (Ibid., p. 11)

This idea of style still allows it to come under the linguisticians' conception of it as deviation from some norm, yet does so without encouraging the faults Wellek puts his finger on in his 'Closing Statement' of *Style in Language*:

We can make a comparison of traits, concluding that certain traits are shown in common, whereas others differ, diverge, or even contrast. Authors nearly related in time, place, and genre will obviously yield very similar grammars. An attempt can be made by statistical methods, to discriminate the frequency of certain devices used by two or more authors: words and their distribution or any other stylistic trait. But we wonder whether the result will be very meaningful for criticism. Statistical frequency necessarily ignores the crucial aesthetic problem, the use of a device in its context. No single stylistic device, I believe, is invariable: it is always changed by its particular context. Literary analysis begins where linguistic analysis stops. The danger of linguistic stylistics is its focus on deviations from, and distortions of, the linguistic norm. We get a kind of countergrammar, a science of discards. Normal stylistics is abandoned to the grammarian and deviational stylistics is reserved for the student of literature. But often the most commonplace, the most normal, linguistic elements are the constituents of literary structure. A literary stylistics will concentrate on the aesthetic purpose of every linguistic device, the way it serves a totality, and will beware of the atomism and isolation which is the pitfall of much stylistic analysis. (pp. 417–18)

The statement that 'the most commonplace, the most normal,

linguistic elements' may be the constituents of literary structure, seems inconsistent with Bateson's idea of 'style' as rhetoric, though what follows tallies well enough. However, there is really no conflict; there appears to be one only because Wellek has spoken of 'deviations from . . . *the* linguistic norm'. In fact there is no such thing as a linguistic norm; what we think of as a norm — by contrast with which a sense of *style* arises — depends (as Wellek puts it) on the particular 'context', the 'totality' — and we might add, the work's relation to reality. We need, in short, to distinguish two broad categories: I. *Situational style*, covering *historical* situations (e.g. Augustan style — sensed by general deviations from a platonic idea of some neutral plain twentieth-century style: an average *Times* leader, say, or B.B.C. news report), *genre* situations (e.g. mock-heroic — by deviations from some accepted sincere-heroic) *group* situations (e.g. 'vulgar', 'polite', and so on), *register* situations (e.g. telephone, advertising, academic) as well as *personal* situations, real or fictional, which condition: II. *Individual style* — that which distinguishes one author from another within any situation or situations, or one character from another within the work of any author. (Individual style is not always equivalent to 'personal' style, since some individual styles may be characterized by impersonality; one then has a sense of style by contrast with some assumed norm of humane warmth, conventional idiom or whatever). Both I and II may be further subdivided into (a) the *essential*, and (b) the *performatory*; (a) being what is given by the integrity of the language and therefore what should be common to all good readers, writers and speakers, and (b) being what the flexibility of the language allows in the way of rendering or interpretation.

Clearly situational style (I) is by definition a more or less general thing, whose recognition therefore requires wide reading rather than close analysis. So the style most studied in literary stylistics will be individual style (II), and within that (a), the essential, will be of more concern than (b), the performatory. And this in practice amounts to the study of Bateson's 'rhetoric' — though one needs to be ready to refer it to wider situations when necessary. Spencer and Gregory sum up the critic's general activity and cogently separate it from the specialized activity of stylistics, as follows:

> The critic's final statement is the result of continually glancing back at his response, as it is checked against the text, with a concentration now

upon one aspect, now upon another; upon its plot, its character presentation its subject matter, its language, and upon the interrelation of some or all of these. This is done in terms of the critic's general experience of literature, life and language, and thus the text is never examined in complete isolation. So too, as the articulation of the critical statement proceeds, the response is constantly open to modification and development, and we are probably never presented with a statement which is simply derived from the immediate response . . . The fundamental difficulty at this point is that different aspects of a work of literature are never completely separable, for it is by means of language that they are all realised and through language that they all impinge upon the critic's sensibility . . . This does not, however, mean it is the language we are primarily concentrating on when we are examining these other aspects of the literary experience. Rather, we are dealing with aspectual abstractions . . .

When the language of a text is examined, not as a source of information about plot or character or thought, but as the major focus of attention in the dialectical process—that is, when the response is primarily to the use of language itself—the critic may be said to be examining the style of the text.

('An Approach to the Study of Style',
Linguistics and Style ed. J. Spencer, London 1964, pp. 62/3)

All these statements make good sense, but it is apparent that no sharp definition of literary stylistics emerges from them. What does emerge, however, is an area of common ground, shading away at the edges. Since wider matters often affect narrower ones situational style will not often be irrelevant, but individual style will be the primary concern of a literary stylistics. A similar relation will hold between structure and texture. What is being said, also, is far from irrelevant—for the quality of the saying very much depends on its aptness[1]—but the way of saying it is the central concern. And that itself will not be a study of the language *per se*, but a study of its

---

[1] A common confusion should perhaps be cleared up here. There *is* such a thing as 'good style' *per se*—some writers are clumsy and even ungrammatical. How can this be reconciled with the obvious fact that since some styles will be right for one sort of work, and wrong for another, there can be no such thing as *a* 'good style'? The apparent dilemma derives from an ambiguity in the word 'good': in the first case we mean 'displaying competence in the handling of language' (a skill that could be inappropriate for some purposes, and not *specifically* apt for many); in the second case, we mean 'suitable for'.

properly derived effects, of the necessary rhetoric entailed by the special relationship Bateson speaks of, between author and audience.

II. Rhetoric 'in its most general sense' is a very subtle and varied business. Wellek and Warren summarize Wilhelm Schneider's scheme in *Ausdruckswerte der deutschen Sprache* (1931):

> According to the relations of words to the object, styles are divisible into conceptual and sensuous, succinct and longwinded, or minimising and exaggerating, decisive and vague, quiet and excited, low and high, simple and decorated; according to the relations among words, into tense and lax, plastic and musical, smooth and rough, colourless and colourful; according to the relation of words to the total system of the language, into spoken and written, *cliché* and individual; and according to the relation of words to the author, into objective and subjective.
>
> (*Theory of Literature*, New York, 1949)

A sensible terminology, for general descriptive purposes. For closer description, we may well prefer I. A. Richards's 'parts of speech', and also find them to be more useful than those used by either old- or new-fangled grammarians; they may be summed up as follows (the first table being derived from *How to Read a Page*, London, 1943, the second from *Speculative Instruments*, London, 1955):

Divisions of Language
1a Words for simple sense-qualities (white, soft, hot)
1b Words for concept-qualities (beautiful, true, good)
2a Words for common objects (table, stone, cloud)
2b Words for concept 'objects' — problem nouns — (relation, quality, energy)
3a Words for acts and their metaphysical extension (shake — literally or in argument, throw — a ball, a fit, or light from a lamp)
3b Words for concept 'acts' — problem verbs — (involve, suppose, know)
4 Logical-linguistic links (in, on, at, you, I, or, now, that, too, but, only, etc.)
5 General verb operators (have, be, do, get, give, make, seem, see, put, etc.)

Activities of Utterances
1 Indicating (points to, selects)
2 Characterising (says something about)

3 Vivifying (wakes)
4 Valuing (cares about)
5 Influencing (would change or keep the same)
6 Controlling (manages, directs)
7 Purposing (seeks, pursues, tries, endeavours to be or do)
8 Venting (releases tension, signalises emotion)

And still more varied lists could be — have been — made. Yet the real subtlety and variety of stylistic rhetoric is likely to slip through the meshes of such nets of classification. It might almost be said that they are more useful for making one aware of the range of language than for actually dealing with examples of it. Richards's list of Activities, is particularly important in this respect, for it indicates that a writer's rhetoric may be intended to hold the reader's attention for many reasons other than entertainment or preaching. It also indicates that while the chief concern of stylistics is with how something is said (by implicit comparison with how it might have been) it certainly cannot be its only concern, for if at one end of the range there is expressive literature that could in principle be expressed otherwise (though not without some alteration of effect), at the other end there is a peculiar kind of argumentative literature that relies more on tricky qualities of language than on logic, and could not be plausibly expressed at all without them, so that what is said is of primary interest. Both kinds may be so subtle that the best reader, unguarded, could be misled. Here is Dr. Johnson, in his Life of Pope, arguing against the idea of sound-effects in verse.

> . . . it may be suspected that even in such resemblances the mind often governs the ear, and the sounds are estimated by their meanings. One of the most successful attempts has been to describe the labour of Sisyphus:
>
>> With many a weary step, and many a groan,
>> Up the high hill he heaves a huge round stone;
>> The huge round stone, resulting with a bound,
>> Thunders impetuous down, and smoaks along the ground.
>
> Who does not perceive the stone to move slowly upward, and roll violently back? But set the same numbers to another sense:
>
>> While many a merry tale, and many a song,
>> Cheer'd the rough road, we wish'd the rough road long.

> The rough road then, returning in a round,
> Mock'd our impatient steps, for all was fairy ground.

We have now surely lost much of the delay, and much of the rapidity.

The point seems to have been conclusively established. In fact, though, what Johnson has unwittingly established is the extra-metrical subtlety of sound-effects.

Let us grant that literature, unlike music, cannot make much of sound apart from sense; given the sense, however, a good writer can make it easy for a good reader to reinforce it sonically. The effects may be slight in themselves but, lifted on the shoulders of meaning, they become a noticeable part of the total effect. Johnson's metre is the same as Pope's; his rhythm is not.

The long vowel and lack of alliteration in 'many a weary' makes easy the slow reading demanded by the sense. 'Many a merry' can be rattled off, with equal propriety. Similarly with the '*st*' and the plosive, 'p', of 'step' as against the plain 't' and the labial, 'l', of Johnson's 'tale'. Again, the extreme degree of alliteration and the fact that 'h' is the sound of panting, taken together with the different sense, makes a genuine difference between 'Up the *h*igh *h*ill *h*e *h*eaves a *h*uge round stone' and 'Cheer'd the rough road, we wish'd the rough road long'.

Johnson continues:

But to show how little the greatest master of numbers can fix the principles of representative harmony, it will be sufficient to remark that the poet, who tells us that

> When Ajax strives — the words move slow
> Not so when swift Camilla scours the plain,
> Flies o'er th' unbending corn, and skims along the main;

When he had enjoyed for about thirty years the praise of Camilla's lightness of foot, tried another experiment upon sound and time, and produced this memorable triplet:

> Waller was smooth; but Dryden taught to join
> The varying verse, the full resounding line,
> The long majestic march, the energy divine.

Here are the swiftness of the rapid race, and the march of slow-paced majesty, exhibited by the same poet in the same sequence of syllables, except that the exact prosodist will find the line of swiftness by one time longer than that of tardiness.

Correct. The exact prosodist will count 'O'er' as two syllables and find that Camilla's line has thirteen syllables to the twelve of Dryden's majestic march. But Johnson's irony is misplaced – the result not only of too quantative a view of the relationship of sound and sense but also of too crude a view of quantity. For surely (among other reasons) it is precisely *because* Camilla's line is *longer* that it does move fast. The reader has to hurry a bit in order to make the rhymes chime, and somewhere along the line (probably at 'o'er') he has to get two short syllables into the time of one to keep the already established metre.

F. L. Lucas, in his justly-praised *Style* (London 1955) also unwittingly demonstrates the need for extreme care in operating any mechanical or quantitative procedure:

Nothing indeed can surpass the *Job* of our own Authorized Version:

> Why died I not from the womb? why did I not
> give up the ghost when I came out of the belly?
> Why did the knees prevent me? or why the breasts
> that I should suck?
> For now I should have lain still and been quiet, I
> should have slept: then had I been at rest,
> With the Kings and counsellors of the earth,
> which built desolate places for themselves;
> Or with princes that had gold, who filled their
> houses with silver.

But this remains far less concise than the Latin:

> Quare non in vulva mortuus sum, egressus
> ex utero non statim perii?
> Quare exceptus genibus? cur lactatus uberibus?
> Nunc enim dormiens silerem, et somno meo
> requiescerem:
> Cum regibus et consulibus terrae, qui
> aedificant sibi solitudines:
> Aut cum principibus, qui possident aurum
> et replent domos suas argento

Forty-six words against eighty-one! No wonder Dr. Johnson would not hear of epitaphs in English.

(p. 77 Pan edition, 1964)

But count what really matters, the number of syllables, and the result comes out as 103 against 93, in favour of English, as so many of the eighty-one words are short ones!

Such examples, different though they are, clearly concern the *how* more than the *what*, and are open to all the normal methods of critical inspection, including the rather neglected grammatical-linguistic one![1]

Some writings—writings that purport to *mean* more than to *be*, to use the modern critical *cliché*—seem to need the methods of philosophical-linguistics, and these surely should come within the purview of stylistics since the argument may well be a *disguised* form of rhetoric (consciously or unconsciously masquerading as logic). Take the following from a copy of the Salvation Army's *War Cry*:

> Even though we have tremendous respect for the animal world, we resent being treated as animals by others. We may not be fully consistent here, in that we may at times treat ourselves as animals, thinking solely in terms of physical needs and satisfactions.

When we speak of prisoners or victims being treated as animals (by others) we mean that they are being *ill*-treated. When this writer speaks of us treating ourselves as animals he means we are treating ourselves *well*. We are therefore perfectly consistent in resenting the one and doing the other. This could not have even appeared to be a good case without the rhetorical exploitation of ambiguity in 'treating as animals'—an exploitation made possible by the fact that both meanings are in fact related to ideas of 'physical needs and satisfactions' (though contrary ideas).

Again, here is Judith Cameron writing on racialism in the *Dudley Express*, a newsletter of the local Conservative association:

> Now let's get this clear. I have not the slightest objection to any colour of skin: I hope I am wise enough to know that the colour of a man's skin is no indication of his character. If that were so, Harold Wilson's skin would surely be as black as a dark night in the coal cellar. (Quoted *Guardian*, 4 May 1968)

[1] See Chaps 14 and 16 for a partial attempt to rectify the balance.

Not precisely a logical-linguistic error, this, but something akin to one: an internal inconsistency of part and whole. (To use the terms given in Chap. 8, the rational *purport* is betrayed by the tonal *implication* of the last sentence.) To end with any 'colour' simile (even 'white as a swan in a snowstorm') would be inconsistent with the preceding statement of utter neutrality. To choose the simile she does, in this particular context, effectively demolishes all belief in the statement (though it may also have demolished Mr. Wilson for her readers, and thus have seemed, in one way, a worthwhile rhetorical extravagance).

The justification for dealing with the intricacies of so intensive a discipline as stylistics seem to be twofold: firstly, to sensitize and alert readers to qualities in a work that might otherwise be imperceptible, that is, to train sensibility; secondly, to warn and safeguard them against the snares of pseudo-reasoning, that is, to train good sense. In short, the discipline can usefully help to *improve perception* and *prevent deception*; and clearly literary-linguistic methods (in addition to the normal critical ones) will tend to be more appropriate for the first task, philosophical-linguistic methods for the second.

Just as various descriptive classifications may be helpful in starting one looking, so various rules, or rather *tips* may be advanced as an aid to dealing with what is found. On the literary-linguistic side, for instance, one may 'improve literary perception and the techniques of describing what is perceived' by distinguishing evaluators and sensibles—the two commonly interinanimating each other in metaphors and similes, where evaluative implication concentrates attention on certain aspects of the concrete vehicle, while the concrete element adds power to the evaluation; but the two may contrast to make an esthetically complex antithesis.[1] It is also useful to pay close attention to patterns of sense, sound, suggestion and grammar (function)[2]—bearing in mind that sound effects may march alongside or across the line of sense, or may be an extra sense. This last can be illustrated by the final line of the first stanza of Philip Larkin's 'First Sight':

---

[1] For a fairly elaborate example v. Rodway 'By Algebra to Augustanism', *Essays on Style and Language,* ed. R. Fowler, London 1966; pp. 57–59.

[2] For examples of syntactical criticism v Nowottny *The Language Poets Use*, London, 1962.

Lambs that learn to walk in snow
When their bleating clouds the air
Meet a vast unwelcome, know
Nothing but a sunless glare.
Newly stumbling to and fro
All they find outside the fold,
Is a wretched width of cold.

Semantically we're simply told what they find, *sonically*, however, —
through the struggle to say 'wretched width' — we're told how it
hampers them; they stumble not only because they are new-born
but (so the sound implies) because their movement is clogged by
fallen snow. Again, one might look out for tensions resulting from
similar forms bearing different meanings (or vice versa). Whether
such tensions — abounding in Eliot's *Four Quartets* — have any
esthetic, or other value will depend on the nature of the whole.
Fourthly, there's the very general class of impressionistic devices,
which range from, say, Auden's use of logicless grammar (v. Chap.
16). or Whitman's use of incomplete participial sentences (noted
by Spitzer) to give the effect of movement snapshot on the wing, to
the use of *absent* rhyme — of which Wordsworth's 'Immortality
Ode' provides a pleasing example:

3.

Now while the birds thus sing a joyous song,
   And while the young lambs bound
     As to the tabor's sound,
To me alone there came a thought of grief:
A timely utterance gave that thought relief,
     And I again am strong:
The cataracts blow their trumpets from the steep;
No more shall grief of mine the season wrong;
I hear the Echoes through the mountains throng,
The Winds come to me from the fields of sleep,
   And all the earth is gay;
    Land and Sea
Give themselves up to jollity,
    And with the heart of May
Doth every beast keep holiday; —

Then child of joy,
Shout round me, let me hear thy shouts, thou happy
Shepherd-boy!

Given the context of 'young lambs', 'happy Shepherd-boy', and
'fields', and still recalling 'throng', a word associated with driven
flocks, can we avoid a subconscious idea of 'fields of *sheep*', the
obvious word to use? By *not* using it Wordsworth loses nothing (we
have the impression of it) and he gains surprise, a sense of mystery,
and an invisible physical support for the metaphysical fields he
actually refers to. Finally—for here we approach logical-linguistics—
we should be ready to respond to various kinds of ambiguity. Empson has analysed many semantic examples, Spitzer some interesting
syntactical ones (such as the many meanings of the word 'of'),
J. L. Austin some which aren't exactly either, in a book that demonstrates how often valid interpretation is impossible without some
knowledge of the situation: 'it is not enough simply to examine the
words themselves; just what is meant and what can be inferred (if
anything) can be decided only by examining the full circumstances in
which the words are used' (*Sense and Sensibilia*, Oxford, 1962, p. 40).

On the philosophical-linguistic side the main things to watch for
seem to be:

Slidings from one meaning to another in the course of argument
(as in the *War Cry* example);

hypostatization ('The Bishop of Exeter, Dr. R. Mortimer, said in
a sermon at Oxford yesterday that fornication was always wrong
because the act of sexual intercourse is intended by nature [Who's
'Nature' to have intentions?] to occur only within the framework of
the lifelong association of marriage' *Guardian*, 21.8.63);

plain logical error—of which Dr. Mortimer's conclusion provides
an example (marriage may imply lifelong association but not all life
long associations need be within the marriage bond);

argument by (possibly misleading) analogy;

the use of imaginary essences ('the Good', 'Truth') as if they
were things;

the failure to distinguish descriptive definitions (*Aristotle* on
the unities) from prescriptive (the *Neo-Aristotelians* on them);

suppressed imagery, latent puns, or subtly pejorative context
which put the reader in a certain mood *before* giving any argument
or reason for it:

The Socialist Party is getting more and more lopsided, with an ominous slant to the left. Like all unbalanced creatures it is apt to be confused and incoherent (*Daily Mail*, 23.6.69)

Here we have the suppressed image of a mumbling, shambling lunatic, reinforced by a pun in 'unbalanced' (lopsided, crazy) and a sliding from physical leaning (slant) to the left and the quite unrelated group of political ideas in 'Left', and of course there's the pejorative context (lopsided, ominous, confused, incoherent. *Do* these apply to a Socialist party that leans to the left? Which way should it lean in order not to be confused and incoherent?)

Then there's the matter of using words without an antithesis, covering everything, and therefore being only apparently meaningful; the misuse of the verb 'to be' (almost any description would answer the question, 'what is X?'; so one aspect can be made to seem *the* reality. Tobacco *is* 'the leaf of a plant', 'an expensive import', 'the chief constituent of cigarettes', 'a carcinogen' and so on). But perhaps the tip most useful to the literary critic would be to watch for the use of blanket words or phrases. In a very interesting article 'Can Buddhists "Read" Dante?' (*Enquiry*, March, 1958), F. P. Gibbon showed that the apparently innocent phrase 'fully appreciates' can mean 'is able to give an account of'

(a) the persuasive techniques of the piece
(b) the attitudes revealed
(c) the possible motives of the writer (propaganda, say, or the desire to share an experience)
(d) the possible effects on groups of readers (specifically defined with regard to *their* intelligence, attitudes, period, beliefs, environment)
(e) the reader-critic's own emotional response, with suggested reasons.

We might add that it can also mean 'evaluates by'

(f) identifying emotionally with the writer
(g) understanding his argument
(h) sympathising with his viewpoint
(i) admiring his skill

The phrase, that is to say, can invite to *descriptive* or *evaluative* criticism of several sorts.

Lists of tips for both the sensitizing and the safeguarding activities of a literary stylistics could be extended indefinitely, but Wellek's remark that 'no single stylistic device ... is invariable; it is always changed by its particular context' is a sufficient reminder of their limited usefulness: they are signposts, not destinations. In the end, one does not see and feel by rule but by the exercise of sense and sensibility – but these can be improved with practice, and some general principles do help one to get started.

It is difficult to see, for instance, what possible rule could enable one to respond to the vastly different sound effects in these two passages from Joyce's *Ulysses* – though the general tip to expect them to be linguistically subtle and subordinate to the sense might help to ensure that they were not overlooked, even when encountered in the course of a long novel rather than in isolation:

> Kind air defined the coigns of houses in Kildare Street.
> No birds. Frail from the housetops two plumes of smoke ascended,
> pluming, and in a flaw of softness softly were blown.

> By Bachelor's walk, jogjaunty, jingled Blazes Boylan, bachelor,
> in sun, in heat, mare's glossy rump atrot, with flick of whip,
> on bounding tyres: sprawled, warmseated, Boylan impatience,
> ardentbold.

How beautifully, in the first passage, the disturbance of normal word-order promotes tonal effects; so that the delicate *quality* of the scene is felt at the same time as the descriptive facts are apprehended. Perhaps one notices first the zephyr-fricatives in 'frail', 'from', 'flaw', 'of', 'softness' and 'softly', then the long open vowels before and after the cotton-wool cluster of 'flaw of softness softly'; next the esthetic effect deriving from a near-pattern of near-assonance: 'kind air' – 'Kildare', 'kind' – 'defined', 'air . . . oi . . . ou . . . –are', 'hou . . . two plume . . . smo . . . plume . . . flaw . . . blown.' And finally, perhaps, the emphasized stillness from the rhythmic pause made by the two-word sentence 'No birds'. There are, obviously, other effects than those of sound – both word-order and the ordering of objects, for instance, carry the inner gaze upward and upward from street level to coigns to chimneys and on into the open sky. This is a matter of *structure* (on a small-scale), something rather neglected, and not our present concern.

In the second passage we are immediately struck by the

conglomerate syntax. Incompatible clauses become appositional phrases by the omission of verbs and connectives ('. . . rump *was* atrot, *as . . . he passed* on bounding tyres'). The main effect is one of fusion: all is part of one instant revealing verbal snapshot. A minor effect is to make from parallelism *additions* of sense not merely repetitions: 'in sun' tells us of weather (and perhaps suggests good luck and happiness, in contrast to poor Poldy), 'in heat' adds to this an idea of sexual excitement — partly from context (Boylan being on his way to the bed of Molly Bloom) partly from the similar ambiguity in 'warmseated'. Given this, and the fact of appositional parallelism, it is difficult not to associate the 'mare's glossy rump, atrot' with Molly Bloom's. Sound, syntax and sense are thus far inextricable; 'jogjaunty jingled', the rapid 'b' alliteration, and the general clipped rhythm — to say nothing of the short 'i's' in 'with flick of whip' — are all clearly very appropriate sound effects.

Such analyses, incomplete though they are, may go some way towards improving 'literary perception'. Do they help at all, though, to improve discrimination 'between variant readings and misreading'? In principle, yes; for the method: general classification, application of 'tips', and finally specific analysis mindful of context and situation, must be the same for any fragment that *can* usefully be extracted, and also for a whole work.[1] In practice, the latter case takes up a good deal more space, and it is unfortunately only in the latter case that the dialectical movement from parts to whole, in the process of analysis, can build a sufficient body of circumstantial evidence to demonstrate a very high probability of rightness of reading. But this present chapter, intended to be theoretical, has already trespassed beyond its brief. However, in Chap. 15 two short complete works are analysed, perhaps sufficiently to carry conviction of rightness of reading, and certainly in a way intended to exemplify Wellek's dictum that 'A literary stylistics will concentrate on the aesthetic purpose of every linguistic device, the way it serves a totality.'

---

[1] If the work is a long one, of course — narrative poem, epic or novel — such stylistic analysis will in practice not only be complementary to broader critical methods (as it is for most short works) but subordinate to them.

5

Crosscurrents in
Contemporary English Criticism

So much criticism has been produced in the last forty years that the presence of numerous crosscurrents need occasion no surprise. What does require explanation, perhaps, is the fact that they have all been contained within one great tide, the movement that has come to be known as the New Criticism. Walter J. Ong has recently defined it as:

> The criticism you get when an academic community supplies an audience for vernacular literature large enough and mature enough and intellectually sophisticated enough to make possible intelligent, and often subtly contrived, talk about literary performance. The New Criticism is, in other words, simply a type of criticism which matures with the emergence of the vernacular full blown on the academic scene . . . Even if you disagree with the New Criticism there is no point in looking back to a conjectural Old Criticism which previously performed the offices of the New. There was no Old Criticism. There were no academic offices for it to perform.[1]

This account allows for the variety within the movement and explains its predominance in the last half-century – the first period in which the study of vernacular literature has been regarded as culturally more central than the study of classical texts, the first period, too, of relatively widespread university education.

That the writer is American in no way diminishes the relevance of his account to the English scene; for, apart from the proportionate difference in quantity, the New Criticism of the two countries has been remarkably similar. Not unnaturally, since all varieties have stemmed from work done in the decade after World War I by T. S. Eliot, an anglicized American, and I. A. Richards, an americanized Englishman. Nevertheless, a closer look at the English scene reveals sharper significances than Ong's larger perspective could.

[1] *The Barbarian Within* (New York, 1962), p. 205.

Two main points stand out: that the modern movement in criticism started in England and that it seems to have been more passionate there than in the States. The earlier start is probably due partly to a greater accessibility to French symbolist ideas (though they had to be imported by expatriate Americans) and partly to a greater involvement in the Great War, which brought about a violent reaction to traditionalism. The matter of passionate commitment seems to have been due partly to the deeprootedness of the tradition reacted against and partly to the interconnectedness of the comparatively small literary world in England. Both facts contributed to the fiercer nature of modern English criticism; the desire for change was greater and harder to achieve, and hostilities in a small world could be focused on personalities. (The divisions in the next section are categories rather than groups; the members were relatively few and might appear in more than one category—and when they did, they often took with them the hostility they had attracted in their first rôle.)

The state of criticism belonging to the old order is indicated by the fact that the Georgians were considered dangerous poetic revolutionaries determined to 'surprise and even to puzzle at all costs', forgetting (as Arthur Waugh put it, in the *Quarterly Review* of October 1914) that 'the first essence of poetry is beauty'. This is the period of graceful impressionism, of new Chairs of English occupied by classical products of an old tradition, trained more in editing than in criticism and not at all in criticism of a living language. The feeling it engendered in the new generation of academics is well captured in Q.D. Leavis's retrospective essay *The Discipline of Letters, A Sociological Note*, which appeared in *Scrutiny* and was provoked by the publication of *The Letters* of G. S. Gordon, who followed Raleigh, the first Merton Professor of English at Oxford.

> The discipline of letters, he proclaims, is . . . twofold. On the one hand, linguistic-philological studies as an end in themselves. On the other, scholarship—the ideal of perfect editing, that is, a frivolous one which is hostile to any real standards in literature, since any text long enough dead is equally meet to be edited; the credit consists in producing the perfect index, etc., to a piece of writing not necessarily worth publishing in the first place. . . . It would be hard to justify a claim that a university school of English, as described by Raleigh, Gordon, Mr. C. S. Lewis, is of value to the community or the individual. . . .[1]

---

[1] *Scrutiny*, XII (Winter 1943), pp. 13, 23.

We noticed, in summarizing this later inaugural lecture, how his position had changed from the complacent insolence of *The Discipline of Letters*. Now he would like to be on both sides at once, and though he cannot conceal his hatred of all that Eliot stood for he makes a great show of openmindedness. . . . This was a cunning move, obviously more serviceable than the last-ditch foaming-at-the-mouth attitude. It kept pace with the quiet ratting that was occurring at this time on the Hopkins controversy. . . .[1]

Not for her the snide urbanities of *The Sacred Wood*, whose author was outside the academic ring! But the criterion adopted by Eliot — also, of course, the editor of the significantly named *Criterion* — was undoubtedly that summed up by Mrs. Leavis:

. . . . for the literary critic and the educationalist will insist that the question they must put to academic authority remains what it always was: are we or are we not to be allowed to apply real standards, to work with real values instead of currency-counters?[2]

The effect of the new criticism on the first recipients — at any rate, of its theoretical side — is recalled by Christopher Isherwood, with a touch of irony for his youthful enthusiasm:

For both of us, the great event that term was the series of lectures on modern poetry given by Mr. I. A. Richards. . . . The substance of these lectures has since become famous through Mr. Richards's books. But, to us, he was infinitely more than a brilliant new literary critic: he was our guide, our evangelist, who revealed to us, in a succession of astounding lightning flashes the entire expanse of the Modern World. Up to this moment, we had been a pair of romantic conservatives, devil-worshippers, votaries of 'Beauty' and 'Vice', Manicheans, would-be Kropotkin anarchists, who refused to read T. S. Eliot (because of his vogue with the Poshocracy) or the newspapers or Freud. Now, in a moment, all was changed. Poets, ordered Mr. Richards, were to reflect aspects of the World-Picture. Poetry wasn't a holy flame, a firebird from the moon; it was a group of interrelated stimuli acting upon the ocular nerves, the semi-circular canals, the brain, the solar plexus, the digestive and sexual organs. It did you medically demonstrable good, like a dose of strychnine or salts. We became

[1] *Ibid.*, p. 22.
[2] *Ibid.*, p. 20.

behaviourists, materialists, atheists. In our conversation, we substituted the word 'emotive' for the world beautiful; we learnt to condemn inferior work as a 'failure in communication' or, more crushing still, as 'a private poem'. We talked excitedly about 'the phantom aesthetic state'.[1]

Some years later (1929) Richards's *Practical Criticism* revolutionized English studies at Cambridge and has since affected such studies at all the newer, and some of the older, provincial universities.

Certainly, then, it is true of academic England that 'there was no old *criticism*'. It is also true, in Ong's general sense, that 'New Criticism' is now predominant. But Oxford, traditionally the home of lost causes, has never radically altered its hostility to real criticism, despite the efforts of the less reactionary dons; and London, together with some of the older provincial universities, still inclines to the old combination of deep, dull, objective philology and superficial, bright, subjective criticism. Meanwhile, the New Criticism, by a natural evolutionary process, has gradually lost its attack and become self-critical, or perhaps it is more nearly true to say, it has turned its passion to internecine warfare and thus given the coelacanths an outside chance of making a comeback. Certainly there are signs of it in *The Literary Critics* (Baltimore, 1962), by George Watson, an Oxford product now established as a fifth-columnist in Cambridge. The book could hardly have come about without the preliminary theorizing of New Critics on criticism, yet in its misrepresentation and misunderstanding of modern criticism it seems to bring the wheel full circle, back to Gordonism.

The diverse currents within the modern movement in criticism, then, are likely to prove as important, for good or ill, as its tidal unity has proved. For good, if they lead to greater wariness about the many critical fallacies theory has pointed out, to increased care for proper critical procedures, and to a clearer awareness of the difference between strictly literary criticism and metacriticism. For ill, if they cause criticism to be discredited and thus lead to a revival of the old academicism.

Both the divisions and the unity, obviously, were inherent in the movement from the start. It began with *The Sacred Wood* (1920), a work of descriptive criticism, using illustrative quotation, and yet, for all its descriptiveness, inventing a new past; with I. A. Richards's

[1] *Lions and Shadows* (London, 1953), pp. 121–122.

lectures, later published as *The Principles of Literary Criticism* (1924), a work of general theory; and with his Cambridge experiments, published as *Practical Criticism* (1929), a work of pedagogical criticism. The differences are obvious; nor are they diminished if we add *The Calendar of Letters* (1925–27, forerunner of *Scrutiny*, 1932–53) and Pound's *Make It New* (1934), a collection of essays written between 1912 and 1931, whose title and tone are perhaps more significant than the content. What they have in common, less obviously, is a certain detachment and a new determination to stick close to the facts and effects of the text. The word 'determination' suggests the seriousness of the attempt, the abandonment of elegant connoisseurship; the word 'facts'—difficult as it is in a context of literary fictions—the desire to make criticism as objective as possible, to abandon subjective impressionism.

Concentration on the text, however, led to the discovery of the many-sidedness of a literary work—a rather paradoxical thing to 'have in common', since naturally some critics concentrated on exploring one side, some another, Concentration on the reader's response, of course (in the *Principles*), led back to concentration on the text, and this in turn led to the desire for some sort of 'objectivity', since *Practical Criticism* made evident the need to establish standards of correctness of response, as well as pedagogical methods of encouraging right readings, as against misreadings. Demonstrating the rightness of right readings was evidently less easy than spotting the wrongness of wrong ones.

Objectivity was required by other critics for several other reasons: to show that criticism could be as much of a 'discipline' as philology or the Anglo-Saxon grind; to show that one really had abandoned subjective impressionism; to show that in education one opinion was not as good as another and taste not a matter of knowing the chic things to say; and finally to show the comparability of arts subjects with the sciences by providing a neutral basis for progress. The chief difficulty of attaining the desired objectivity lay in the immaterial nature of literary works. As we have said, their material existence is insignificant—mere paper and squiggles; their significant existence is immaterial. In short, they do not really exist; they take place (when read). Equally obviously, in the light of *Practical Criticism*, what does take place in reading is often not what ought to take place. And this raises the key questions: What are the limits of variation in a 'correct' reading? And how can criticism help to steer readers, reasonably, into those confines and away from eccentric, private readings?

Both questions involve enormous difficulties and complexities which are still engaging the attention of theorists on both sides of the Atlantic, but now seem on the verge of solution. Inevitably, however, the easier ways were tried first—looking before and after, rather than at the work itself. After all, the work's effects on social groups or even on individuals are objectively there to be examined; so are its causes in the writer's period or his life, at least if you can get enough documentary evidence together. Moreover this sort of work seems scientific. Indeed it often is scientific, and that is why, as theorists in rival categories were to point out, it is not strictly literary criticism but metacriticism: a specialized form of sociology or psychology, history, biography or anthropology. And the real difficulties of assessing what interpretations the nature of the language properly allows and what the right response is, have been by-passed. At any rate, almost by-passed, for in fact biography, history, philology, anthropology, sociology, psychology, and all the apparatus of scholarship may give the critic valuable tips, by indicating what to expect and what not to. It is *relying* on any of these extraliterary disciplines to answer the key literary questions that leads to the numerous misconceptions we group as subdivisions under the inclusive heading of the Intentionalist and Affective Fallacies (see Appendix A).

In England, the partially abortive attempts of New Critics to put criticism both on the map and on a sounder footing can be categorized, for diagnostic convenience, as follows: moralistic criticism, psychological criticism, sociological criticism, symbolic criticism, and, most recently and most hopefully, stylistic criticism. These are by no means exclusive categories: moral criticism shades off into the sociological on the one hand, through its concern with environmental health, and into the psychological on the other, through its concern with individual quality. Again, D. W. Harding, as a psychologist and a *Scrutineer*, features in two categories. The Empson of *Seven Types of Ambiguity* (1930) and *The Structure of Complex Words* (1951) is a stylistic critic; the Empson of *Some Versions of Pastoral* (1935), a psychological one; and the Empson of *Milton's God* (1962), a moralist. Furthermore, Orwell, as an anti-Marxist, and Caudwell, as a Marxist, naturally both come within the sociological category. But, bearing such *caveats* in mind, we can briefly note under these headings the virtues and limitations of what has been on the whole, for all its rancours and theoretical failings, by far the most vital English criticism of this or any other century.

Moralistic criticism: René Wellek has recently, and rightly, said:

> The impulses from Eliot and Richards were most effectively combined, in England at least, in the work of Frank Raymond Leavis (born 1895) and his disciples grouped around the magazine *Scrutiny* (1932–53). Leavis is a man of strong convictions and harsh polemical manners. He has in recent years sharply underlined his disagreements with the later development of Eliot [*towards the subordination of literary to theological criticism*] and Richards [*towards purely linguistic and pedagogic studies*]. . . . Leavis's concern with the text is often deceptive: he quickly leaves the verbal surface in order to define the peculiar emotions which an author conveys. He becomes a social and moral critic who, however, insists on the continuity of language and ethics, on the morality of form.[1]

The effectiveness of the combination of influences referred to is evidenced by the fact that moralistic critics far outnumber those of any other category, and Leavis has been easily the most influential critic of the century in England. What Wellek might perhaps have stressed more is the fact that the *Scrutineers* have generally been sufficiently scrupulous in their close attention to the text to avoid the charge of naïve moralism (i.e., judging crudely in terms of paraphrasible content): they have focused rather on the quality of life revealed by style. This is, however, a difficult poise to sustain, particularly under attack. One wonders if, for instance, it has been sustained in Leavis's John-the-Baptist championship of Lawrence or even in L. C. Knights's recent work on Shakespeare. Furthermore, such an approach, even at its best, must lead to a literary undervaluing of certain works. True, morality is being carefully associated with literary merit. But what about the purely literary merits of works not, in the critic's view, tending towards even so broad a concept of morality as the 'life-enhancing'? Frivolous works, say, or pornographic ones? Yet such works may be dull, mediocre, or brilliant creations of their kind; and not to consider this is to be narrow in one's literary-critical outlook. At some point, in short, even the most subtle and enlighted moralism confuses essential

[1] *Concepts of Criticism* (New Haven, 1963), p. 358.

differences, a confusion which has been increased in this case by Leavis's refusal to interest himself in theory and the consequent readiness of *Scrutineers* not only to move from description to evaluation a little too quickly, but also to be tempted into allowing unconscious, preliminary evaluations to affect the descriptions.

Psychological criticism: More obviously metacriticism—a form of psychology—than moralistic writing, this category of work nevertheless owes much to Richards's perfectly correct perception that a literary work exists significantly only as a response in the reader, though Graves's *Meaning of Dreams* (1924) and *Poetic Unreason* (1925) were first in the field. Richards's own development of his insight was immensely influential, but rather for its scientific tone, its astringency (poetry as mere pseudo-statement!) than for giving a working theory. The *Principles*, in fact, turned out not to be scientific (no one has measured an isolated esthetic impulse, let alone compared sets of them) and also not to be critical, since *anything* producing a harmonious balance of multiple impulses must count as good. But Richards also described the psychology of the artist and linked it with a theory of value—the artist being the man with a wider area of experience readily available—and this in turn was linked with a social ambition to improve society through literary culture, to train sensibilities so that more people would be more like artists, and fewer people stock-responsive to commercial and political bait. This aspect of Richards's work, of course, leads on to Leavis and the moralists in one direction; in another, though, it combined with the scientific tone to lead to a revival of Coleridge's interest in the psychology of the creative process. D. W. Harding, once a *Scrutineer* and now a Professor of Psychology, has recently published a most interesting collection of essays of this kind, under the title *Experience into Words.* It is significant, however, that the least literary-critical essays, those dealing psychologically with preverbal experience and feelings of 'social' kinship with dead authors, 'speaking' to us through their works, are the most completely satisfying. The others, inevitably, tend towards the intentionalist or affective fallacies when they are literary-critical, towards metacriticism when they are psychological. F. L. Lucas's *Literature and Psychology* (1951) covered more relationships—social, biographical, sexual, and so on—but rather surrounded literature than took its citadel. Empson, as always, was dazzlingly brilliant in the Freudian analyses of *Some Versions of Pastoral* (1935), but nevertheless was necessarily open to the objection that the literary quality of a work is irrelevant to its suitability for such analyses and is rarely illuminated by it.

Romantic criticism tends to be inspirational and intuitive, but in so far as it concerns itself with the discovery of Jungian oppositions and integrations or Adlerian desires, it is closely allied to psychological criticism and is therefore open to the same objections. Maud Bodkins's *Archetypal Patterns* (1934) was one of the most important examples; and it did undoubtedly help to explain how certain works move us, though they are not realistic or even obviously applicable to real life in any way. But the 'how' of such works must be very general and superficial, for *Macbeth* is as archetypal in comic strip as in blank verse; so the demonstration of archetypes has nothing to do with specifically literary quality.

G. Wilson Knight, Lord of the Symbol-hunters, has been less psychological than mystical in his romanticism, somewhat associating himself thereby with J. Middleton Murry, while Herbert Read links up rather with Miss Bodkin. Nevertheless, since Knight's symbols are always of an archetypal kind (Life and Death, Time and Eternity, Sex and Spirit, Light and Dark), his criticism ultimately runs into the same dead-end; and in fact he has, quite logically, claimed greatness for an amazing number of second-rate works, such as Byron's dramas and Eastern tales, on the ground that they reveal 'Eternity'. Other objections are that in his view translations must be equivalent to the originals; that no writer can protect himself, since anything, however naturalistically tested, that such a critic approves of can be made symbolical, given sufficient ingenuity; and that categories so general leave practically nothing a work is *not* about, and are thus uninformative. Admittedly, Wilson Knight's first book, *The Wheel of Fire* (1930), did give a new direction to Shakespeare studies, turning attention from 'character' and 'plot' to 'theme' and 'image-pattern', but the increasingly erratic quality of his later books clearly reveals the uncontrolled element in his critical theory. Perhaps one should rather say 'interpretative' theory, as the introduction to *The Wheel of Fire* claims to be interpretative but not critical. Criticism, it allows to be equal with interpretation but different (at the same time always associating the word 'criticism' with pejoratives). However, this simply seems an excuse for doing criticism without the usual safeguards against eccentricity of interpretation.

Sociological criticism ranges from Empson's minute analyses of the implications of Gray's 'Elegy' (in *Some Versions of Pastoral*, called *English Pastoral Poetry* in the United States) to Christopher Caudwell's heady Marxist mixture of brilliance and nonsense, in the form of general ideas, in *Illusion and Reality* (1937), of which a non-Marxist socialist critic, Raymond Williams, has aptly written:

> Christopher Caudwell remains the best-known of the English Marxist critics, but his influence is curious. His theories and outlines have been widely learned, although in fact he has little to say, of actual literature, that is even interesting. It is not only that it is difficult to have confidence in the literary qualifications of anyone who can give his account of the development of medieval into Elizabethan drama, or who can make his paraphrase of the 'sleep' line from *Macbeth*, but that for the most part his discussion is not even specific enough to be wrong. On the other hand, he is immensely prolific of ideas, over an unusually wide field of interest.[1]

Caudwell and other Marxist critics, however, can be contrasted with Arnold Kettle, a communist whose training in the Literature-Life-and-Thought complex of the Cambridge English Tripos is more evident in his criticism than communism is. In this way there is a direct line from Leavis (an anti-communist) to the communist critics. However, communist criticism in England has never been important or influential. Much more vital are critics like Raymond Williams, Richard Hoggart (*Uses of Literacy*, 1957) and George Orwell, all of whom have used literature, with stimulating and valuable results, as a means to an end: the metacritical extension of our insights into social culture, particularly as it is affected by the mass-media. Like Leavis, but in a different direction, they pass rather rapidly from close attention to the text to a more general concern. In between, come former *Scrutineers*, like the L. C. Knights of *Drama and Society in the Age of Jonson* (1937) or *Poetry, Politics, and the English Tradition* (1954), or non-Leavisite products of Cambridge and those provincial universities that set literature firmly in its age and ethos, who differ from older historical critics only in their closer focus on the verbal surface of the text.

Stylistic criticism springs from the combination of this belief in the primary importance of the words on the page with a knowledge of the fallacies lurking in reliance on other approaches. The historicist, personalist, romantic, biographical, or intentionalist and

[1] *Culture and Society* (Baltimore, 1961), p. 269.

affective fallacies all somewhat discredit the non-stylistic modes of criticism, particularly in so far as any one is taken as a sole touchstone of merit. If one assumes the assessment of specifically literary facts and qualities to be the critic's chief job—while not denying his right (sometimes indeed, his duty) to push out into surrounding fields in which he is an amateur, providing he acknowledges what he is doing—then it seems to follow that close attention to language should be his first concern. From the beginning, of course, such attention had been given by Empson and Richards. But this was almost entirely a matter of the semantics of ambiguity and overtone. What is new is the development of adding to this semantic interest a concern with syntax, musical effects, and matters open to philosophical linguistic analysis.

Empson's brilliant *Structure of Complex Words* (1951), an analysis of the operation of key words in a larger structure, was first in the field. Donald Davie's *Articulate Energy* (1955) provided a theoretical argument for investigating the 'poetry' of syntax, and incidentally put a bomb under the established modernist dogma, first stated by Richards, that creative literature should *be* not *say*, which led to the cult of the image, the omission of grammatical filling, and the consequent typical obscurity of modernism. This point was reinforced by Graham Hough in *Images and Experience* (1960); and finally Mrs. Nowottny, in *The Language Poets Use* (1963), demonstrated the strictly literary illumination to be derived from a critical practice which took the linguistic facts, especially those of syntax, as its primary, but not exclusive concern.

Undoubtedly, this approach, too, has its dangers. Already a linguistic fallacy seems due for exposure: the belief that certain syntactical structures must entail parallels of sense or suggestion. They may, but since structures in English are finite (and in practice rather limited) while possibilities of meaning are infinite, it is obvious that such a method must be used carefully. There is, in short, no substitute for sense in criticism, no automatic method. Nevertheless, the sheer commonsense of the basic idea of this approach—that verbal artefacts are usually most profitably approached through their use of language first rather than through the mind or the society that produced them or through the minds and groups that they affect—seems sufficient to warrant the feeling that this is now the growing point of a maturing New Criticism.

6

Fictions and Fallacies

THE Tree of Fallacies (*Appendix A*)[1] acts as a reminder of what the body of this chapter amounts to when reduced to the bare bones of argument. Skeletal remains, perhaps, that might seem also to act as a *memento mori* for this book as a whole, since they give a logical spread over all the main kinds of criticism and show them all to be fallacious. Looming up, so to speak, might seem to be the grisly moral that Critical Theory is a suicidal murderer of Critical Practice. Not so. One moral only is properly deducible: the need to bear in mind the multivalence of magisterial views and the multifacetedness of masterpieces.

The point is, that there *are* standards and values, but all relative ones; and good critical practice is a juggler's art. To sharpen the point to the extent of paradox: adopt *any* one standard as your sole criterion of literary merit and you fall into a fallacy; commit all the fallacies and you near perfection of method. What is fallacious is the magisterial assumption of one proper mode of being for literary works or one proper way of assessing them, for all works are multi-faceted in principle (though in practice one facet may predominate), and all assumptions, however magisterially stated, are in principle multivalent (one always could assert against, say, the assumed standard of closeness-to-life that realism was bad for art, or was not central, or that what usually passed as such was not really realistic).

Now, we have earlier seen that extrinsic and intrinsic criticism (or metacriticism and criticism) are interconnected in various ways. They differ in principle but overlap in practice. This fact complicates applied criticism, but in order to get clear about the theory it should be set aside, though borne in mind. For in principle it is self-evident that *ex*trinsic criticism as a whole must be fallacious as a method of judging *literary* merit—that is, if we take it not in Hirsch's narrow sense but in Wellek's wider one as referring to movement outwards, the relating of the literary work to things beyond itself in order to understand *them*. By definition, metacriti-

[1] P. 95

cism cannot provide criteria for *in*trinsic assessments (in which, if a relationship is made with matters beyond the work itself, it is in order to understand *it*). Since there is no point in expatiating on the self-evident, we shall not be concerned with extrinsic or meta-criticism, save in passing; and it is therefore important to note that the two main branches of the Tree, the *External* and *Internal* are *not* equivalent to 'extrinsic' and 'intrinsic', despite the verbal simi-larity—a similarity that has been responsible for reams of critical misapprehension. Internal evidence may be used extrinsically (for example, to give inwardness to the author's biography) and external evidence may be used intrinsically (the author's biography giving a tip towards the elucidation of a crux in the work). Since intrinsic criticism is certainly not self-evidently fallacious as a whole, it is worth expatiating on the fact that every single kind of it—whether stemming from the internal *or* the external branch—does seem to be fallacious. We can, of course, account for this in a general way by pointing out that, if the facts of multifacetedness and multi-valence are accepted, what is fallacious is the assumption (often half-conscious, and muddling criticism and metacriticism together) of one standard as the sole standard. But so much of the history of criticism has been vitiated by such assumptions that more particular discussion seems warranted.

The External branch, as we see, divides logically into *Causal* (study, whether for purposes of extrinsic or intrinsic criticism, of what comes before the work) and *Consequential* (what comes after it, its effect on reader or society). Adherence to causal criticism, even if inescapable metacritical elements in it are consciously placed and controlled, may lead to the Intentional Fallacy and its variants; adherence to consequential criticism, to the Affective Fallacy and its variants.

Intentional Fallacy. In their seminal essay of this title in the *Sewanee Review*, 54 (1946), William K. Wimsatt, Jr and Monroe Beardsley wrote as follows:

> . . . this is a principle which goes deep into some differences in the history of critical attitudes. It is a principle which accepted or rejected points to the polar opposites of classical 'imitation' and romantic expression. It entails many specific truths about imagination, authen-ticity, biography, literary history and scholarship, and about some trends of contemporary poetry, especially its allusiveness. There is

hardly a problem of literary criticism in which the critic's approach will not be qualified by his view of 'intention'.

Some of these points are implicit in what has been said in earlier chapters. Whether they are true or not has been a matter of discussion for the past twenty years; but there is little use in rehearsing it here, since most of it comes from misapprehension of what the original essay in fact maintained. In particular, the authors omitted to use a separate term—such as our 'purport'—to distinguish the apparent intention found within the work itself from that imported from outside (by scholarly deduction or the author's own statement), though the distinction was in fact made in the essay. And, of course, only the second sort of intention was declared to be fallacious as a measuring-rod.

Why should that be so? At first sight intentionalism seems a good answer to the main critical questions: how to decide whether an interpretation is valid or not, central or eccentric, and then how to evaluate it. Find the author's intention, and surely you can go on both to interpret and evaluate the work objectively by the degree of his success in embodying that abstraction? Yet there are three reasons for rejecting this standard. Suppose, firstly, an author were to fully realize a silly and trivial intention. Are we to say such a work is better than one that has not quite succeeded in realizing a more difficult, profound and important intention (in the same kind)? Obviously there would be several ways in which the second was 'better' and only one in which the first would be. Secondly, what about the numerous cases in which the author has left no clue to his intention? Either we deduce it from within the work and are in fact operating intrinsically with the concept of 'purport' or, striving for the imagined objectivity of external evidence, we try to deduce it from the period background or from biographical evidence. But can we be sure the author was typical of his period? And might he not for once have written uncharacteristically? Thirdly, is it not possible that an author might do something other than he intended but, by some standards, better? It is true that most authors revise, and in doing so take pains to make the actual effect match the intended one. But writers of an inspirational tendency are apt to be chary of conscious revision; and they have on their side a good deal of psycho-analytic support for the idea that subconscious creation should take precedence. In cases where a subconscious intention is at odds with a conscious stated one, the final result is likely to be patchy, but who is to say that patchy brilliance is *indisputably* inferior to the flawless competence of a perfectly realized conscious intention?

This causal branch may be subdivided into the *Personal* and the *Historical*. The former is related to the critical notion that art is self-expression, the latter to the notion that it is a product of 'race, milieu and moment', to quote Taine. The former leads to the *Bio-graphical Fallacy* (looking to the life to find a measuring-rod for the work) and the *Romantic Fallacy* (using the work of art as a way into the life—not fallacious, of course, if undertaken as a conscious act of metacriticism, by a biographer). Both critical fallacies seem to be exemplified in this passage by Coleridge:

> No one can rise from the perusal of this immortal poem without a deep sense of the grandeur and purity of Milton's soul, or without feeling how susceptible of domestic enjoyments he really was, notwithstanding the discomforts which actually resulted from an apparently unhappy choice in marriage. He was, as every truly great poet has been, a good man; but finding it impossible to realize his own aspirations, either in religion, or politics, or society, he gave up his heart to the living spirit and light within him, and avenged himself on the world by enriching it with this record of his own transcendent ideal.

> (*Lectures of 1818*, Quoted by Hugh Sykes Davies,
> *The Poets and their Critics*, Pelican Books, 1943, p. 113)

Suppose *Paradise Lost* does lead us to conclude that Milton had a grand pure soul and a taste for domestic life, are we any nearer to an objective assessment of the poem? Perhaps a little: the writing was powerful enough to make us wonder about the author. But the same might be said if it had led us to a deep sense of priggishness and bigotry of soul, and a detestation of domesticity. Yet clearly Coleridge would not, in that case, have been so enthusiastic about the work. In any case this sort of evidence of literary quality is so slight as to carry very little critical weight—certainly not enough to act as sole criterion. Besides, what of writers of whose lives we know nothing, or those who did nothing interesting because they were too busy writing to have much time for living? Are their works therefore to be considered unassessable?

Judgement by a work's revelation of race, milieu and moment, was the first purportedly scientific criticism. It is not scientific, since it cannot lead to prediction and does not spring from experiment (and very often is merely circular argument, the work itself being the chief evidence for the intangible historical qualities it is supposed to be corresponding to). Furthermore, this assumption makes the quality of the work dependent on the quality of its time and place, and might well seem to rule out, say Jane Austen, in advance. Perhaps more important is the paradoxical effect that historicism has had on certain modern critics, who have convinced themselves that as the pastness of an age is irrecoverable, and as literary works are the expression of that pastness, no literary work of the past can be understood in its original sense; it can be interpreted, if at all, only in terms of the meaning, if any, that its words have at the present day. The confusions involved, between meaning and significance, limitation and impossibility, immediacy and understanding, are too complex to tease out here, but the job has been thoroughly done by Hirsch (*Validity*, especially pp. 40/44).

The other main branch of the two External ones, the *Consequential* leads to the Affective Fallacy and its variants.

Affective Fallacy. If art cannot be assessed in terms of its causes, surely it can be assessed in terms of its effects? If we confine 'effects' to emotional or cognitive responses, leaving aside actions, the case seems unanswerable, for as we have seen literary works exist significantly *only* as responses in the reader. In addition, this position can claim distinguished support from authority: Aristotle, Longinus, Shaftesbury, Addison, Santayana, Richards and others. On the other hand, it is quite clear that the reader's response is not *necessarily* a quality of the work. It might be a product of misunderstanding, misinformation, bias, stupidity or insensitivity. Clearly for 'the reader's response' not to be a fallacious measuring-rod, we must stipulate that the response be *justifiable*, and postulate the right reader. 'Justifiable' does not imply conclusive proof; it does imply good reason, sufficient publicly demonstrable circumstantial evidence to bring a conviction of high probability. 'The right reader' is one sufficiently well-informed, sensitive and sensible to be able to see the evidence and sufficiently unprejudiced to accept it for what it is. (The main value of such a book as this may well lie simply in its tendency to promote looking round, which gives some chance of objectivity, rather than leaping to conclusions; the difficult part of the trick is to retain at the same time a sense of immediacy.)

The Consequentional branch subdivides first into *Personal* and *General* approaches. The former, taking personal pleasure as a standard, involves the *Hedonistic Fallacy* — a fallacy because pleasure is a by-product of other experience and therefore a variable (compare the 'pleasure' of tragedy and comedy for instance). There is also the objection noted above, that it might be based on misunderstanding or personal peculiarity. So while it may be all right as a criterion for a purely private reader wanting only a daydream it is no use to the critic. The latter, *General*, branch covers sociological and anthropological investigations — reports on the effects of television on delinquents, Hoggart's *Uses of Literacy*, Maud Bodkin's *Archetypal Patterns in Poetry*, and so on — which lead to the *Scientific Fallacy*, dealt with in Chapter I. I. A. Richards made a valiant attempt in his *Principles of Literary Criticism* (London, 1924) to provide a scientific basis for intrinsic criticism. That work was best which harmonized the greatest number of neural impulses. Unhappily no one has yet been able to measure a single neural impulse indisputably provoked by literature and nothing else let alone measure and compare the sets from, say, *Alice in Wonderland* and *King Lear*. If anyone did — well, *can* one sensibly compare these two books? Isn't the standard irrelevant to literature? (After all, some drug might well harmonize many more disparate impulses than any work of literature, for all we know.) Of the subdivisions of the *Personal* branch — *Self/Others*, *Pleasure/Emotion/Physiology* — little needs to be added to what has already been said, save that scientific experiment has demonstrated that we do possess an innate esthetic sense of a rudimentary sort, in so far as rectangles are instinctively preferred to squares, and the like; but this is of no help with the complex esthetic effects of literature — and in any case there are no grounds for supposing esthetic standards to be the only, or even the most appropriate standards for all kinds of literature. Perhaps it is worth remarking in passing, too, that so far as 'emotion' is concerned the matter is complicated by the fact that in life and art alike we usually feel, *not* mainly a pale replica of the emotion witnessed, but a complementary emotion: in fact we *perceive* more than directly feel, anyway, and achieve emotionally enlarged understanding rather than simply feeling an emotion.

A little more, however, ought to be said about the subdivisions of the *General* branch, since they link up with the 'Internal' side of the Tree, thus showing that in literary criticism external and internal evidence, though obviously different in principle, are not entirely separable. Judgement by a work's *moral,* political or *religious* effects involves the *Paraphrastic* and *Didactic* fallacies. Poetry may support morality and religion in the way Sidney suggests, Shelley may be right in calling poets the unacknowledged legislators of mankind, and Arnold in preferring literature that is a criticism of life, but it is clear that all works of literature *could* be judged by other, esthetic, standards, and that *some* positively demand to be. And on what grounds do we cast these lighter kinds into the outer darkness? Within the most trivial kind there will presumably be good, bad and indifferent works to be critically distinguished, for some audience, some purpose . . .

At this point, we pass over to the 'Internal' side, which logically divides into *Contentual* and *Formal.* It is, of course, almost a dogma of modern criticism that content and form cannot be separated. A dogma, it may be suspected, largely dependent on the fact that until very recently most modern criticism was concerned with short lyric poems, from which it *is* usually pointless trying to extract a paraphrasable content. However, the same point is made about the novel. Raban, for instance speaks of:

> . . . the unrealistic assumption that one can in some way discriminate between the 'subject matter' of the novel and the language used by the novelist to 'convey' this independent entity. But the reader has no power to separate, say, the personal history of Isabel Archer from James's elaborately structured presentation of it in *The Portrait of a Lady.* All we can know of Isabel consists of what James has invented, and the manner in which he renders her character is part and parcel of her character itself.
>
> (J. Raban, *The Technique of Modern Fiction,* London, 1968, p. 135)

A difficult case to dispute, because James is stylized rather than plainly realistic, and because he succeeds in what he is doing so that no obvious gaps are betrayed. But suppose in an otherwise realistic mining novel the author had made his miners talk like bank clerks. Surely all we should have to concede to Raban would be this: strictly speaking, we couldn't assert that *these* miners would not speak so, for in fact this is how they *do* speak in the book; but we could say that *such* miners don't speak so. And of course it is precisely such gaps that authors try to eradicate by revision. They believe in a content that can be given an improved form, if critics don't. Indeed, it is quite evident from the fact that synopses can be given, or that we can say 'twice two makes four', 'two times two is four', 'two multiplied by two equals four', and so on, that to all intents and purposes an identical content can be conveyed in different forms. As one moves through the spectrum from purely informational writing towards pure lyric poetry, of course, it does become increasingly necessary to distinguish between a work's full meaning (inseparably contentual *and* formal) and its paraphrasable meaning (deriving from, or perhaps expressing, content alone). It is not, then, this division, of form and content, that leads to fallacious criticism. Indeed, without it, esthetic appreciation, distinction of kinds, and the operation of the concept of 'purport' would all be impossible; and so, therefore, would criticism. Indeed if we could not start by being able to make this division, we could not talk about even those works in which the form is said to be part and parcel of the content. Moreover, it is clearly right in the case of many didactic works to concentrate on discussing their content, since their verbal excellence is likely to be a negligible part of their total value. Where fallacious criticism is likely to arise is in confusing the two subdivisions of the Contentual, *Truth about* and *Truth to*. The former is propositional truth, which taken as a sole criterion leads to the Paraphrastic and Didactic Fallacies (and thus links up with the 'External' side of the Tree). The latter refers to the imitation of reality (already dealt with). It also covers the creation of attitudes to a subject or situation. Truth-to statements are subject only to indirect verification by observation or introspection or experience of life; truth-about statements are verifiable by logic, in so far as they are propositions deriving from certain premises, or by observation, in so far as they are statements about matters of fact. That observation comes in both lists may be the chief cause of confusions that go back as far as Plato. Properly taken, however, *Truth to* leads to the *Naturalistic Fallacy*, when closeness to life is taken as the sole standard of judgement, realism the sole proper mode of being. Of course, little fallaciousness is involved if the work clearly purports to be a work of realism (though it does no harm to bear in mind that *in principle* even such a work could be considered from other angles: moral, linguistic, sociological, and so forth). Often enough, however, works which make no pretence of realism are simply disparaged as absurd or fantastic or not 'true to life'.

That leaves 'Formal' criticism—surely the one mode that must be indisputably literary and intrinsic? True, but there is more to be said. It is not the whole of intrinsic criticism (if it is taken to be so, as Hirsch does, it limits the intrinsic to the trivial); painting and music can achieve greatness as pure form, but as words are essentially carriers of meaning literature cannot. Archibald MacLeish asserted in a poem of the 'twenties that poems should not *mean* but *be*. I. A. Richards put this idea in a prose form in *Science and Poetry* (New York, 1926), and it became a universally accepted critical view; yet it is obvious that MacLeish's statement is open to logical attack, for merely by being itself a statement of meaning it made the poem self-contradictory. It is also falsified by observation, for poems (and prose works) through the ages have *meant* as well as *been*. If you say, well in that case they don't count as poems, you merely shift verbal counters, you don't alter the facts: they count as *something*, and it's something open to literary criticism. Formal criticism, then, has no more than a part to play—though an important one if it is not separated from criticism of content. The attempt to separate it invariably leads to triviality, and almost invariably to one of the three fallacies shown in the Tree, *Linguistic*, *Autotelic*, or *Reification*.

The Linguistic Fallacy is the notion that refined grammatical analysis can provide a standard of literary judgement, whereas in fact it is with difficulty made to provide supporting evidence, since grammatical forms are finite, possible meanings infinite. Hirsch covers this admirably in *Validity in Interpretation*:

> The norms of language are neither uniform nor stable but vary with the particular sort of utterance that is to be interpreted.
> A single principle underlies what we loosely call 'the norms of language'. It is the principle of sharability. Because sharability is the decisive element in all linguistic norms, it is important to conceive of them, despite their complexity and variability, on this fundamental level. We thereby place emphasis not on the structural characteristics of the linguistic medium, but on the function of speech, which is our central concern. Theory of interpretation need not and ought not describe linguistic norms merely in terms of syntax, grammar, meaning kernels, meaning fields, habits, engrams, prohibitions, and so on, all of which are extremely variable and probably incapable of adequate description. It is more important to emphasize the huge and unencompassable areas of meaning—including emotional and attitudinal meanings—that language actually does represent. Considering this

immensity taken as a whole, the restrictions imposed by all the different varieties of linguistic ground rules do not require special emphasis. It is by no means a denial of these restrictions to say that the capacity of language to represent all conceivable meanings is ultimately limited only by the overarching principle of sharability.

(*Op. cit., p.* 31)

Wellek, too, is typically shrewd on this issue:

> The question of the correlation between style and philosophy cannot be solved, it seems to me, by the fundamental assumption of German stylistics that a 'mental excitement which deviates from the normal habitus of our mental life, must have co-ordinated a linguistic deviation from normal linguistic usage'. [*Spitzer.*] One must, at least, admit that stylistic devices can be imitated very successfully and that their possible original expressive function can disappear. They can become, as they did frequently in the baroque, mere empty husks, decorative tricks, craftsman's *clichés*. The whole relationship between soul and word is looser and more oblique than is frequently assumed.
>
> (*Concepts,* pp. 112/13)

In short, the linguistic approach to a literary work can give useful *tips* to interpretation, and even towards evaluation. But ultimately standards are chosen, not given, and any assessment will be relative to some standard or standards from elsewhere—philosophy, experience, genre—and *could* in principle be related to other standards, critical or metacritical. Though some works may seem positively to dictate their own criteria, at least, for intrinsic assessment, it would always be logically possible for a perverse reader to adopt some other standard, and culturally possible for someone from an alien culture to do so.

It is the doctrine of Art-for-Art's-sake that leads to the Autotelic Fallacy. This was a good counter to the Victorian doctrine of Art-for-Morality's-sake, but it doesn't hold water any better. As we've said paintings may exist, like prettily marked pebbles, as objects of beauty in their own right, related to nothing in the world outside nor to any content within themselves, but not works of literature. In practice, the doctrine tended to produce vapid verses about paintings, statuettes, and other poems; in principle it could provide no measuring-rod of formal quality. What *is* excellence of form *per se*? Can it be the same for any subject matter? or for none?

The Reification Fallacy has already been touched on. It springs from the idea that works of creative literature must Be, not Mean. This is almost impossible to achieve in practice—though the Imagists tried hard, and H.D. succeeded once or twice—and when achieved is rarely worth the effort. Clearly, a doctrine that pushes a writer towards the narrowest imitation of the physical surface can hardly provide a dogmatic criterion for 'Literature' as a whole; and in any case it links up with mimetic theories (and therefore with our *Truth to* branch—thus providing a little evidence for the view that the formal and the contentual are not *finally* separable). This link, of course, means that it is also connected with the Naturalistic Fallacy—a piquant thought since modern Reifiers have normally considered themselves to be reacting against naturalism or 'naïve realism'.

In addition to the *Tree of Fallacies*, *Appendix A* also gives a brutally schematized outline of M. L. Abrams' full and brilliant book, *The Mirror and the Lamp* (New York, 1953). It is compared with the scheme of fallacies, not because Abrams is concerned with that subject, but rather because, approaching criticism in an entirely different way—historically, not logically—he gets the same full sweep over all the main kinds. His book shows, too, how easy it has been in practice for critics unwittingly to assume fallacious standards—especially didactic ones—that perhaps seem too elementary to be credited when dealt with *in vacuo*, as here, rather than in the concrete circumstances of life.

Abrams divides criticism into two main types: *Mirror* criticism, practised by those who believe that art holds a mirror up to nature and judge it accordingly, and *Lamp* criticism, practised by those who believe that the artist casts the illumination of his genius upon nature, and accordingly judge his work by different standards. Each of the main types is subdivided; and as it happens the divisions follow a historical sequence. So we have:

Mirror—corresponding generally to our *Contentual* branch

(a) Mimetic (Greek period)—our *Truth to*

(b) Pragmatic (Medieval and Augustan periods)—our *Truth about*.

However, the critic of content very easily slips into becoming preoccupied with *effects* on the audience (mirrors reflecting bits of nature that might have a bad influence get a bad press, unless they manage to add wholesome comments).

Lamp—corresponding to our *Causal, Consequential,* and *Formal* branches

(a) Expressive (Romantic period)—our *Personal* branch (Causal or Consequential)

(b) Objective (French Symbolist, Art-for-Art's sake, Russian Formalists)—our *Formal* branch.

Again, it has proved in practice easy for critics of this kind to slip into becoming preoccupied with effects, either from the (inspired) author or from the (objective) work, and thus running into the didactic or naturalistic fallacies. In fact, critics clearly have an inveterate desire to draw a moral, to see Nature, or Genius, or Art as teaching lessons. Nor is this wholly a bad thing—authors certainly share this view, 'pure' literary art being a rare thing—; it is dangerous only if we forget the multifacetedness of all works of literature and the multivalence of magisterial views.

APPENDIX A—TREE OF FALLACIES

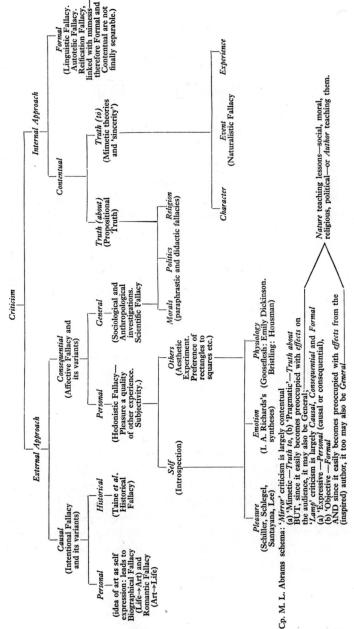

Cp. M. L. Abrams schema: *Mirror* criticism is largely contentual
(a) 'Mimetic—*Truth to*, (b) 'Pragmatic'—*Truth about*
BUT, since it easily becomes preoccupied with *effects* on
the audience, it may also be *General*;
'*Lamp*' criticism is largely *Causal, Consequential* and *Formal*
(a) 'Expressive —*Personal* (causal or consequential),
(b) 'Objective —*Formal*
AND since it easily becomes preoccupied with *effects* from the
(inspired) author, it too may also be *General*

7

Truth in Fiction

PLATO'S view of the world as an imperfect imitation of some ideal reality may well have sprung from his interest in geometry, where material lines and points (especially if drawn in sand) are obviously imperfect—and thus in some sense untrue—representations of ideal figures. At any rate, it led him, committed as he was to a mimetic theory, to condemn literature as the doubly unreal imitation of an imitation and therefore the expression of lies. Sidney, of course, pointed out that if fictions do not pretend to be mimetic they can hardly be accused of lying; the concept of 'truth' is simply irrelevant to them. However, that leads immediately to the question: What use are they then? And to this Shelley seemed to have the answer when he wrote in *The Defence of Poetry* that creative writing 'awakens and enlarges the mind itself'. Yet discussion, and confusion, have continued, for the fact is that Plato, Sidney and Shelley are all partly right and partly wrong; the subject has more ramifications than those mentioned, and it is further complicated by the ambiguities and persuasive prestige of the word 'truth'.

J. R. Brown points out in *Shakespeare and his Comedies* (London, 1957) that Elizabethan vocabulary is not particularly helpful for discussing Elizabethan works; in particular *truth* may refer to sanity (being then the opposite of 'folly'), or to sincerity (the opposite of 'falsity'), or to constancy (the opposite of 'faithlessness'), or to loyalty (the opposite of 'traitorousness'), or to reality (the opposite of 'appearance'). All these meanings are sanctioned by usage and none is absurd, yet it is clear that when a word's range is so extended it has become critically useless. Far better to use 'sanity', 'sincerity', 'constancy', and so on, and let the interconnections within this complex look after themselves.

However, the Gordian knot can't be cut simply by banning the word 'truth' from the terminology of criticism (though that ought to be done), for the vague, shifting complex of ideas covered by the word touches on all sorts of literary problems that deserve discussion, or at least recognition. W. H. Auden, for instance, writes as follows) to justify exclusions from his Collected Poems):

> A dishonest poem is one which expresses, no matter how well, feelings or beliefs which its author never felt or entertained. For example, I once expressed a desire for 'New styles of architecture': but I have never liked modern architecture. I prefer *old* styles, and one must be honest even about one's prejudices.
>
> (*Collected Shorter Poems, 1927–57*, London 1966, Foreword)

Surely a dishonest *poet* rather than 'a dishonest poem' is in question? But, of course, this does raise the question of the relationship between the man and his work, and therefore questions of intention (already dealt with) and sincerity. Then there is the fact that the frame of reference or 'universe of discourse' may well be relevant to both truth and meaning in literature. Something may or may not strike 'a false note' according as it is consistent or inconsistent with the rest—and this brings in the question of the validity of Eliot's standards of coherence and comprehensiveness for judging literature. And so one could go on.

Possibly the most important of the critical concerns covered by 'truth' in fictions are illustrated by the story of the lunatic in a lie-detector. Asked if he was Napoleon he answered 'No' and the lie-detector recorded that he was lying. Shakespeare, of course, lumped the poet with the lunatic (and the lover). If we take that hint for an analogy then we see that what is the case in *fact*, the literal truth, may in *fiction* be a lie, detected as such by the critic (lie-detector), whereas sincere delusion in fiction would ring true. When the creative artist says, not what he 'knows' in his bones (that he is Napoleon, so to speak), but what he thinks his readers wish to hear (that he is not Napoleon), the lie in the soul, the insincerity may be betrayed by inconsistencies and small incoherences in the work. In theory, this need not be so; the lie could be perfect, therefore undetectable and the fiction none the worse for it. Indeed, all we have to go on are the inconsistencies and incoherences; and the impression of insincerity they give rise to (if they do) is in the fictional narrator, the persona. Whether that tallies with the author, whether he is sincere or not in his private life, is none of our business as critics.

From this we might go on to argue that truth and falsehood are not relevant to most literary creations, in the sense of direct reference to daily reality; rather they create their own terms of reference, even as the lie-detector judged the lunatic by its own 'mental-moral' standards of 'reality'. Russell's famous sentence, 'The King of France is bald', a philosophic example of a case to which criteria of truth and falsehood just don't apply, seems equally apposite to literature. The statement has *sense*—we can analyse the linguistic elements and assess their meaning—but it has no *referent* (there is no king of France) and thus is not open to any sort of verification. And Frege has added that the 'question of truth would cause us to abandon aesthetic delight for an attitude of scientific investigation'. This is correct, but does it settle the matter? Perhaps we *should* abandon aesthetic delight in some cases, or at least let it take its chance—in particular in cases where a work clearly purports to reflect life? It creates a frame of reference that mirrors nature, and thus items in it can perfectly well be compared with their counterparts in life and checked as true or false to them. Moreover, in certain works, like *Macbeth*, although the work as a whole does not have reference 'the "utterances" of characters within these works may. Such "utterances" possess, in a secondary or fictional sense, the same characteristics as those of normal speech' (A. G. Pleydell-Pearce, 'Sense, Reference and Fiction', *British Journal of Aesthetics*, July 1967, p. 234). On the other hand, even a work purportedly, and actually, highly realistic is unlikely to be adequately dealt with in terms of verisimilitude alone, for what Harold Osborne says of paintings applies equally well, *mutatis mutandis*, to literature:

> When the pictorial image emerges and we see the field with cows we still see simultaneously the textured and pigmented surface of the canvas . . . This 'dual' seeing, and the seen relation between the painting as a pigmented surface and the pictured image, enhance the aesthetic interest . . . This reciprocal relation of the real surface and deep illusion is apparently inexhaustible.
>
> ('On Artistic Illusion', *British Journal of Aesthetics,* April, 1969, p. 121)

But what if a work purports to be realistic, betrays no insincerity (that is, remains free from inconsistency or incoherence), and is otherwise formally satisfying (stylish), yet by the check of experience is found to be clearly mistaken about the nature of the reality it purports to be portraying (that is to say, is characterized by the incoherence of a discernible gap between purport and achievement, though not by any gap between tone and statement)? Do we approve its sincerity? And if so, on moral grounds? or on esthetic ones, because it avoids discrepancies of tone and statement? Or do we say that purport and achievement should match, above all else? The only clear answer seems to be that moral grounds are irrelevant to such a case; the other two judgements are not inconsistent and should probably both be given to make clear that such a work must be seriously flawed by one relevant standard or another. We are left, though, still uncertain of the relative importance of truth, of one sort or another, in works of one sort or another, and of the relation of truth to value.

Some of the problems will perhaps dissolve if various notions and aspects of 'truth' in fictions—some related, some not—are teased out. Of those mentioned so far, emotional 'truth' sincerity, seems the most tricky; the main problem here seems to be to spot it and talk about its significance in the work as a whole without getting morally indignant with the author. It's all right if we are perfectly clear that 'author' is merely a convenient shorthand term for characteristics of the work. It probably helps to be clear if we con-centrate on the fact that truths like this are recognized rather than proved or verified. In fiction they seem roughly akin to appraisal statements in life—statements by people who do *not* think they are merely reporting personal preferences, and who do produce reasons (but not proofs). Such statements, dealing with dispositions and propensities rather than sharply specifiable single characteris-tics are more subject to error—and therefore to discussion—than propositional (truth-about) statements, which are tested by the standard of accuracy (once the complication of *sense* and *reference* has been taken into account). What T. D. Weldon says of appraisal statements seems transferable to literary critical concerns:

> The reason why we seem to find difficulty over appraisal statements that we do not find in metrical statements is . . . partly that neither 'X is important' nor 'I like X' gives a specifiable new bit of information about X, and partly that there is not and could not conceivably be any general answer to the question, 'Precisely what does it mean to say "X is important"?' We can give reasons for saying it . . . but we cannot deduce it from a general principle . . . [such phrases] assume some context . . . They are 'more or less' not 'either-or' phrases.
>
> (*The Vocabulary of Politics*, Penguin Books, 1953, p. 155)

It is perhaps worth adding that in literary criticism reasons given may be emotional ones; emotion is not always subconscious; it may be quite conscious and perfectly relevant to the discussion of matters, like sincerity, associated with tone.

Both emotional and propositional truths are in reciprocal relations with perceptions of form, in fictions—a fact more clearly evident in connection with illusionistic truth (truth-to), as Osborne showed[1]. This fact itself is but one aspect of a more general characteristic of literary works: that nothing stays still. Such works are systematic syntheses, variable constellations of qualities held together by fields of force; so elements may function in one way when the work is seen in relation to one set of other elements, and in a different way when in relation to another set. All works are in different—and, according to one's viewpoint, varying—proportions conceptual *and* referential *and* experiential. What follows from this is that it is always permissible to look for different kinds of truth. One danger is that we may mix truths of significance and truths of meaning (to use Hirsch's terms) and in doing so both misestimate the evidence and miss the obvious. Is William Empson falling into such a trap in this tiny extract from his brilliant essay on *Alice in Wonderland*?

> It is tempting to read an example of this idea into the poem that introduces the *Looking-Glass*.
>
> > *Come, hearken then, ere voice of dread,*
> > *With bitter summons laden,*
> > *Shall summon to unwelcome bed*
> > *A melancholy maiden.*
>
> After all the marriage-bed was more likely to be the end of the maiden than the grave, and the metaphor firmly implied treats them as identical

Perhaps it is significant that Empson speaks of reading *into* the poem, not of reading in it, 'this idea' (that there was a connection in Dodgson's mind between death and the development of sex). At any rate, he certainly ignores what a more simple-minded reader would see in the poem, that it is light verse about children's dislike of being made to go to bed when they wish to stay up longer; the discrepancy between tone and content being a matter of kind: the mock-tragic. Of course, Empson might be quite correct about Dodgson's mind, but this particular tonal discrepancy does not seem to be a subconscious betrayal, but a conscious literary device;

[1] See quotation on p. 98

so it is not good metacritical evidence of a biographical truth. On the other hand, if the idea has external support from psychological theory, can it be used intrinsically to bring out a subtle underlying propositional truth in the work? Not here surely; the metaphor is not 'firmly implied', it is 'read into'.

Among other things literature does in fact convey knowledge, and often, along with the knowledge, values (for certain values are estimated as such by acquaintance, by being 'proved on the pulses'):

> Literature offers us the raw material for moral judgement, and it offers us *far more* material than any one life can do . . . literature offers us an extension of our moral experience.
>
> (Graham Hough, *An Essay on Criticism*, London, 1966, p. 28)

Knowledge and values, it may be argued, are connected with truth but not identical with it. No doubt this is so, and we should not add them to the list of relevant meanings of 'truth'. But at least it is very important that we should be able to estimate the *accuracy* of the 'raw material', to *recognize* (by whatever effort of imaginative extrapolation from our own limited experience) the emotions deriving from it, and to check the *correctness* of any propositions the author might deduce or imply himself—a task rendered less difficult if the word 'truth' is avoided.

In other circumstances—e.g. in connection with mimetic assessments—other words will be appropriate: 'common experience', 'psychological insight', 'reportage', 'verisimilitude'. If we are concerned with a work's truth to itself (with an esthetic assessment) then words like 'consistency' and 'unity' will be appropriate substitutes. But genre theory is likely to be relevant, since certain kinds imply certain criteria.

There remains what is apparently the most difficult case of all: that of works which seem to purport to rely on facts—sincerely believed to be so by their authors—yet which are unverifiable by any of the criteria so far given. The most obvious examples are works, written from the standpoint of an established, dogmatic religion, though symbolic and mystical works that purported to be reports of something more than purely personal experience would also qualify. No problems arise if religious poetry is treated extrinsically, to see what the age believed, how certain sections of the public felt; or poems could be considered in terms of the correctness of their dogma or their likely effect upon a congregation if they were being considered, say, for inclusion in a hymnal. This is not, how-ever, the usual treatment of religious poems; many of them stay firmly in the canon of English literature even though few today, believers or sceptics, would be found to share all the writer's beliefs. Sharing the writer's beliefs, as we found in considering Stylistics, can be as much of a drawback as an advantage for a critical assess-ment; what you gain on the swings you lose on the roundabouts. Yet any critic who would rank, say, Herbert's 'The Window' higher than 'Lead Kindly Light'—and who would not?—must be neglecting the absolute unverifiable fiats of religion in favour of some contingent qualities of literature. But what are they, and are they verifiable, or at least justifiable to 'right' readers of all beliefs or none?

Clearly, statements about 'God' or 'Eternity' cannot be checked in any obvious way by such standards as emotional recognizability, accuracy, or correctness, for these are not statements with any mimetic or logical reference, and the mere sincerity of the writer will hardly be held to have much value. No piece of sincere non-sense, with no apparent bearing on life, is likely to continue to be valued (save for purely devotional reasons, and by the writer's fellow sectarians). It seems to follow that intrinsic criticism of such works must often ignore the obvious meaning and the apparent purport, and seek for underlying ones—a dangerous procedure as the 'Alice' example shows. It also seems to follow that the intrinsic 'truths' of religious writings will all in fact be values, or rather qualities that carry some value-weighting for most men, or most men in a given culture or cultures. Such writings, in other words, if they are not to become mere documents for metacriticism, or devotional aids for fellow-believers, must be obliquely expressing some recognizable form of common—or at any rate potentially available—human ex-perience, giving knowledge by acquaintance (and thus giving 'truths' indirectly verifiable by reference to experience). When Vaughan speaks of seeing Eternity 'the other night' we cannot know what (if any) sort of entity he meant, nor can we assume that any reader will share his idea of it. But we can have some literary assurance that he is saying something—which may turn out to be apprehensible and valu-able—about his own experience. In that case, by virtue of our com-mon humanity we remain in the realm of the verifiable, however roughly and indirectly so. Critical analysis, with constant reference to the subtleties of experience, and allowance for 'period', may then genuinely enlarge perception, without any cheating by rhetoric, or blackmailing by authority. It is probably the case that sincerely held irrational convictions are more likely than others to make manifest certain truths about the recesses of human nature—witness the Romantic Movement in general. The truths revealed, however, may not seem of value, or may be so much at odds with the ostensible meaning and purport as to ruin the piece as a literary artefact. Somewhat after Donne, and at much the same time as Vaughan, the Reverend John Norris wrote 'The Aspiration'—a clear example of a poem ostensibly purporting to be about religion, but really about sex. However, as the unconscious Freudian imagery indicates, it is the expression of erotic fantasy, so that what it says, what feeling it shows, is not particularly valuable or educative, and the way it says it is so incongruous with the surface meaning and ostensible purport as to be farcical. Here, is the climactic stanza:

> How cold this clime! And yet my sense
> Perceives e'en here Thy influence.
> E'en here Thy strong magnetic charms I feel,
> And pant and tremble like the amorous steel.
> To lower good and beauties less divine,
> Sometimes my erroneous needle does decline,
> But yet, so strong the sympathy,
> It turns, and points again to Thee.

Scholarship will tell us that there was a seventeenth-century tradition of religious poetry using erotic imagery; this poem may have been influenced by it—but pretty soon the tail was wagging the dog, for this imagery makes of God the Father a woman faced by an exhibitionist! Take, on the other hand, an acknowledged masterpiece which is in that tradition:

> Show me deare Christ, thy Spouse, so bright and clear
> What! is it She, which on the other shore
> Goes richly painted? or which rob'd and tore
> Laments and mournes in Germany and here?
> Sleepes she a thousand, then peepes up one yeare?
> Is she selfe truth and errs? now new, now outwore?
> Doth she, and did she, and shall she evermore
> On one, on seaven, or on no hill appeare?

Dwells she with us, or like adventuring knights
First travaile we to seeke and then make Love?
Betray kind husband thy spouse to our sights,
And let myne amorous soule court thy mild Dove,
Who is most trew, and pleasing to thee, then
When she is embrac'd and open to most men.

This certainly reveals deep feeling and conflict of an emotional sort, but there is nothing unconscious about it. It is violent but coherent; its apparent incoherences are all carefully controlled and appropriate. It is one of Donne's most celebrated divine sonnets, yet it neither asserts nor denies the 'truth' of his religion—nor does it seriously question it. What really comes through, and gives the poem survival-value, is not its recognition of the paradox that there should be one Christian Truth and one True Church purveying it, yet that it should seem not possible to prove which of three it is; rather is it the poet's expression of his feelings about this recognition—which are analogous to those of people faced by any such shocking paradox (compare Shakespeare's Troilus: 'This is, and is not, Cressid!'), and are therefore apprehensible regardless of the reader's acceptance or rejection of the particular beliefs that the poem takes for granted. To appreciate it we are not required to have any attitude to Christian beliefs, only to know of them. Works like Greene's *The Living Room* and Eliot's *Cocktail Party*, on the other hand, tend to fall between two stools. This is no doubt why they seem strangely out of focus for perceptive admirers of the authors' earlier works. Both start with human problems, but more and more towards the end shift to problems of dogma, almost of dogma for its own sake—and thus lose general interest, and lose contact with any verifiable truth. But perhaps these examples are too easy, since they all touch on problems of dogma, and therefore approach propositional statement. To come to grips with a mystical poem such as Vaughan's 'The World' is probably a trickier task, and one that can't be fully accomplished here. It is after all a longish poem. But as a start one should react innocently to it as if its words were strange—for a stock reaction will bar the way to any experiential truth it may have to offer under its literal, strictly meaningless, surface. (How can 'Eternity' be *seen*?)

What, then, is the human experience the poem deals with? A dream, in which the world is symbolically seen as dark, struggling, and nightmarish for lovers, statesmen, and misers, whereas it may become calm and light for those who 'weep and sing', for they can soar into the ring 'Eternity'. Obviously, Eternity is a state of mind (whatever Vaughan's metaphysic may have been). The nature of this state is given by implication in the line on the statesman whose light is *eclipsed*: 'Condemning thoughts—like sad eclipses—scowl/ Upon his soul.' This is confirmed by the sense and movement of the opening lines, and probably, by what seems to be *latent* imagery in them:

> I saw Eternity the other night,
> Like a great ring of pure and endless light,
> > All calm, as it was bright;
> And round beneath it, Time in hours, days, years,
> > Driven by the spheres
> Like a vast shadow mov'd; in which the world
> > And all her train were hurl'd.

These lines seem to obtain their effect not so much from the period idea of a *primum mobile* or unmoved mover of the planetary system (no longer believed by anyone) as from a remembered vision of the Milky Way, transmuted in dream to a vast silent clock without figures or fingers; the path of time without its tick or turning. Beneath it is the clock of the moving universe of spheres in their orbits. Behind this one glimpses a hinted picture of Eternity as a *halo* above the world of time (that reeling head where clouds of crying witnesses without/Pursued him with one shout./Yet digg'd the mole, and lest his ways be found/Work'd underground). Perhaps some of this is fanciful. But at least it is on common ground where we can argue meaningfully as to whether it is fanciful or not, and if not, what it is worth. As ordinary propositions, subject to the test of truth-value, Vaughan's statements in this poem would be null and void. But in fact these are extraordinary 'propositions', subject to a different test, that of value-truth. Criticism could start from here. The poem evokes and judges certain classes of men and states of mind (makes statements akin to Weldon's 'appraisal' statements), and contrasts them with that sense of Nirvana which the most worldly may momentarily have captured in some still night or in a dream. If we do find that there is a point of contact, verifiable in our experience, that it is not mere uncontrolled fantasy, then we are led to questions about this 'truth'. Does Vaughan enrich our comprehension of these human states, 'awaken and enlarge the mind itself'? Does his embodiment of them provide evidence of the value he claims for them? And is all this combined in an esthetically pleasing verbal whole? The last stanza, of course, makes the orthodox suggestion that the Church is the way to the possession of the Nirvana-state; and it is probably at this point that we should properly pass from criticism to metacriticism, from discussion of truth in the world of fiction to truth in the world of fact.

8

Coming to Terms

To have maintained that the literary critic's *prime* concern is with *literary* (intrinsic) criticism may well have seemed truistic: it is not, however, necessarily trivial. Such a critic must also be able to assess literature in the light of its correspondence with actual or ideal moral, social or psychological states, but his special competence is in the field of verbal analysis and the examination of literary techniques, not in the psycho-analysis of dead authors, nor even in the dissection of his own emotional responses to literature. He should, of course, be eager to accept the help of textual scholars, literary historians, biographers, sociologists, and indeed almost anyone who offers it. But he must on no account misconstrue the objects of his own essentially self-contained discipline.

In order to discover the strategies of the artist and articulation of the work of art, and to elucidate its full meaning, a critic's first qualification will be a sense of relevance. Without this, it is as easy on the one hand to fall into the trap of passing off comma-counting for criticism, as it is on the other to promote one's obsession with the life of the artist: ultimately the work under examination is his special concern, not the context in which it was produced nor the units of language used in its production. A sense of relevance is a function of intelligence, unlike taste, the second item in the critic's equipment, which is more dependent on general culture. Taste depends too upon the critic's total experience and the quality of his response to it. The superficial mind of the minor critic unerringly selects the potentially fashionable works of his day, whereas the judgements of the great critic outlive fashion. Without good taste one cannot even begin to be a critic.

It hardly matters what these two qualities are called. Some may prefer the word 'discrimination' to 'a sense of relevance' and 'sensibility' to 'taste'. Granted that a critic has them, he will still need to write coherently and, if possible, elegantly. It is with one part of coherence that this chapter, and *Appendix B,*[1] *The Table of Terms* that goes with it, is concerned.

[1] Pp. 123/6

On every level of criticism the failure to define terms leads inexorably to muddle and unnecessary disagreement. Besides, the more comprehensive, concise and communicative one's critical language is, the more one can usefully say about a poem, play or novel. Every teacher has suffered the student of literature whose critical vocabulary is almost exhausted by the one word 'effective'. It would be foolish to imagine that critical activity consists of nothing more than finding satisfactory niches for the obstinate particulars of art, but a proper concern for names and classes is an indispensable preliminary to fruitful analysis and comparison.

What is needed then, and what the *Table of Terms* outlines,[1] is an inclusive, coherent and consistent terminology which will be sufficiently near to current usage to be fairly easily assimilable and to have some chance of general acceptance. Of course, some theorists have been coining their own more or less esoteric terms for some time, and where it seemed appropriate they have been borrowed; there is no point in novelty for its own sake. In some cases, especially among the 'Local' terms' where the field is vast and complex, only samples are given—the samples chosen being among the commonest but including those terms that seemed most to need or deserve some comment. Indeed, though one purpose of this chapter is to put forward a basic terminology for general acceptance, another equally important one is to use it as a means of, or excuse for, talking about various aspects of literature and criticism.

The suggested terminology is given in three groups (v. *Appendix B*), Global, Regional and Local, the items in each being briefly commented upon. The terminology, of course, is no more than a set of tools. Were it generally agreed a great step forward would have been taken (a step scientists took long ago), but the important question of what critical procedure the terminology should be used with would still remain open. One idea of an appropriate procedure is to be found in the concluding chapter (17). In so far as some of the terminology would not suit metaphysical systems of criticism, it does imply certain, exceedingly general, limits. But its acceptance would not entail acceptance of any *particular* theory of critical procedure, and acceptance of the limits in question is already a fact for

[1] It makes no claim to completeness, but rather provides a skeleton of basic terms, the discussion of which may be of critical interest. It can be filled out from such a *Dictionary of Critical Terms* as that by Barnet, Berman, and Burto (London, 1964).

nearly all the academic world. This encourages a faint hope that the terminology, or some of it, may be seriously considered by teachers in higher education for eventual acceptance—no doubt with modifications—rather than as a provocation to individualism. *Some* terminology must ultimately be agreed upon, some definitions, if literary criticism is not to founder in ambiguity and cross purposes.

I. GLOBAL

The first items here seem to need little comment and do not pretend to much practical importance. The reason for their presence is theoretical. For the terminological framework to be *potentially* all-inclusive—capable of providing whatever degree of delicacy may be required at any stage of the critical procedure—it must extend from extreme to extreme: from 'Language', defined with the greatest degree of generality, down to 'overtone', possibly of a single morpheme, or 'reverberation', the effect of interacting overtones, i.e. the overtones of overtones (III. *Local*, Eiii, Diii). It is perhaps, too, worth repeating here that outside such a terminology as this we have at one side, so to speak, *principles*: unity, emphasis, coherence; the difference between meaning and significance; criticism and metacriticism; the need to discriminate between the demand for accuracy, recognizability, correctness and value often confounded under 'truth'; and the 'multifacetedness of literary masterpieces and the multivalence of magisterial views'. And at the other side we have the need to use *personal*, even metaphorical language in the last stages of critical delicacy, since our terms necessarily name properties that are of a class, whereas works of art are, if of a class, significantly unique within it.

The definitions of 'prose' and 'verse', which come next on the list, seem fairly unobjectionable if we bear in mind the fact that some universally accepted 'prose' is more strongly rhythmical and metaphorical than some universally accepted free 'verse' (and the fact, too, that to be acceptable a terminology will have to accommodate itself to such irremovables wherever the demands of consistency, clarity and reason permit). However, what is likely to seem wantonly provocative is the devaluation of 'poem' and 'poetry', though it is right in line with popular usage. But evaluative definitions seem to have no merit, whereas devaluation has both a negative and positive virtue. It rids us of all those endless, fascinating and inevitably fruitless attempts to seize and define an intangible spiritual essence, 'poetry', which can then be used as a crumbly touchstone in any field. As well as wasting time, this quest leads to confusion and evasion. If 'poetry' is defined so, then critics shouldn't speak of bad, or even flawed poems, but this is difficult to avoid and in fact is not avoided. There *are* poems of varying merit and it is easier to say so than to speak of, say, 'badly failed *failed-poems*', 'just failed *failed-poems*', and 'nearly failed *poems*' when speaking generally. More positively, to use poetry in our neutral technical way forbids such evasions as the reviewer's ascription 'poetic', or 'here Lawrence achieves a profound poetry', and so forth; the critic has to be more precise and discriminating in bringing to the reader's attention exactly what quality he senses or thinks he senses.

Of course, *Verse, poem and poetry*, as defined, are not all logically necessary; and further, it might be argued, they should not be necessary in practice since we manage with only one word, *prose*, in the other camp. But these three words are also irremovables; all we can hope to do is to adjust and regularize their use. Furthermore there is the practical point that nearly all kinds of prose have names; but this is not the case with verse, particularly modern verse, so we should often find ourselves having to speak cumbersomely of 'this complete set of verses' if we dropped 'poem'.

The definition of the next term, 'Art', may seem to incline to vague Beauty-worship. It should be emphasized, then, that lower down the *Table* it is maintained that the distinction between the purportedly factual and the purportedly fictional is more important for the critic than that between art and non-art. It is more important not to criticize an historical novel as if it were history—letting it stand or fall, in the last analysis, on its facts—than to register the esthetic pleasure given by a well-made historical work and class it as a work of art. Furthermore, it is nowhere implied that a work of fiction is to be damned if it turns out not to be a work of art; for it may have merits of interest, information, or amusement which more than compensate for the lack of esthetic pleasure. With 'art', as with 'poetry', some devaluation is desirable; it is here reduced to a technical term.

However, literary works do often have an esthetic dimension, and sometimes it is important as well as merely essential (i.e. merely the defining characteristic). To indicate that esthetic criticism need not be so vague as it usually is, the term itself has been subdivided. The 'esthesis of composition' is most obvious in paint-

ing. It is the disinterested (non-moral, non-utilitarian, non-preju-
diced) delight that comes from the perception of the relationship of
parts to the whole and other parts. In literature it might come from
the structuring of a novel or long poem, the complex patterns—like
a formal dance—of a Jonsonian plot, the interweaving of *terza rima*
or, in little, the elegant play of antitheses; it is almost purely formal.
'Complementarity' refers to pleasure resulting from a sense of the
perfect matching of form and content; akin to the mathematician's
'beauty', it is seen most clearly when the development of a theme is
matched by matters of rhyme, rhythm, syntax, plot, time-shift and
so on. Finally, the term 'condensation' is intended to cover local
instances, within the parts—though with sufficient logical rigour
such instances could always be seen as minimal examples of the
esthesis of composition or complementarity. 'The *multitudinous*
seas' might be an example. Apart from any consideration of the
relations of parts and whole in *Macbeth*, or theme and image, there
is the pure literary delight of one's sense of the perfection, unexpectedness and inevitability of this epithet.

It is probably worth remarking, in connection with esthetic
pleasure, firstly, that a synoptic view is better for the apprehension
of esthetic qualities than a discursive one—and is a function of
'compactness' (not equivalent to brevity, though in practice it is
true that complementarity and composition are easier to appreciate
in short works in which memory is less taxed); secondly, the degree
of 'coercion' in a work (to accept only relevant meanings and implications) is a good guide to its merit as texture: and thirdly, the
'insistence' of parts, to give them more prominence, is a guide to
structural merit.

Why esthetic pleasure should be considered important at all is
perhaps outside the scope of such a book as this; it is simply a fact
that it often is. However, R. W. Pickford, by implication, gives
an interesting explanation of the odd force of esthetic feelings in an
article on 'The Psychology of Ugliness', which concludes as
follows:

> As for the question of ugliness, in so far as it is purely negative, it is
> the absence of esthetic quality. In so far as it is a positive attribute, it is
> caused by the activity or effects of destruction, aggression and fear,
> and guilt due to the influence of the super ego and consequent action
> of ego defences, when these impulses and emotions are or might be

excited and experienced. The esthetically satisfying is found in a positive way where there is mental restitution and the resolution of absence of conflict.

(British Journal of Aesthetics, July 1969, p. 269)

If this article gives reasons from depth psychology, Guerin, Labor, Morgan and Willingham add something from surface psychology. Pickford accounts for the power, so to speak, and they account for the pleasure. Discussing motifs, they say:

> The evocative power of steadily repeated images and symbols makes the experience a part of our own consciousness and sensibility. Thus the image satisfies our senses, the pattern our instinctive desire for order, and the thematic statement our intellect and our moral sensibility.
>
> . . . Coleridge suggests the double principle of recognition and surprise . . . Extending this double principle to the study of motifs, we see that the recurrence of thematic statement, image, or symbol comes to be a pleasure whenever we find a new instance of a motif. Conversely, when we recognize the motif in a *different* manifestation, our pleasurable recognition is augmented by the pleasurable perception of difference. Nor is this all, for the perception of sameness and of difference [*cp the esthetic principle of variety-in-unity*] is more than mere pleasurable stimulus, a play of mind. It opens out to the richness and truth of a given experience by gradually revealing its essence to the reader.
>
> (*A Handbook of Critical Approaches to Literature*, New York and London, 1966, p. 154)

Like everything else in literature, it would seem, the esthetic shades off at the edges into something else—and it is these hidden connections, this being part of a field of force, that provides its surprising vitality.

'Anti-art' applies to the two poles of complete surrealism (which proclaimed itself to be against art and beauty) and complete realism. In each case the reader is so drawn into the fictional world that he has no room for either judgement or esthetic appreciation—extreme cases being those addicts of radio or television serials who write in to warn, blame, or condole with characters. For them the set is obviously a *keyhole* or *window*.

Little needs adding to what is already given under 'Fictional' and 'Non-fictional'—a more important distinction than that between art and non-art—save to note that the former can be conveniently subdivided according to *method*, the latter (equally appropriate to its nature) according to *matter*. (These are the basic MODES of the fictional and non-fictional):

F. *mimetic*—realism, naturalism, romance with lifelike texture.

metaphoric—symbolism, allegory, significant fantasy.

rhetorical—lyric of shared experience, lampoon, satire. (In so far as the last includes works that *mean* or *say*, but are not factual, it merges with the last non-fictional category, the *controversial*; some satire, for example, is rightly judged in part by the accuracy of its facts.)

N.-f. *factual*—history, report, biography.

abstract—scientific exposition, analysis, philosophy.

controversial—polemic, forensic rhetoric, sermon.

All the foregoing items, however, pale into insignificance beside 'Purport', for this term might be said to bring Intention back through the window after Wimsatt and Beardsley had thrown it out of the door. All logic is on their side, as we have seen, yet critics have never been quite easy about rejecting intentionalism. In part this may be because it is psychologically, if not logically, reassuring to find as a scholar, after you have said as a critic that a work is *x*, that the author had said he intended it to be *x*. But mainly it is because practically all criticism, even of a descriptive sort, becomes impossible without some sort of hypothesis. What is needed is to get one from *within* the work.

It might be argued that 'purport' is no more than what a work *is*, and could therefore be eliminated in favour of 'Mode'. But Mode is a very fluid concept. Furthermore, to say straight away what a work is begs most of the critical questions; a dialectic of hypotheses and evidence is required for a just estimate of both a work's generic and its specific nature. And works may purport to be other than, on close sensitive examination it turns out they really are. Hence the need for 'Implication'—the inner counsel behind the official front—that reveals itself through minor inconsistencies and incongruities: the big boots under the dress of Purport that give the game away. Another point is that the concept of Purport counters the tendency set up by many critical terms (like 'structure' and 'texture', and to some extent 'Mode') to take the work as an *object*, whereas it is more importantly an *action*.

As soon as the critic passes from the most elementary matters he

THE TRUTHS OF FICTION

needs the concept of purport. How can a work be said to be flawed (or anything else) unless what it purports to be has been decided, and therefore what constitutes a flaw? How do we assign it to a kind (and thus refrain from inappropriate criticism) unless we have an idea of its general purport. How indeed do we describe its various characteristics without a rough idea of *what* they are characteristic, since they can change if read in one light or another? Sometimes it may be useful to split the concept of Purport into *Contentual* (to classify, assess appropriateness of elements, or demonstrate organic textural form giving rise to small-scale esthetis of complementarity) and *Formal* (to distinguish failed organic textural form from imposed textural form—a matter relevant to esthetis of composition and of complementarity). But this is already to trespass on the regional terminology.

II. Regional

In this section there is inescapably some overlap; the terminology is intended to match the material it will have to deal with, and literature only rarely divides itself into mutually exclusive categories. In particular, as Chapter 2 argued, Mode and Kind are neither sharply definable, nor mutually exclusive categories (the *Table*, *Appendix B,* gives the most generally useful division only). Nevertheless one can only deplore the indiscriminate use of a multiplicity of terms—mode, type, genre, kind—all used indiscriminately over large areas of meaning. Where the present terms overlap, they do so deliberately and from different worlds (v. Chaps 2 and 9). The terminology of Mode, Kind, Type, Mood and Variety is meant mainly to encourage, as a start—and the whole thing is no more than a basis for making more delicate discriminations, without preliminary misunderstandings—the habit of triangulation from psychological or impressionistic and technical viewpoints.

If the generic words have been fairly thoroughly dealt with elsewhere, the matter of 'Form' has not: and it is here that the real difficulties begin. But the current chaos of usages is such that those given, if accepted, could hardly fail to be an improvement. The division into structural and textural seems the least questionable, and little seems to need adding to the *Table*'s definition of those terms save the remark that they do not correspond to Ransom's pairing of 'logical structure and local texture' (in *The World's Body*, New York, 1938), where the word 'logical' is misleading and the idea as a whole—roughly that of general theme and particular irrelevances—is not very helpful, though it does point to the truth that there is room in literature for a certain degree of freedom or play within the overall plan. Our division gets rid of one of the main confusions of usage; that between the 'form' that is, crudely speaking, *shape* (sonnet-form, plot, and so forth) and the 'form' that is everything other than content (imagery, syntax, rhythm and so forth). Both have in common the fact that they are ways of saying, not what is said (the paraphrasable, translatable meaning). They differ in being large-scale and small-scale respectively. But obviously they overlap—and ultimately 'structure' can be reduced to selected bits of 'texture'. Met for the first time an image makes a local, textural impact; met for the second or third time, as part of a motif, it is apprehended as structure. This point of intersection is nicely indicated by C. H. Rickword:

> Schematic plot is a construction of the reader's that corresponds to an aspect of the response and stands in merely diagrammatic relation to the source. Only as precipitates from the memory are plot and character tangible; yet only in solution have either any emotive valency.
> (Quoted by John Kilham, 'Autonomy Versus Mimesis?',
> *British Journal of Aesthetics*, July 1967, p. 279)

'Texture', then, is just how the writing hits you as you read. Most generally, it can be placed (a) on an *incarnation-scale*, ranging from the transparent (sentences simple and informative, words directly linked with referent) to the opaque (sentences enacting their meaning rather than abstractly stating it, words carrying the full charge of their etymology, past history, and present context), and (b) on an *elaboration-scale*, from simple (in vocabulary, syntax, rhythm or presentation) to complex or figurative. Clearly texture can be regarded as the narrowest version of 'Style'. The difference between stylistics and the study of texture is one of viewpoint; the latter is concerned simply with immediate impact and the relationship with structure, the former with rhetorical quality, the relationship with some assumed norm.

Since 'Style' has been discussed at some length in Chapter 4 it will be enough here to indicate that the relationship with a norm may be viewed positively as well as negatively, according to the critical requirement of the moment:

. . . every literate person is prepared to distinguish a host of norm-defining features in a number of styles. Such features may be stated in terms of metre ('heroic couplets') time ('Elizabethan style'), place ('Yankee humour'), language, dialect, writer ('Byronic style') or literary work ('Euphuism'), school of writers ('romantic style'), genre ('poetic style, journalese'), social situation ('Sergeant-Major of the Guards addressing recruit') and so forth. Again, all such norms seem to be roughly circumscribed by context, including time, place and situation. And all of them presuppose definition of a norm. Here the emphasis is put on similarities, not differences, between the given text and the norm; otherwise this approach is identical with that described above as comparison of the text with a contextually related corpus.

(Nils Erik Enkvist 'On Defining Style',
Linguistics and Style ed. J. Spencer, London 1964. pp. 25/6)

Both structural and textural form can be either 'organic' or 'imposed'. To decide when either is the case, however, is usually a psychological decision not a technical one. Imposed form, then, is that which is apparently — or actually, in the case of 'given patterns' — predetermined, and thus seeming to take precedence over content. Works with imposed form are more noticeably verbal *forms* — and therefore most easily susceptible of esthetic effects — and not merely forms of communication by words. Organic form on the other hand arises when there *is* form, not amorphousness, but it seems to grow naturally out of the content and to be inseparable from it. Space forbids any extended comment; perhaps some of the potential comment may be deduced from a list of the risks these forms run:

(1) Organic structural forms risk amorphousness (where the content itself has little potential form; it is arguable, e.g., that despite the demands of mimesis anything entitled *A Dream* needs imposed form).

(2) Imposed structural forms risk incongruity and therefore unestheticism, or overestheticism (of composition).

(3) Organic textural forms risk documentary (and consequent loss of esthetic distance) and diffuseness.

(4) Imposed textural forms run the risks under (2) but the overestheticism will be of *condensation*.

Linear and fugal forms are those of large-scale arrangement of time, and are therefore structural only. Traditional works almost always use linear time, apart from minor exceptions in the way of flashbacks of one sort or another. The word 'fugal' was coined to cover such modern works as *Ulysses*, *Point-Counter-Point*, or *The Alexandria Quartet*, works in which it has been realized that as fiction is not reality time can be treated like space and shifted about kaleidoscopically; it can be layered, as in counterpoint (hence 'fugal' —'contrapuntal' being already in use for themes and scenes). This matter—along with 'Author-time', 'Narrative-time', and 'Reader-time'—is more fully dealt with in Chapter 11. What is not mentioned there is the need to distinguish between time as *form* and time as *content* (either 'history' or—a preoccupation of the German novel—'Time' itself). That the subject is Time in no way compels an author to use any particular technique—though it may encourage him to be experimental with his formal time-schemes. Further, though a book such as this is concerned with basic things—the fictional concept of time itself rather than practical methods of handling time in relation to pace, character, point-of-view, or scene—it may not be amiss to bring these less abstract points to mind, if only as a tiny element of transition to the lesser generality of our PART II:

Some categories of fiction create their own distinctive time schemes. The 'history' or 'chronicle' (Trollope's *Barsetshire Chronicles*, Galsworthy's *The Forsyte Saga*, Anthony Powell's *The Music of Time* series) deals with many years of change and development in the lives of a large group of characters. The 'anecdote' (many short stories fall into this class) seizes upon a single illuminating incident that may take only a minute to enact. The 'journal' (Gogol's *Diary of a Madman*, Sartre's *La Nausée*) consists of a day-to-day commentary by a single character on the events of a period. The 'assembled evidence of witnesses' (William Faulkner's *As I Lay Dying*, Julian Mitchell's *Imaginary Toys*) is made up of a series of individual accounts of the same incidents, in which the reader is repeatedly sent back to the beginning of the story, each time from a different character's point of view.......................
......flexibility of tempo is one of the novelist's major instruments: he can indicate the relative value of each occurrence by his handling of pace ... narrative tempo is largely determined by the amount of detail. But syntax too has an important part to play. Short clauses, strung together with connectives like 'and' or 'then' tend to convey an impression of greater speed than elaborate dependent constructions ...

But all these structures and devices must be tested in the light of the 'macro-narrative', where the novel is located in terms of historical actuality and possibility.

(J. Raban, *The Technique of Modern Fiction*, London, 1968. pp. 57/8)

The wisest remark on the whole matter of pace in fiction remains E. M. Forster's. He says that human beings lead two lives, 'the life in time and the life by values'. In other words, two clocks run on, the regular chronometer and the eccentric clock of the emotions. 'He waited for her only half an hour, but it seemed like forever' is a familiar example. Thirty minutes is real time, forever is value-time. As noticed earlier, the technique of direct narrative severely condenses real time, while the extended scene gives value-time. And nothing differs more drastically among individual authors than value-time . . . Thus at the very beginning of a work of fiction the writer should be prepared to record actual time so that the work makes sense; but, more than that, he should be prepared to make his stresses, his meanings, his pattern of life occur in accordance with value-time. And to do that he must know his values.

(R. Macauley and G. Lanning,
Technique in Fiction, New York, 1964. pp. 156/7)

Everything else in this Regional section is probably clear enough —at any rate when taken in conjunction with Chapters 2 and 9— save the words 'romance-' and 'report-' which appear with each type of kind. They derive from the long-attempted distinction between novels and romances. The distinction is well-founded in the facts, but it has never quite taken; people go on referring to both as novels. In any case, it ought to be extended to dramatic and lyric literature as well, since works of all types can in principle tend to lifelikeness or to fantasy and myth. It seems preferable then to speak of romance-novels (-stories, -plays, -poems) and report-novels (-stories, -plays, -poems).

III. LOCAL

Again, there is deliberate overlapping here in order to make the analytic tool many-handled and easy to use. No new method of analysis is implied, only provision for existing ones. If the divisions begin to look crude and mechanical, it should be remembered that they are skeletons which the critic can flesh out as he chooses.

Section *A* Seems largely self-explanatory ('Epigram' comes here as well as in *B* because epigrams have the formal characteristic of being short; the four types of narrative are taken from Northrop Frye's *Anatomy of Criticism*.) So too with section *B* ('Ode' is a doubtful case perhaps—but odes do have in common some 'high' subject, or at least a high tone). Although some of the same textural elements are found in all kinds of literature, it will easily be seen that the more elaborate textural devices will be most often associated with the complex forms of literature. The introverted kinds of narrative, the confession and the romance-novel, tend as one might expect towards the formal complexity of even the more introverted lyric. A writer who aims at comprehensive reportage will obviously eschew the more blatantly rhetorical figures.

Puttenhan's division of figures into Auricular, Sententious and Sensable is incomplete and confusing in its coverage. Division into Musical, Lexical and Syntactical (*C*) is more logical and complete, though there is bound to be some overlapping. The exemplary terms given here may all be found in any dictionary of literary terms. Metaphor and metre, however, are very important and much misunderstood; so, one or two apposite quotations:

> A very broad distinction can thus be made between metaphors which work through some direct resemblance between the two things, the tenor and vehicle, and those which work through some common attitude which we may (often through accidental and extraneous reasons) take up towards them both...
> ....
> Let us go back to *leg* for a moment. We notice that even here the boundary between literal and metaphoric uses is not quite fixed or constant. To what do we apply it literally? A horse has legs literally, so has a spider, but how about a chimpanzee? Has it two legs or four? And how about a starfish? Has it arms or legs or neither? And, when a man has a wooden leg, is it a metaphoric or a literal leg? The answer to this last is that it is both. It is literal in one set of respects, metaphoric in another. A word may be *simultaneously* both literal and metaphoric, just as it may simultaneously serve to support many different metaphors, may serve to focus into one meaning many different meanings. This point is of some importance, since so much misinterpretation comes from supposing that if a word works in one way it cannot simultaneously work in another and have simultaneously another meaning.

I   119

Whether, therefore, a word is being used literally or metaphorically is not always, or indeed as a rule, an easy matter to settle. We may provisionally settle it by deciding whether, in the given instance, the word gives two meanings or one . . . if we can distinguish at least two co-operating uses, then we have metaphor.

(I. A. Richards, *The Philosophy of Rhetoric*,
New York 1965, pp. 118/20)

The truth is, that with a poetic metaphor the actual content of the reader's mental imagery doesn't matter. The author can't control the reader's mental images — castings-around of the rat in the maze — he merely provides the linguistic maze itself, with its entrance and exit. What matters about poetic metaphors is their structure — which is both the logical structure of a process of reasoning, and the architectural structure of words in a line of verse — for that is what the author can control. And just as no two lines of verse have the same rhythm, though they have the same metre, so no two poetic metaphors have the same structure. What differentiates one metaphor from another is the kind of effort — the length and complexity and particular character of the effort — that trying to 'realise' it demands of the reader . . . For a metaphor is not something heterogeneous in the texture of a poem, like a sixpence in a pudding; the words composing it have all sorts of other functions as well — acoustic, rhythmic and associative. It is not *only* a metaphor, any more than a rhyming word is *only* a rhyme.

(P. N. Furbank, 'Do We Need the Terms "Image" and "Imagery"?'
Critical Quarterly, Winter 1967, p. 342)

Certain modern stylistics men, notably Trager-Smith, have endeavoured to supplant the traditional idea of metre by something more subtle, some system of stresses, or intervals or musical notation. Wellek and Warren put their finger firmly on the flaw:

Yet laboratory metrics obviously ignores, and has to ignore, meaning
....

The whole assumption that the findings of the oscillograph are directly relevant to the study of metrics is mistaken. The time of verse-language is a time of expectation. We expect after a certain time a rhythmical signal, but this periodicity need not be exact nor need the signal be actually strong so long as we feel it to be strong. Musical metrics is indubitably correct in saying that all these distinctions of time and stress as well as pitch are only relative and subjective. But

acoustic and musical metrics share one common defect or, rather,
limitation: they rely exclusively on sound . . .

(Theory of Literature, New York 1949, p. 171)

All that is needed for metre is the regular recurrence of more and
less stressed syllables; it is their proximity not their actual weighting that matters; a syllable in one part of a line may require more
breath than one in another part, but what will determine whether
we feel either to be stressed or unstressed will be its weighting relative to the syllable(s) next to it, and this will be largely determined
by meaning.

Local terminology may be used, like regional, to differentiate the
various types of literary work. But very often such works share their
most important characteristics, and this is nowhere more apparent
than in the use of larger elements of literary structure. Lyric poems
as well as novels and plays are frequently built on the plan of
Oedipus Rex as expounded by Aristotle. Sonnets and ballads, as well
as novels and tragedies may have a more or less long complication
followed by reversal and the relatively swift resolution. Within this
large framework, however, there is room for wide structural variation. Where literature achieves lifelikeness the events portrayed will
appear to be causally related to each other, but quite independent of
the narrator. The seeds of a work's development will be planted at
the beginning and from them everything will appear to grow naturally. The difficulty for the artist, as James points out, will be knowing where to stop; where he should draw a line round the spreading
relationships and yet have his narrative appear naturally self-
contained. In works which do not have lifelikeness as an end, the
structure will appear altogether different. Structural symmetry will
replace fidelity to observed particulars, repetition, parallelism and
convolution will be substituted for the logical developments of
report literature. At its furthest extreme this kind of structure is
represented in the short lyric whose articulation approaches stasis.
Certainly there is no deliberate step-by-step movement here, but on
close examination a certain structural vigour is given to the lyric by
the reverberation of connotations.

In section *E* are shown the devices used in the manifestation of
this structure—primarily symbolism, ambiguity and play on words.
If lyric provides the poet with the subtlest strategies, for narrative
complexity we must turn to the novel. At the heart of its narrative

technique is manipulation of the point of view. It is this manipulation that accounts for most of the special effects of prose fiction. One has only to examine a few representative plays with their small store of verbal presentational devices to appreciate the greater flexibility of novel narrative. All the great innovators—Richardson, Jane Austen, Henry James, James Joyce—have been so because they confronted their material in a new way. The complicated strategies of such narrative are examined in great detail by Wayne Booth in his *Rhetoric of Fiction*, Chicago 1961, and this section of the *Table of Terms* owes a good deal to it. Macauley and Lanning (*Technique in Fiction*) also have an excellent, and less theoretical, section on point-of-view.

Criticism at present seems to be in the state reached by science in the eighteenth century; and a great many empirical facts have been gathered and classified; what is lacking is a complementary theory. For the reasons given earlier, this must be different from scientific theories; but a prerequisite for any usable theory is an agreed terminology.

APPENDIX B

TABLE OF TERMS

I GLOBAL CONCEPTS   II REGIONAL CONCEPTS   III LOCAL CONCEPTS

I GLOBAL CONCEPTS

'Language' – Any system of communication by signs.

'Signal' – Any communication by signs without system.

'Verse' – Any writing in which line-length is part of the expressive form.

'Prose' – Any writing in which it is not.

(A poem is a complete structure of verses. A 'prose poem' is a contradiction in terms. The content of Verse is 'poetry'; the content of Prose is 'prose').

'Art' – Work characterized by a strong esthetic element: i.e. an element dependent on form and disinterestedness:
   (a) esthesis of *composition*
   (b) esthesis of *complementarity*
   (c) esthesis of *condensation*

'Anti-Art' – Work that opposes 'beauty', the esthetic, the quality of disinterested appreciation. The wilfully ugly and/or over-involving.

'Non-Art' – Work not characterized by a strong esthetic element; content counts for almost all, form for little or nothing. However, a more important distinction, for literary work, is that between the *purportedly*

'Fictional' – (e.g. autobiographical novel, but not autobiography) and the *purportedly*

'Non-Fictional' (e.g. history, though it may be fanciful, but not an historical novel though it may be faithful)

This leads on to:

'Purport' – the apparent intention of a work as it reveals itself to the reader from the title onwards. This concept is required not only for evaluation but even for description.

'Intention' – the writer's stated purpose, or a purpose deduced from evidence outside the work. A fallacious criterion for evaluation, but may provide tips on what to look out for, or psychological support of it turns out to tally with what the purport seems to be.

'Implication' – unconscious intention deducible from gaps in the work, between purport and achievement. Ideally – if we accept as desirable the principles of unity and coherence – intention, purport and implication should coincide (i.e. there should be no implication, in this sense; the underlying meanings of irony and allegory would be part of a 'compound purport')

– – – – –

123

II Regional Concepts

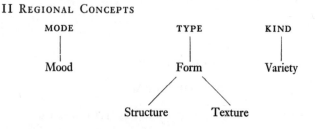

'MODE'—Basic genre-name defining the nature *of* the constituent kinds in terms of their most general aspect or effect

(PSYCHOLOGICAL conclusion resulting from all factors—unless the Mode has been predetermined by some special interest)

Examples, running from the more to the less inclusive—the last being interchangeable with 'kinds':

(a) Fictional/non-fictional.

(b) Mimetic, metaphoric, rhetorical/factual, abstract, controversial.

(c) *(Northrop Frye)* Mythic, Romance, High mimetic, Low mimetic, [Ironic]

(d) Tragedy, comedy, tragi-comedy, farcical comedy, farce, sentimental work, celebration, thriller.

'Mood'—Secondary class-name defining the nature of works *within* a kind (PSYCHOLOGICAL—mainly from style).

Examples: heroic, reverential, satirical, humorous, cynical, wistful, erotic, pastoral (if one follows Empson in assuming this to be a matter of tone rather than subject).

'Type'—Basic genre-name defining the general nature of the constituent kinds in terms of presentation (TECHNICAL):

Dramatic—typically the Play. Author disappears behind characters; usually all dialogue. Author's relationship with audience, indirect.

Narrative—typically the Tale. Author usually uses both narration and dialogue, and is partly visible. Relationship with audience, mediate.

Lyric—typically subjective utterance. Author speaks for, or as if for (persona) himself. Usually all narration, and usually a poem. Relationship with audience, direct.

'Form'—Secondary class-name covering all elements *within* a word other than those covered by 'Content'. Of two sorts:

Structural ('form' as contrasted with 'amorphousness')

Textural   ('form' as contrasted with paraphrasable content)

Both structural and textural form may be *organic* or *imposed* (relation with content). Structural form will also be either *Linear* or *Fugal* (ordering of content, in time). (TECHNICAL).

'Structure'—The ordering of the work, the way its elements are related to each other (Plot and story are structural elements of form; Theme is an aspect of content; leitmotif is equally structural and contentual—and, in so far as it is apprehended sensuously as concrete imagery, it is textural)

Note also the 'given pattern'—sonnet, rondeau, etc.,—a specialized example of imposed structural form. (TECHNICAL).

'Texture'—The rendering of surface detail; mainly a matter of the way language is handled—and therefore a narrow aspect of 'style'.

'Style'—Any *characteristic* handling, textural or structural. A concept wide enough to include the 'situational'—the style of a mode or period—and narrow enough for the 'individual'—the characteristic speech of fictional personages. 'Style' is a matter of relation to some norm (and is most readily conceived as deviation from, or particularizing of a more general, assumed norm). 'Texture' is a matter of immediate impression (in contrast with the dependence on memory required for 'structure') (PSYCHOLOGICAL)

'Kind'—(major or minor). In general, best regarded as species and sub-species of a TYPE (Definition therefore mainly TECHNICAL, from structure; but partly PSYCHOLOGICAL, from purport):
Dramatic: Play (stage- radio-), Filmscript (cinema-, TV-), Dramatic monologue (ritual, recitation). All these may be 'romance-', or 'report-'. (See III, Local Concepts, *A*).
Narrative: Short story (plot, mood/romance-, report-), Chronicle 'pretended or real; of theme, place or character), Novel (romance-, report-), Poem (epic-, romance-, report-)
Lyric: Song, Elegy, Epigram, Panegyric, Meditation, Ode, Sonnet. (All may be more or less patterned or free, more or less public or private in tone) [For particular purposes, *any* classification—not only this one by Type—may constitute a Kind]

'Variety'—A form of KIND (A TECHNICAL judgement, by formal presentation]:
Dramatic: Prose or verse, expressionist, masque, opera.
Narrative: Letter, biographical, point-of-view, omniscient narrator.
Lyric: Couplets, quatrains, etc., metrical, free, 1st person or 3rd, persona or 'real' voice.

Note: Hypothetically any of these presentations could be *oblique* (symbolic allegorical, ironic, parodic), and thus of compound purport, OR direct (mimetic, literal, plain) and thus of simple purport.

III Local Concepts

A. *Kinds described by (Imposed) Form (or partially by Form)*
  i Drama: One, Three, Five Act play, Masque, Monologue.
  ii Narrative: *Report*—(novel, nouvelle, short story)
  Romance—(novel, Gothic tale, fairy tale, short story)
  Confession—biography, autobiography, journal.
  Anatomy.
  iii Lyric: Sonnett (Petrarchan, Shakespearean, Miltonic), Villanelle, Rondeau, Carol, Epigram, Triolet, Ballade, Ode, etc.

B. *Kinds described by content (or partially by content)*
  i Drama: History, Tragedy, Comedy, Farce, Religious and Secular Autos.

ii Narrative: Report-novel Social, Moral, (Psychological)
                  Romance-novel (Supernatural, myth)
                  Confession (Physical or mental development)
                  Anatomy (Ideas, Theories, Feelings)
iii Lyric: Religious, Panegyric, Complaint, Epigram, Pastoral, Elegy, Ode.

C. Kinds described by Texture:

For the most part all textural elements may be found in all kinds (and types). The three sections below give a logical spread over all possible figures of speech, only some of which are more characteristic of one kind (or mode or type) than another (as rhyme and metre are of Lyric, hyperbole and personification of Epic).

  i Musical: *Examples:* Onomatopoeia, Rhyme, Rhythm, Metre, Alliteration.

  ii Lexical: *Examples:* Metaphor, Paronomasia, periphrasis, Metonymy Litotes, Simile, Personification, Hyperbole.

  iii Syntactical: *Examples:* Rhythm, Chiasmus, Anaphora, Zeugma, Syllepsis, Polysyndeton, Periphrasis, Parallelism, Climax, Antithesis, Inversion, Co-ordination.

D. Kinds described by (Temporal) Structure

Again only some structures are especially characteristic of a particular kind.

  i *Continuous Structure:* Chronological development of the subject. Story (Sequential), Plot (Consequential). Linear time. [Narrative, Drama]

  ii *Discontinuous Structure:* Counterpointed, or convoluted development. Double Plot, Parallelism, Flashback, Inversion, Time-shifting. Fugal time [Narrative, Drama]

  iii *Static Structure:* No development; structure by reverberation, the interior hum of implication; gestalt effect. Mood, or short experience-sharing, lyric. Complex whole, seized at once [Lyric]

E. Kinds described by Strategies (Ways of using devices for given effects)

  i Drama: Privileged character as semi-narrator. Alienation effect. Effects from different settings: open stage, picture frame, etc. Commentator.

  ii Narrative: (a) *Showing* unmediated reality or undramatized narrator). Stream of consciousness, montage, cutting, time-shift.

      (b) *Telling*   i Narrator distant from author (morally, intellectually or temporally)
               ii Narrator distant from character
               iii Narrator distant from reader's norm

  iii Lyric: Strategies for expressing the unmediated thoughts and feelings of the (supposed) speaker—typically, symbolism, ambiguity, overtone, metaphor.

  iv Universal Strategies: (a) *Oblique* (compound purport) Symbolic, Allegorical, Ironic, Parodic
                      (b) *Direct* (simple purport) Mimetic, Literal, Plain.

PART II

9

Terms for Comedy

THAT criticism of comedy lags far behind that of tragedy and indeed of most other forms of literature, will occasion no surprise to anyone who has attempted it; for in this field every tool breaks in the hand: even the commonest terms turn out to have been damaged by inconsistent use.

To criticize any particular work it is necessary to have in mind three major questions: (i) *Is it comedy at all?* Is the work, that is to say, an example of purposive art working in a detached yet accommodating way through laughter, holding judgement in one scale, geniality in the other? (ii) *What sort of comedy is it?* Humorous, cynical, satirical, celebratory? Is it using the right methods for that sort? Using them well? (iii) *Is it good comedy of its kind, mode, or type?* Technically? Socially, in its own day? Psychologically, in ours? In tendency *and* actual effect? Though some of these questions have a different logical status from others, in so far as they relate to descriptive or evaluative criticism, it is probably important to bear in mind the undesirability, in the last analysis, of compartmentalized criticism for what one hopes will be artistic unities. However, so far are we from the possibility of any last analyses, that only passing apology is required for what many may feel to be the rather humdrum list of definitions to follow; it is a primary requirement. What does need apology is the fact that the most important term, 'comedy' itself, must be dealt with inadequately—simply because it *is* the most important and therefore, properly dealt with, would take up more space than it can have.

The present study, then, sets out briefly to distinguish comedy as an art-form from other forms; to distinguish between the modes, moods, and methods of comedy; and to define sufficiently for critical application the words appropriate to each division.

Lexical definitions in this field would be impossible, since terms

---

[1] Fuller discussion will be found eventually in Rodway, *The Character of English Comedy*, in preparation for Chatto and Windus.

relevant to the discussion of comedy are, and always have been, used in hopelessly confused and contradictory ways. Logical definitions, if they could be formed, would be impracticable, since neither comic art nor common usuage is reducible to tautology; both—to have any merit at all—must reflect living experience, however obliquely. The definitions to be put forward, therefore, are admittedly stipulative, and claim no validity save that of usefulness. However, though stipulative, they are not arbitrary, since they are adaptations of, and selections from common usage, designed to make it critically manageable.

In common usage, the word 'comedy' carries more overtones of approval than the word 'farce'. Since there are different sorts of funny literature, and since one sort is nearer to art and another sort is nearer to entertainment, the difference of emphasis is right, and should be clarified into full consciousness. There are bad comedies and good farces, but the one mode may be said to be 'higher' than the other, since it both gives and demands more. Not that there is anything which is inherently comic (so definitions by subject-matter are useless), or that there are any clear-cut distinctions (comedy of psychological release shading off into farce at one end of the spectrum, just as corrective comedy shades off into tragi-comedy at the other). At the heart, though, differences of *genre* are clear enough, or may be made clear enough, as follows.

Historically speaking—or perhaps anthropologically speaking—comedy seems to have originated as an expression of man as Cultivator, tragedy as the expression of man as Warrior. Tragedy emphasizes inflexible courage to defy a remorseless Fate; comedy emphasizes flexibility to get by it, round it, or on with it. In Aristophanes, farce and comedy are still merged in one form. In English literature, however, three modes can be distinguished almost from the beginning. Farce, divertissement and comedy seem appropriate words for these different forms, 'comedy' being used for that sort of amusing work which is a mode of psychological warfare, deploying laughter purposively—usually to insinuate certain values. Sociologically speaking, comedy may be of an *innovating* or a *conserving* kind. Psychologically speaking, *restraining* or *releasing*. Farce can only be 'releasing'. To the statement that 'comedy' is to refer to writings produced by a purposive attitude inseparably linked with laughter, we can add that such writings are further distinguished from tragedy by their gregarious quality (and this will prove to be helpful in determining more clearly what 'farce' should cover).

The tragic hero is invested with his isolation; though it may cause his downfall, it does not reduce his stature. In comedy (as defined) such extreme individualism is seen as eccentric or abnormal. Again, the comic writer, unlike the lyric poet, has an audience in view when he composes; and more than the writer of tragedies he seems concerned to have the audience accept his values, for they tend to be social rather than individual ones.

Those values are by no means always fully explicit or systematized, they may often be muddled in fact, for the undidactic mode of comedy necessarily leads the writer to insinuation rather than exposition. Though laughter is compatible with attitudes other than the comic—and may be a mere physical reflex, as in the case of tickling—it is not compatible with what we normally think of as didacticism. In short, comedy is purposive in a uniquely accommodating way, and thus produces more complex, if less perceptible effects than the exhortations of didactic or sentimental works.

Now 'farce', for all its backslapping, lacks this sort of sociability. In so far as it reaches to the depths of the psyche it is more akin to tragedy than comedy. Potts[1] neatly defines farce as 'comedy with the meaning left out'. In comedy, that is to say, laughter is a means to an end; in farce the means *is* the end: it is purposeless—but not therefore motiveless. Knockabout farce is often unconsciously motivated: the expression of instinctual impulses of envy, aggression or hard feeling. So patches of such farce may serve comedy well *as one of its means*, both in giving psychological depth and in relieving the diplomatic mode by the acrobatic. But farce on its own draws one into a primitive private world, where conscious awareness, particularly of a social kind, is relatively absent. It is thus different from the sort of writing to deserve the title of 'comedy'.

The definitive qualities of comedy, then, must include a considerable degree of conscious control, in the whole if not in every part. Though value-judgements must be insinuated *un*didactically the audience should not be allowed to lose itself in the laughter. A certain 'distance' is a requisite characteristic. Neither writer nor audience is or should be so involved in a comedy as in a farce.

Yet it is often possible to feel for the characters of comedy, but never for those of farce. The point is that we feel for them as

[1] Potts, L. J., *Comedy*, 1948 (p. 152).

characters separate from ourselves, whereas in farce we are involved with uncontrolled fragments from an inner world. In existentialist terms, we are *pour soi* (dominating and contemplating the subject) or *en soi* (submerged and thinglike).

There remains one sizeable class of amusing works which is not covered by either of the general terms considered. 'Divertissement' may serve to describe works which, like farce, leave the meaning out (sometimes, as in the miscalled 'sentimental comedy', the laughter too), and like comedy abjure the acrobatic. In a word they are frivolous rather than farcical or comic. At their best they manipulate current verbal counters with skill sufficient to disguise their superficiality for many decades. Lyly, Steele, Wilde and Fry have thus coruscated with this sort of *intellectual farce*.

Any further clarification of words referring to modes and their psychological *causes* or moral or social *ends* would probably prove unnecessarily restrictive. But some elucidation of the vocabulary of *means* is urgently needed.

In common usage the distinctions between such indispensable terms as parody, burlesque, satire, invective, irony, cynicism, wit, and humour are so blurred as to make them almost useless without some reworking. Since yesterday's usage was no more consistent than ours, no 'right' meaning can be borrowed from history. (Coherent evolutions, particularly of 'Wit', have, of course, been made, but only by leaving out the inconvenient usages proliferating in most periods.) If we start from today's usage we start with something known, if not clear, and it should be possible, guided by principles of sense and usefulness, to work out concepts that are neither so tight that they hurt nor so loose that they come down.

The need for clarification is apparent from the sort of questions that spring to mind in connection with any one term. For instance, ought we to consider satire as a mode, distinct from comedy, like farce and divertissement? If it is a mode, is it so always or only sometimes? Or should it be looked at from a different angle altogether.

If comedy is accommodating, does it therefore follow, as almost all critics suppose, that it must be a different *genre* from satire? Certainly, satire can be savage and laughterless, but need it be so? Or it may have laughter but no human feeling—only perhaps such feeling as the female mantis has for her mate. In Pope's lines on Lord Harvey (Sporus) there is this sense of a cannibalistic affection as the victim is mangled; the poet gains strength in a vampirish way.

Could this possibly be comedy? On the other hand, in the satire on Addison (Atticus) surely, for all its bite, there is a less dreadful feeling involved? And if there were not, could we possibly exclude the whole of the *Epistle to Arbuthnot* from the realm of comedy because it is satirical? . . .

At this point, though, it is necessary to take stock, as we are obviously approaching the field of wit, humour and irony: words that tend to gravitate towards any discussion on satire. It is an old-established critical custom to offer contrasting definitions of humour and comedy, wit and humour, comedy and satire, satire and ridicule, ridicule and humour. . . . Something is clearly amiss when one's definitions go round in circles. That is what comes of pairing items from different logical categories. In brief, a necessary distinction between methods and attitudes has hitherto been overlooked. This not only leads to a critical merry-go-round but also has the effect of hiding much that deserves notice. For instance, it may hide the fact that it is very questionable indeed whether humorous wit or comic satire *are* contradictions in terms. Certainly if we are to be forbidden by definition to use those terms we shall have to invent others that mean the same thing, for they fit some literary facts. Some such schema as this, however, seems workable:

Comedy, farce and divertissement are to be taken as MODES;

Irony, invective, parody, incongruity, slapstick, nonsense[1] *and wit* as METHODS:

Satire, humour, cynicism and celebration as MOODS.

The mode of a work is the widest category—of a psychological, not a technical sort—into which it can be placed. The moods are a refinement or subdivision of a mode: the prevailing climate of that region. They represent the spirit, or tone, in which the methods are used. The methods are the writer's technical means of incarnation.

Enough has probably been said about the distinguishing characteristics of the modes, comedy, farce and divertissement. Before passing on, however, to the distinguishing characteristics of the moods and methods most relevant to comedy, it might be as well to investigate a little further the notions of mode, mood and method themselves—if only as a reminder of their ultimate inseparability.

First, though, it ought to be repeated that such classifications can

---

[1] Nonsense might seem better placed among the modes, but any complete nonsense work could be considered either farce or divertissement, according to the sort of nonsense.

make no claim to absolute truth, only to critical usefulness. Had we been concerned not with comedies but satires it might have proved more convenient to take 'satire' as the mode and 'the comical' (slightly redefined) as one mood that might give it a predominant tone, to make a 'comic satire'. For such an investigation would require the separation of *all* satire from all that is not satire, and therefore kinds of satire would need to be distinguished.[1] Orwell's *Animal Farm*, then, might be called a comic satire to distinguish it from 1984, a horrific satire. As we are dealing only with 'comedy', 1984 cannot come within our purview at all, and *Animal Farm* would be more conveniently termed a 'satirical comedy' to distinguish it from humorous, cynical and accepting comedies that we might be dealing with.

Like a human being, and unlike a machine, the work of art is a continuum; so the mode may alter with alterations of mood and methods—just as, for instance, an aggressive mood in a man will affect his method of behaviour and his total being: colour, shape (posture of attack perhaps) and internal relationships (heartbeat, blood pressure, glandular activity, muscular tension)—but these are inseparable from his mood. The continuum is unbreakable. A work is technically good or bad according to its success in embodying the purport. But the purport iself is deduced from what the work does as it goes on.

Normally, we may suppose, the mood or attitude to the subject comes first (but, of course, some subjects prompt certain moods more than others), and then mood and subject together call for that handling of the subject which *in total* distinguishes one mode from another.

Mood is obviously more fundamental than method: a witty tragedy is not impossible, but a humorous tragedy would be a contradiction in terms. Yet sometimes structure—large-scale method—does come first. This is one of the harmful effects of tradition: the provision of set moulds into which authors obediently pour their feelings (it is helpful when it provides formal models of the failure and success of various methods of embodying different moods).

It is in farce that such an order of precedence is probably most

[1] Such an investigation has in fact been very successfully undertaken by A. M. Clark in a long essay, 'The Art of Satire and the Satiric Spectrum' in *Studies in Literary Modes* (1946), which anticipates and expands some of the points made here.

common and least harmful. Since farce is largely mechanical any way, the writer can decide, let us say, to have one act of a play complicating relationships of ABC and D; a second of slapstick, containing one jelly-slapping scene, two in undies (female nylon, male Jaeger), and to wind up with a third act leading to an in-and-out-the-windows denouement—and then think of suitable characters, style and unifying tone.

This possibility may seem to imply that *Situation* ought to have been listed separately. In fact, situations are not separately classifiable, though it may sometimes be convenient to speak as if they were. They partake of both moods and methods, as part of the system of relationships determining modal class. What that mode is depends on the handling, and conversely the handling will be affected by what the author intends the mode to be: farce, or comedy, for example.

Suppose an adultery scene in a bedroom farce. Lover A is hiding in the cupboard, lover B is cowering in the bedroom, C, the wife, is trying to head off D, her husband, who wants to get his dressing-gown out of the cupboard and go to change in the bedroom.

The mood, communicated largely by style, will be humorous; no moral judgement is required. Moreover, as the aim of farce is simply to arouse laughter, the emphasis will be on action, not character. Dialogue, save for the sake of tone, will be unimportant and probably deliberately implausible. Timing, of word and deed, will be of first importance. All this will affect the future of the situation. For us to remain part of this apparitional world, it must steer clear of sense and sensibility. Perhaps, as the wife turns her husband's attention elsewhere, A will slip out of the cupboard and dive under the table (where the husband stands on his hand, the wife giving a loud hiccup to account for the yelp of anguish). While the husband is at the cupboard getting his dressing-gown, B will tiptoe from the bedroom, and meet A, for the first time, under the table (where the husband stands on *his* hand, and the wife has to hiccup an octave lower).

Were this initial situation to be part of a comedy, the dialogue would have to be more plausible, and there would necessarily be less dodging about—partly because comedy has more care for character, but mainly because a comedy should not be so funny as to allow the audience to miss the point. Too much belly-laughter is bad. If the mood were satirical (about marriage) the dialogue and action would be angled to show both wife and husband as knaves or fools or victims of the law, or all three. Irony would probably be prominent among the methods. If the mood were satirical about wifely hypocrisy, she might be given wily, loving speeches to her husband, to be exposed by the eventual discovery of the lovers. If the satire were on masculine vanity, the treatment would be different again. Were the tone cynical, the two lovers under the table might be made to come to agreement, and thereafter to lock the husband in the cupboard and share the wife in the bedroom. All this, in sharp contrast to previous protestations of singlehearted love from all three. Finally the husband might be shown willing to take money in compensation, and to forgive his wife provided she promised never to do it again—for nothing.

About the farce, no complaints would be heard (rightly, for its fantasy world has no meaning), but the cynical comedy would probably produce a crop of complaints about its immorality. Such complaints would have been justified had the tone been *humorous*, in this case; but the cynical tone in fact implies a 'realistic' (and defeatist) morality, opposing to the orthodox one disillusioned views on Right & Might, Love & Money. . . . It is clearly time to go on to discuss the nature of such moods and methods.

That all the methods listed are no more than means is proved by the fact that they can all be used in tragedy as well as comedy (save possibly slapstick, the chief method of farces). It is the formal end to which they are used, the way they are deployed for a given purpose, which makes them 'comic'.

That the moods or attitudes are sensibly so described gains support from adjectival usage. We do speak of a man's having a humorous, satirical, or cynical attitude, but not of his having a witty or parodic one. Admittedly, we do sometimes speak of an 'ironic attitude to life', but this is one of the places where common usage has to be rather arbitrarily tidied up for critical purposes, for though the grammatical form is parallel to that for the attitudes the sense is not. We use this phrase more vaguely, to denote the detached, cynical or satirical attitude of which the irony is an *expression*. If greater precision is needed—and it is—irony must be thought of as a technique.

THE MOODS:

Satire, the manifestation of a satirical mood, may be subdivided *ad infinitum*. Professor Lawlor,[1] for instance, distinguishes the Augustan or urbane variety from the traditional rough one, and minor from major modes. Such refinements, however, are more useful in actual practice than for general definition. For the moment, satire can be sufficiently characterized as entertaining but corrective attack on vice, with intellectual weapons or a tone of superiority (though occasionally the element of correction may be so slight that the satirical mood almost evaporates, leaving a work of intellectualized humour or clinical naturalism).

Satirized characters are dealt with extrinsically: revealed not as they would see themselves, but as they would be seen by prefects in an upper form.

The commonest methods of a satirical mood are wit and irony; and while it uses them it may remain within the bounds of comedy. When invective becomes predominant, however (as in the last book of *Gulliver's Travels*) the satire parts company with laughter and detachment and therefore passes from comedy into the less sunny realm of the lampoon or flyting—a realm of attack with unintellectual weapons, chiefly ridicule.

The *humorous* mood seems to be fundamentally one of self-defence. (To have a 'sense of humour' usually means to be able to shrug off one's mishaps.) Often, however, it assumes the guise of a good-natured attack on another character with whom we have some underlying cause for partial identification. Then our tolerant laughter at him protects us, in much the same way as our laughter at ourselves protects us, by forestalling the probably less indulgent laughter of others and burking further criticism. Thus humour is a tone indicating amusement without judgement, attack without malice.

Cynicism is easier to recognize than define, but its nature becomes more apparent if we take it to be the opposite of humour: essentially a form of self-attack. There are certain feelings or beliefs—those sponsored by 'conscience'—which we cannot ignore unless we are hypocritical. But we can snub them; we can devalue our sterling qualities. The cynic thus pretends to be bad, much as the hypocrite pretends to be good. Irony is the chief means of maintaining a cynical attitude, for it enables us to accept what we emotionally dislike, by taking both sides of the ironic statement as of equal value

---

[1] John Lawlor, 'Radical Satire and the Realistic Novel', in *Essays and Studies*, *Vol.* 8 (1955).

so that it cancels itself out. By cynicism we bring about an uneasy truce between the forces of theory and practice. It is not peace but an armistice; we have inwardly agreed to differ. That writers of cynical comedy, like the early Huxley or Isherwood, sometimes become mystics is not accidental. Such comedy is based on despair and its purpose is not so much to defend values as to defend defeat.

All this means that cynicism is psychologically expensive, and may become ruinously so. Therefore it gets itself condemned as immature, immoral and destructive, and so artistically valueless. Yet in certain circumstances it may in fact be a mature and responsible mood, the only way of preserving integrity, and therefore suitable for bitter comedy. Such circumstances, for instance, might arise when the general populace was being taken in by inflated values actually manipulated by pressure-groups for their own end, and opposition was rendered impracticable. For a one-eyed man in the kingdom of the blind, cynicism is mature, moral, and (if only for him) integrative—a way of still seeing and surviving. In comedy that is not cynical as a whole, too, cynicism may play a valuable part by deflating sentimentality: to the angel-face it opposes a baboon's bottom (cf. Touchstone in *As You Like It*).

A mood of 'celebration' seems inappropriate for a purposive mode like comedy, and perhaps a better word might be found.[1] All the same, it may serve as a reminder that 'comedy' is not being implicitly equated with 'humorous satire'. Its purposiveness may stop at revealing absurdity without trying to correct it—either because the writer likes the absurd with some part of his nature, or because he does not think it can be corrected, or because he thinks it is a necessary element in the individual or society, regrettable but amusing, which once corrected would leave life duller and colder than it was. Hence the prevailing climate of his comedy may be that of the celebration of inescapably unideal common humanity, despite squalls of satire and bright periods of humour. Or, people may be shown overcoming their weaknesses.

Some such notion seems to be needed to cover great comedy like Chaucer's 'Marriage Group' in the *Canterbury Tales*, Shakespeare's *Twelfth Night* and *As You Like It*, and Joyce's *Ulysses*. All these are shotsilk comedies, the product of myriadminded men, who seem

[1] 'Festive' would serve admirably, save that it seems a little too gay in its implications for a comedy tinged with sadness, like *Twelfth Night* (though the title and the name Feste do indeed tend to justify the description).

conscious of the complexity of experience and the limitations of every view, so that one mood tends to be given depth by a shading of some other.

Such writers relish the absurd at the same time as they expose it, and have a good deal of charity for the failings of human nature. Thus, though they place what is laughable by some implicit norm of sanity and balance, they also seem to accept it as a concomitant of human nature—and none of them thinks human nature itself can be changed. So they are not too severe, not too wholehearted in their comedy, for behind the effort to change particular manifestations of human folly lies the feeling, *Plus ça change, plus c'est la même chose.*

Such writers tend to be empirical humanists rather than systematic moralists. Their comedy tends to be tinged with sadness, and the shotsilk quality of their vision tends to make the comic point less apparent. Indeed there may be no one point—apart from the general trend in favour of benevolent discrimination. Thus against a gain in human richness must be set a loss in force. So the established preference for Shakespeare's comedies rather than those of Jonson has no objective validity. Shakespeare has more depth, but then Jonson has more direction. For comic purposes, neither strength seems universally or necessarily more valuable than the other.

THE METHODS:

Among methods *Irony* needs fairly extensive consideration, even for such a general characterization as this. Fortunately, it is one of the few words whose etymology proves helpful. So many critics today, especially in America, find irony under every stone that a reminder of its original meaning may not come amiss—*eirōneía*, 'assumed ignorance', from *eirōn*, 'a dissembler'. The sense of a dissembling that is meant to be seen through must remain fundamental if the word is to have any consistent function. And Brower,[1] for instance, is misguided in extending the term to cover Keats's *Ode to Autumn*. 'Irony' is not synonymous with 'ambiguity'; though it is ambiguous, as the ironic vision is bifocal. On that last point, Brower is right; irony is not merely a matter of seeing a 'true' meaning beneath a 'false', but of seeing a double exposure (in both senses of the word) on one plate. The fact of opposition must be as apparent as the fact

[1] R. A. Brower, *The Fields of Light* (New York, 1951), p. 27.

that it is overcome. Only then will there be an effect of laughter, usually inward laughter, through the release of tension.

The inevitable risk run by an ironist, of course, is that his dissembling will *not* be seen through. One recalls the story of the dear old lady who re-read Mr. Gibbon for the sake of all the pious reflections in his footnotes. Irony needs a discerning audience. But given such an audience it may prove the most profitable of means.

Where primary states like hostility subdue, irony, more complex, may reform. Hence its prevalence in satirical comedy. Such comedy combines strong feelings with didactic purport by means of barbed laughter.

The operations of irony are too multifarious to be dealt with fully, but a few of the more important may be indicated. Probably Deflation is the commonest: the apparently indifferent introduction of the physical, perhaps, when we are concerned with the moral, or the apparent equating of ideals with mundane facts, or the humbling of a proud style by a bastard content. Pope's *Rape of the Lock* is full of such deflations:

> This day, black omens threat the brightest Fair
> That e'er deserv'd a watchful spirit's care;
> Some dire disaster, or by force, or flight;
> But what, or where, the fates have wrapt in night.
> Whether the nymph shall break Diana's law,
> Or some frail china jar receive a flaw;
> Or stain her honour, or her new brocade;
> Forget her prayers, or miss a masquerade.

There is a sequence of deflation in Swift's *On the Death of Dr. Swift*:

> My female Friends . . .
> Receive the News *in doleful dumps*,
> 'The Dean is Dead, *(and what is Trumps?)*
> 'Then Lord have Mercy on his Soul.
> '(Ladies I'll venture for the *Vole.*)
> 'Six Deans they say must bear the Pall.
> '(I wish I knew what *King* to call.'
> 'Madam, your Husband will attend
> 'The Funeral of so good a Friend.
> 'No, Madam, 'tis a shocking Sight,
> 'And he's engag'd To-morrow Night!

'My Lady *Club* wou'd take it ill,
'If he shou'd fail her at *Quadrill.*
'He lov'd the Dean. *(I led a Heart.)*
'But dearest Friends, they say, must part.

The technique of Inversion—of roles, ideas, or values—is so often found in the works of Shaw, with his dustman-philosophers and the like, that it hardly needs illustration. It depends for its effect, of course, on our idea of the normal being constantly implicit. Again, there is Fusion—usually of appearance and reality. Witness Robert Ferrars, who is adorned in the first style of fashion and has 'a person and face of strong, natural, sterling insignificance' (*Sense and Sen-bility*, chap. XXXIII).

Finally, it should be noted that where irony is used not for satirical but for cynical comedy it is often masochistic. The author identi-fies himself with the bad, the impotent or the defeated. Possibly some of Henry James comes into this category. This sort of irony was presumably at the back of Kierkegaard's mind when he wrote that irony ends by killing the individual—a dubious judgement, though provocatively near the mark for some cases. He also writes, on the same page:

> An individuality full of longings, hopes, wishes, can never be ironical. Irony (as constituting a whole life) lies in the very reverse, in having one's pain just where others have their longings. Not to be able to possess the beloved is not irony. But to be able to possess her all too easily, so that she herself begs and prays to belong to one, and then not to be able to get her: that is irony. Not to be able to win the splendours of the world is never irony; but to have them, and in profusion, within one's reach, so that power and authority are almost forced upon one, and then to be unable to accept them: that is irony. In such cases the individuality must have a secret, a melancholy, or the secret of a melancholy wisdom. That is why an ironical individuality cannot be understood by one who is full of longing, for the latter always thinks: if only one could have one's wish.[1]

Certainly, if such an individual is aware of the contrast between his state and the normal one, there is irony, and his wisdom must be of a melancholic, or even masochistic kind. But is he worse off than if

---

[1] *Kierkegaard*, ed. W. H. Auden, 1953, p. 49.

he suffered unaware, and therefore without irony? Ironical, such a man is (so to speak) his own audience mitigating his tragedy with the wry enjoyment of 'dramatic' irony; unironical, he is the tragically possessed protagonist.

An author's reasons for using irony may be very varied. In addition to those implicit in the foregoing account, there is its use to blame without seeming to, by divorcing tone and statement, as in Fielding's *Jonathan Wild (passim)* or Beerbohm's glancing blow at scholars: 'To give an accurate and exhaustive account of that period would need a far less brilliant pen than mine' *(Eighteen-Eighty)*. This use tends to give the impression that the writer is more polished and urbane, more 'polite' than possible opponents, and is a common motif of Augustan irony. Irony may also be used to give the impression that an unarguable case is so foolproof that only a reminder of it, a hint, is needed—anyone thinking otherwise convicting himself of proven foolishness. Henry James provides a nice example of a double-take in this kind, with his irony about the crude irony of Mr. Wentworth (the Jamesian irony being set in motion by the preceding speech given to that worthy):

> 'I don't know what her manner of life may have been,' he said; 'But she certainly never can have enjoyed a more refined and salubrious home.'
>
> Gertrude stood there looking at them all. 'She is the wife of a Prince,' she said.
>
> 'We are all princes here,' said Mr. Wentworth; 'and I don't know of any palace in this neighbourhood that is to let'
>
> *(The Europeans.* Chap. IV)

Argument can be answered; irony cannot, for it undermines a position in the very act of defending it. Again, irony is a form of flattery for the intelligent reader, and a veiled threat to hypothetical opponents, who had better be careful in dealing with so level-headed a fellow. There is the suggestion, too, of dispassionate objectivity; the ironist has obviously not been misled by passion or prejudice. Since in all he writes there is an implication as well as a statement, it seems to follow, however illogically, that he sees both sides of a question. And lastly, among the commoner reasons for using irony, is that of substituting a tone of reasoned contempt for an expected indignation—witness Swift's *Modest Proposal*, the Letters of Junius, or, in little, Pope's brisk dismissal of the Universities and the Stuart question:

May you, my Cam, and Isis, preach it long!
'The right divine of Kings to govern wrong.'

(The Dunciad. IV)

The ironist seems to give light instead of heat, since he has maturity enough not to be blinded by wrath. It remains only to remark that when irony passes into *sarcasm*, its crudest form, it is usually to be found keeping bad company with invective in a non-comic satire.

Of *invective* little need be added to what has already been said. Its place in comedy appears to be small, and is in fact smaller than it appears to be, for much of what might be taken for invective turns out to be humorous hyperbole. Falstaff's bravura passage on Bardolph's nose, for instance (1 *Henry IV*, III, iii), is less biting, and more comic, than a shorter and intenser attack on the drunkard's debasement would have been. The swelling takes away the sting:

FAL. Thou art our admiral, thou bearest the lanterne in the poope, — but 'tis in the nose of thee; thou art the knight of the burning lampe.

BARD. Why, Sir John, my face does you no harme.

FAL. No, I'll be sworn; I make as good use of it as many a man doth of a deaths head, or a *memento mori*: I never see thy face, but I think upon hell fire, and Dives that lived in Purple; for there he is in his robes, burning, burning. If thou wert any waie given to vertue, I would sweare by thy face; my oath should be, By this fire that Gods Angell. But thou art altogether given over; and wert indeede, but for the light in thy face, the sonne of utter darknesse. When thou ran'st up Gadshill in the night to catch my horse, if I did not think thou hadst been an *ignis fatuus* or a ball of wildfire, there's no purchase in money. O, thou art a perpetual triumph, an everlasting bonefire light! Thou hast saved me a thousand Markes in Linkes and Torches, walking with thee in the night betwixt taverne and taverne: but the sacke that thou hast drunke me, would have bought me lights as good cheape, at the dearest Chandlers in Europe. I have maintained that Sallamander of yours with fire, any time this thirty yeares; God reward me for it!

The general tone is sufficiently indicated by the movement from the genial 'I think upon hell-fire' (which could have been bitterly indicting) to the not-completely-ironical 'Heaven reward me for it!'

On the satiric scale, true invective is generally to be found at the opposite end from detached irony. And invective-satire is of a lower order than ironic-satire, if only because it does not work so well. The follies of big-enders and little-enders in Lilliput seem follies indeed, for they are presented with a detached irony. But at the end of *Gulliver's Travels* few readers can help siding with the loving wife who is called 'that odious Animal' and the children who have the misfortune to smell more like human beings than horses. That satire is unsweetened by laughter, and its bitterness leaves a nasty taste behind. Furthermore, its effect is neurotic rather than integrative. Ultimately, it is man's inescapable humanity that is denounced.

Parody need present no difficulties, provided that it is distinguished from its near relations *burlesque* and *mock-heroic*. According to Boileau and Dryden there is burlesque when a high theme is treated in a low style; when a low theme is treated in a high style, there is mock-heroic. A simple, useful and adequate distinction for most critical purposes. Parody is a form of mimicry that is just off the note, and it may therefore approximate to burlesque or mock-heroic, according as it is sharp or flat. The pleasure we take in parody is that of seeing the mighty fall, to our own level or a little below it; so that it is generally a means of 'releasing' comedy. It acts as a preservative, keeping sentiment from going sugary, solemnity from becoming pompous. All good qualities are in danger of losing vitality or relevance and hardening into mannerism. Parody indicates the end-product of such a process. It is unique among methods of comedy in that it usually mocks not the bad but the good, holding up a glass in which its worst potentialities are seen realized. Amongst modern parodies, Henry Reed's *Chard Whitlow*[1] stands out as both clever and salutary comedy, finely evoking the prim precision latent in T. S. Eliot. So many spoof lines, too, carry a momentary air of admonitory authenticity: 'As we get older we do not get any younger', 'And I cannot say I should care (to speak for myself)/To see my time over again—if you can call it time', or 'The wind within a wind, unable to speak for wind'—a clear warning of the disguised emptiness to come in *The Cocktail Party* and *The Confidential Clerk*.

Parody could, perhaps, have been subsumed under 'Incongruity' —in this case, of content and manner—but *incongruity*, like *knockabout*, hardly warrants much discussion. Both are immediately

[1] From *A Map of Verona* (1946).

recognizable and primarily are means of arousing *un*thoughtful laughter by surprise. Knockabout, in particular, is far more often a means of farce than comedy.

Nonsense is more interesting. In her sensible book on the subject[1] Miss Elizabeth Sewell maintains that nonsense is a game in which the forces of logic play—and beat—the forces of dream and disorder. However, if one is not going to concentrate on Lewis Carroll and (unlike Miss Sewell) has no theological axe to grind, there seems no need to follow her in deciding that the worlds of dream and disorder are not be be considered as Nonsense. Why, after all, is the mind able to receive nonsense in only '*one* of three ways'? The common use of the word covers all three ways, and all three have this in common: they are not of the world of the senses and commonsense. Logic, like algebra, is independent of it; dream transforms it; and disorder denies its laws. The last species would seem to be of no value in itself and of no use for comedy. As Miss Sewell says 'nothing is more boring' than 'an endless succession of random events'. Dream-nonsense, however, may well be of use for comedy, since it can symbolize realities of the world of sense and commonsense in a striking way, or obliquely comment on them.

Where there is much condensation but comparatively little distortion of everyday reality, we have not nonsense but *wit*, the most important and inclusive of all our terms. Historically, there is perhaps good reason for the traditional contrast with humour—*wit* being once thought of as a mental quality, as opposed to *humour*, a bodily fluid. And doubtless there lingers still in modern usage an echo of that fundamental distinction. However, there is certainly no contradiction today in speaking of a humorous man as an intelligent one also. Moreover, Freud,[2] who has given by far the most satisfactory modern account of wit, shows that there is such a thing as humorous wit. Thus the idea of a contradiction between wit and humour is shown to be itself contradictory. The puzzle is solved by taking the one to be a method, the other a mood.

Both fact and theory make it apparent that wit may be used to convey *any* comic attitude (and also, as in *Hamlet* and *Lear*, attitudes that are not comic). Its intellectual quality and its indirectness

---

[1] *The Field of Nonsense*, London 1952.

[2] Freud, S. *Wit and its Relation to the Unconscious* (1914), translated by A. A. Brill. A brilliant analysis to which the present account is much indebted, though it differs in many minor respects.

render it peculiarly fitted for comedy, which is a civilizing agent, an alternative to violence as a group-weapon. Of this sort of use Clough's *The Latest Decalogue* is a deservedly well-known example, and its most famous couplet is not only a biting comment on the economic orthodoxy of a sanctimonious age but also an accidental description of the satirical wit's own attitude: 'Thou shalt not kill; but needst not strive/Officiously to keep alive.'

Wit taps the deeper levels of the psyche; it is the only civilized equivalent of those 'releasing' elements of primitive ritual which in most developed societies—particularly Christian ones—are considered too aggressive, too irreverent or too indecent for open expression. This, indeed, seems to be intrinsic to wit: that though it is made *by* the intellect it is made *from* the unconscious. Irony on the other hand is intrinsically conscious. The ironist applies his technique quite consciously; wit comes 'in a flash'. Brevity is the soul of wit, which must, as it were, shortcircuit the civilized mind's censorship system; whereas irony can be leisurely. There are, then, two layers in wit: an intellectual veneer which varies as the culture changes, and a primitive substratum always effective regardless of changes in outward fashion.

Even if we ignore Freud's separation of word-wit and thought-wit, as a distinction without much difference, we are left with two broad categories of wit that differ importantly. Though the two are not entirely separable, the distinction between *Play-Wit*, as we may call it, and *Tendency-Wit* seems both valid and necessary.

Play-wit is probably a form of regression to the freedom of childhood, an escape from the repressions required to maintain adult dignity, reason and responsibility. In consequence, it is primarily associated with ingenuity rather than intellect, and is more useful for farce or divertissement than for comedy. Almost by definition, what is playful is not particularly purposive, though it may release pent feelings and be brilliant—witness Whistler's remark that photography was a *foe-to-graphic* art, or Keith Preston's neat couplet:

> A modernist married a fundamentalist wife,
> And she led him a catechism and dogma life.

Next to the pun, dream-nonsense is perhaps the chief expression of play-wit. Often it may occur briefly in a complex pseudo-pun in the clinching phrase, as in the incongruous sexual-moral-economic-vocational complex in the word 'frontage' below:[1]

> There was a young lady from Wantage
> Of whom the town clerk took advantage.
> Said the borough surveyor:
> 'Indeed you must pay her;
> You've totally altered her frontage'
>
> (Anon.)

Significantly, England's great age of nonsense is that of the first three quarters of the nineteenth century; an age too authoritarian to be ideal for comedy but for that reason needing the more a harmless way of retreat into farce and fantasy. In Lewis Carroll's case, of course, to the strain of living up to the standards of Victorian respectability were added those of being a mathematician, a male spinster, and a clergyman who dared not allow his logic to impinge on his religion. In the twentieth century, America has been the land of nonsense, for it has resembled nineteenth-century England not only in its wealth and accompanying sense of virtuousness but also in the degree of pressure exerted by its conformism:

> . . . You crush all the particles down
> into close conformity, and then walk back and forth on them.
>
> Sparkling chips of rock
> are crushed down to the level of the parent block.[2]

Where pressures are too great, comedy is apt to be replaced by indignant revolt or regressive retreat.

It is apparent that much play-wit shares with tendency-wit its kinship to the dream. But it is obviously nearer the surface, dealing with material that is little repressed—under the surface only because a fully conscious mind tries to work sensibly. Such wit more often chooses *de jure* subjects, and is limited to comedy of mild release. It tends, moreover, to rely much more on the associations of words than idea. Wodehouse's description of a character as

---

[1] That this *is* play-wit is confirmed by the fact that the joke will not stand up to analysis. The wit is merely verbal legerdemain. For, of course, the value of property to which a bay window has been added is increased, not diminished, and therefore invites not compensation but extra tax.

[2] *To a Steamroller*, Marianne Moore.

'meadowfied'—'cowed and sheepish'—is typical play-wit. Typical of tendency-wit, on the other hand, is that ancient joke (instanced by Freud) of the prince who noticed a slave resembling himself and asked patronizingly, 'Was your mother ever employed in the king's household?' 'No, Sire,' came the reply, 'but my father was'. Here, quickness of the wit deceives the emotions. The brevity and complexity of the largely implicit statement enables expression to be given to thoughts and feelings that would otherwise have had to be repressed. A retaliatory impulse, a forbidden insult degrading the mighty, and a lightning piece of logical reasoning are compressed into that six-word answer. In that disguise they pass muster, expecially since the tension gathered for understanding is released in the hearer not through wrath but through laughter; at any rate when all the points are taken *at once*—not quite consciously—*together* with a recognition of the cleverness of the wit-work and of the incongruity of rude implication and polite tone.

As Freud points out, a dream, too, uses disguises—such as Inversion, Substitution, Symbolism, Representation through Opposites, Indirect Expression (as in this joke), and so forth—in order to smuggle into consciousness tendencies to aggression or other forbidden behaviour. All these mechanisms are to be found in tendency-wit too.

The correspondence between dream-work and wit-work, however, is not exact. Visual symbolism, the chief mechanism of the dream, is of much more service to the cartoonist than the writer. Again, a dream is usually personal and unintelligible. Wit is social, and to be so must be intelligible; the disguise must not be impenetrable. Further, if wit is in words there is a natural tendency to coherence (unless a Dodgsonian logic-game is being played), as words are normally the agents of consciousness and sense: a late product of evolution; whereas the language of dreams is mainly pictorial: scarcely less primitive than the repressed impulses it works on. However, wit and dream share the kindred characteristics of latent significance, unexpectedness, disguise and compression. So although wit is made, not found, a good deal of its making, though not all of it, must be unconscious. The speaker often surprises himself, and yet is not quite so surprised or amused as his hearer. It is difficult to believe that the schoolboy author of the following tendency-witticism was either completely conscious or completely unconscious of his full meaning:

During my first period of religious instruction this term (a teacher wrote to *The Manchester Guardian*) I was asked, 'What are the Seven Deadly Sins?' whereupon I enumerated them with brief explanations. Later in the morning I caught the questioner loafing and brought him out before my desk.

'Smith,' I began in ominous tones. 'Earlier this morning I enumerated for your benefit the Seven Deadly Sins. Can you remember any of them?'

'Yes, sir,' he replied. 'Wrath.'

(*M.G.* Miscellany, 10.9.53)

It seems needless to multiply examples, enumerate tendencies, or subdivide mechanisms. Indecency and aggression are the forbidden tendencies most obviously served by wit, and all the mechanisms can be subsumed under the one term, *Condensation*. Whether there is play on sound, as in Whistler's pun, or on sense, as with the word 'rest' in the epitaph Dryden is said to have written for his wife:

> Here lies my wife, here let her lie.
> Now she's at rest—and so am I;

whether there is telescoping of form, as in De Quincey's remark that in old age one drops into anecdotage; or of ideas, as in Johnson's comment that second marriages represent the triumph of hope over experience; or of tone and implication, as in the husband's comment on his wife's epitaph:

> As I am now, so you must be,
> Therefore prepare to follow me . . .
>
> To follow you I'm not content;
> How do I know which way you went?
> (Anon.)

—in each case there is condensation, and in each case some craving, playful or purposive, is gratified despite the potential hindrance of reason, respect, or politeness. Johnson's remark, however, is obviously not play-wit, and the element of tendentiousness in it— undermining the sacred and sentimental views of marriage—is so slight that we seem to be nearing the *epigrammatic*. If wit is defined as the marriage of intellect and abandon, begetting surprise and delight, then epigram is a chess-playing widower.

To confuse 'What oft was thought, but ne'er so well express'd' with the sort of wit that serves psychological needs was pardonable in Pope's day but is not so now. When La Rochefoucauld writes:

Qui vit sans folie n'est pas si sage qu'il le croit

(*Maximes*, No. 209) our satisfaction lies only in the recognition of a truth expressed with the utmost point and economy. This is even more apparent in No. 228. We all know, perhaps rather vaguely, that pride is not precisely the same as self-love, but could we define the difference so as to reveal their distinct essences? How swiftly and brilliantly La Rochefoucauld pierces the mist:

L'orgueil ne veut pas devoir, et l'amour-propre ne veut pas payer.

No desire, save that to understand, is here gratified. The case is different with some comments whose tone seems equally detached — so different as to require another name. Thus Gibbon's footnote on the Empress Theodora's banquet for ten nobles and forty slaves is witty, not epigrammatic. 'Her charity,' says Gibbon, 'was universal.' By doing so he intimates, demurely enough to pass the wards of decorum, that she took fifty men in one night; the word 'charity', however, recalls Christian attitudes to 'love' and implicitly praises the Empress (for charity is a ruler's Christian duty); he smiles at Christian chastity (for the Church's charity, too, is 'universal', though not so literally loving) and excuses Theodora (who after all, was putting precept into practice). Moreover, in the context, one is made aware of the smug Emperor Justinian, a *persecuting* Christian, deceived and given an object lesson in the love of one's fellow men by his pagan wife. Tendency-wit could hardly go further or be more briefly complex. It is as civilized and delicate, too, as it well could be in the circumstances. After all, it just *might* refer only to the feast.

With this polished weapon Gibbon fought against the forces of barbarism and fanaticism that, in his view, had destroyed Augustan Rome, and were then menacing Augustan England. The polish of high civilization, however, is not to be attained without exiling some part of human nature. There is a loss of depth and wholeness: a loss rarely made good by the following reaction, which usually tips the scale the other way. In England, a divorce of mind and body, of 'higher' and 'lower' faculties, is evident in most of the literature between Urquhart's translation of Rabelais and Joyce's *Ulysses* — a divorce responsible, at least in part, for the movement from Shakespearian richness of texture, though Congrevian urbanity, to a comedy of urban sentimentality. However, there is some gain too. 'Deformity' headed Bacon's list of objects of merriment (*Nat. Hist.* viii, 721); 'infirmities' were emphasized by Hobbes (*Human Nature* Ch. 9) but in his case the word was not restricted to a physical sense; and Congreve at the beginning of our Augustan age is to be found objecting even to the mockery of fools if they are not self-made but born so (Dedication to *The Way of the World*).

He is, of course, in advance of his age. But then so is all comedy in one way, for whether innovating or conserving, releasing or restraining, it works humanely and without fanaticism, tending always rather to persuasion than persecution; and it must rank high among the many social factors which contributed to that one indisputable gain between the sixteenth and eighteenth centuries: the gradual humanization of laughter and social life. By its nature comedy is a humane way of influencing public opinion. In the very act, even, of bringing a disciplinary vigour to a culture it contributes to a civilized growth.

Minimal Comedy: *Waiting for Godot*

Waiting for Godot has established itself as a masterpiece of the modern theatre, yet few of its public can have failed to share Estragon's multiple bafflement: 'I don't know why I don't know.' Indeed only Beckett's own later plays are less unpromising material for dramatic success. What other dramatist would have begun by jettisoning plot, motivation and characterization, proceeded by leaving us in ignorance of where the action was, when it took place, and whom it concerned, and concluded with one of his protagonists wondering, 'Was I sleeping while the others suffered? Am I sleeping now?'?

That last awkward question, posing an insoluble philosophic problem (how can you prove you are not dreaming when you think you are awake?) may give a clue to the right modal approach. It would be easy to read, and produce, *Godot* as farce (note the circus clowning, the business with boots, hat, and breaking rope, the release of primitive impulses), or as divertissement (note the apparent play-wit of *non-sequitur* and paradox), or as tragedy (the suffering, the hopelessness, and the carrying-on despite them). On the title-page, it is in fact described as a tragi-comedy. Certainly, if its mode is comic it is only just so—and only a philosophic purport could make such a mixture so: by absorbing the farce into a larger whole and giving sufficient detachment to eliminate tragic feeling. In fact, there is a good deal of evidence, in addition to the teasing question with which the play ends, to suggest a philosophic purport. The primitiveness of the impulses released, for instance, is significant; it makes a point. Much of the apparent play-wit turns out to be tendency-wit. The work, in fact, is purposive in the manner of comedy. Yet it is purposive in the most minimal way: its purpose is to show that there is no purpose, or that all supposed purposes are pretences, or, rather, defences against having to acknowledge the only ultimate, the Void. The mode, then, is comic—but it is comedy at the end of its tether. And, in that, it is admirably attuned to its philosophic purport, for if the purposiveness is negative, the mood is cynical: all actions, noble or ignoble, are merely games, ways of passing the time (which would pass anyway). The methods are— again appropriately; this play offering considerable esthetic pleasure, of complementarity—those of symbolism, inverted logic, and anti-religious, anti-humanist scepticism. And it is suffused with implicit irony, since the characters, alas, always behave as they would, while we are made aware that it is never as they conventionally should.

Both structure and texture throughout support this complex of ideas. There are two acts, covering two days—the minimum re-quired to suggest the main types of personality and the basic class-division of boss and bossed. Vladimir, in so far as he is anything, is optimistic, extravert and resilient; Estragon, pessimistic, introvert and defeatist in so far as he is anything (but both are near to being nothing: man as Lear's 'poor bare forked animal'). Pozzo is domi-neering, and a master; the ironically named Lucky is submissive, and a servant. The names are Russian, French, Italian and English. So we seem to have a play which has deliberately abandoned the usual localized action, motivated plot and personalized characters, for the grander concerns of metaphysical philosophy: Mankind Anywhere and Always. A very appropriate activity for a former secretary to James Joyce. Various repetitions and recurrences, which take the place of plot, also recall Joyce's belief in history as a cyclic reshuffling and superficial reshaping of basically unchanging elements, and thus act as further confirmation of metaphysical purport.

All this however merely passes us into a further set of puzzles. The action ought to be grand, but in fact is trivial; it is incon-sequential yet seems loaded with vague significance—not *in spite of* but *because of* the inconsequence (*why*, one is impelled to ask, does that tree have leaves today when it didn't yesterday?). Almost every single idea expressed is noncommittal (or promptly cancelled by the next) yet the idea of the whole is violently biased. On the other hand, one could say with equal justice that it is in general a philosophical play, but pointless in every particular. It is described as a tragicomedy, but it seems more often a mixture of depression and farce. It is, in short, philosophical but hardly reasonable.

Faced with all this, what can one do? Why, what else but walk out or accept it as it is? 'All this' is so much, and is so carefully all it is and not all it is not, that we are obviously not faced with an *obscure* play, which would be clear to superior minds. Rather we are faced with a clear play which is obscure to unquestioning minds; the puzzles are its answer to complacent clarities, its pointlessness is Beckett's point. The philosophy, in short, is nihilism; the play, a brilliant embodiment of total scepticism or agnosticism, whose unprogressive action, barren setting, logical structure and illogical texture perfectly render its plausible and perverse theme: 'They give birth astride of a grave'—and *all* their activities are merely ways of passing the time till they drop in.

This key image is itself typical of the literary quality, as well as the nihilistic theme, of the work. When Pozzo utters it, in Act II, it seems clear enough, if a little melodramatic (but then a man who has gone blind is entitled to be melodramatic):

> They give birth astride of a grave, the light
> gleams an instant, then it's night once more.

Quite. We come from darkness and then, like an extinguished light, are claimed by the dark again. But when Vladimir echoes the remark (thus raising its status from image to motif) we discover that grim clarity to have been too easy:

> Astride of a grave and a difficult birth. Down in the hole, lingeringly, the gravedigger puts on the forceps. We have time to grow old. The air is full of our cries. But habit is a great deadener.

Life is *at once* a long painful birth to the end and a long painful dying from the beginning. Moreover everything else becomes ambiguous: 'time to grow old' (while we're being born—and thus *bad*? Or before we die—and thus *good*?), 'the air is full of our cries' (hopeful sign of new life? Or hopeless sign of painful dying?), 'habit is a great deadener' (Of the pain of prolonged birth or dying, and thus *good*? Or a great killer, and thus *bad*?). And could the image not imply that it's only when we die that we're finally and fully born— i.e. the opposite of Pozzo's implication? There is no answer to these puzzles, no right way of interpreting the motif. *Waiting for Godot* may be a philosophic play but, however improbably, it is a *play*, so what comes over is not so much an idea as an experience. These words get prominence because they are not colloquial, not really in character, and therefore suggest a symbolic significance, but the suggestion is immediately dispersed among the ramifications of uncertainty and ignorance which constitute the perverse and hilarious texture of the play and render, as a phantom experience, the other half of the main theme: that all our activities are merely ways of passing the time, and thus of uncertain status:

VLADIMIR: That passed the time.
ESTRAGON: It would have passed in any case.
VLADIMIR: Yes, but not so rapidly.

One is forced to apprehend the dark profundity of both uses of the image and then is prevented by ambiguities and cancellations from taking either seriously.

This indeed is a characteristic technique of the whole play. Despite the grim situation of the protagonists, and the depressing viewpoint of the author, the work is outrageously funny; and much of the amusement comes from our recognizing human truth in the midst of logical absurdity, while being absolved from responsibility for or to it:

VLADIMIR: One is what one is.
ESTRAGON: No use wriggling.
VLADIMIR: The essential doesn't change.
ESTRAGON: Nothing to be done.

Thus the following dialogue, in Act II, reveals amusingly—but not satirically—truths of human nature within an absurdity of expression which absolves us from pity or horror or the duty of condemnation.

POZZO: Well to begin with he should pull on the rope,
as hard as he likes so long as he doesn't
strangle him. He usually responds to that.
If not, he should give him a taste of his boot,
in the face and privates as far as possible.
VLADIMIR: *(to Estragon)* You see, you've nothing to be afraid
of. It's even an opportunity to revenge yourself.
ESTRAGON: And if he defends himself?
POZZO: No no, he never defends himself.
VLADIMIR: I'll come flying to the rescue.
ESTRAGON: Don't take your eyes off me.
(He goes towards Lucky)
VLADIMIR: Make sure he's alive before you start. No point
in exerting yourself if he's dead.
ESTRAGON: *(bending over Lucky)* He's breathing.

VLADIMIR: Then let him have it.

> *With sudden fury Estragon starts kicking Lucky,*
> *hurling abuse at him as he does so. But he hurts*
> *his foot and moves away, limping and groaning.*
> *Lucky stirs.*

ESTRAGON: Oh the brute!

Much else appears to be satirical but, since no reformist intention manifests itself, is really just comedy of the Absurd—or, more appropriately, as Beckett is Joycian rather than existentialist, of the Void.[1] Indeed every character manifests some of the basic human faults: egotism, arrogance, self-pity, self-deception, servility, callousness and so on. But these are all presented simply as characteristics: part of the general lack of sense or consistency in existence. This is not to assert a nonsense-principle, but to acknowledge that *if* there is any order one couldn't possibly know it. The sceptical agnosticism is complete. Sense or order is like Godot (who is not 'God'—according to Beckett, who first wrote the play in French anyway—but apparently any sort of millennial hope—or fear); he never comes, his nature is unknown, but he sends messengers—who might or might not be reliable.

One thing, however, Beckett can be satirical about, namely assumptions of certainty or validity. Like Joyce—especially in the parodies-chapter of *Ulysses*—he assumes that humanity is always hiding from itself the poor bare reality under a garment of style. Hence the parody of the jargons of religion, law and scholarship—and of 'thinking'—when Lucky is made to *think*, in a flow of empty verbiage:

> Given the existence as uttered forth in the public works of Puncher and Wattmann of a personal God quaquaquaqua with white beard quaquaquaqua. . . .

These, after all, are not the important activities the practitioners take them to be—just games to pass the time. Since most of the

---

[1] 'He [Stephen] affirmed his significance as a conscious rational animal proceeding syllogistically from the known to the unknown and a conscious rational reagent between a microcosm and a macrocosm ineluctably constructed upon the incertitude of the void' [*Ulysses*. Chap 17.] But for Beckett there is less of the known and more of the void (cp. Estragon's answer to 'Where were we yesterday evening?'—'How should I know? In another compartment. There's no lack of void.')

activities of the protagonists of *Waiting for Godot* (including that of waiting for Godot) are shown to be similarly empty forms there is often an effect of satire upon such activities in life. But this effect is mitigated by leaving open the possibility that believing the games to be authentic activities may be as good a way of passing the time as believing them to be merely games, or having *no* beliefs like Lucky. (Perhaps he really *is* Lucky?) However, even if taking the business of life seriously is not quite satirized it is at least shown, by comic exaggeration, to verge on the absurd. Here, for example, are the forms of politeness:

POZZO: I'd very much like to sit down, but I don't quite know how to go about it.
ESTRAGON: Could I be of any help?
POZZO: If you asked me perhaps.
ESTRAGON: What?
POZZO: If you asked me to sit down.
ESTRAGON: Would that be a help?
POZZO: I fancy so.
ESTRAGON: Here we go. Be seated, Sir, I beg of you.
POZZO: No no, I wouldn't think of it! *(Pause. Aside.)* Ask me again.
ESTRAGON: Come come, take a seat I beseech you, you'll get pneumonia.
POZZO: You really think so?
ESTRAGON: Why it's absolutely certain.
POZZO: No doubt you are right. *(He sits down.)* Done it again! *(Pause.)* Thank you, dear fellow. *(He consults his watch.)* But I must really be getting along, if I am to observe any schedule.

Here, language as ritual:

VLADIMIR: You must be happy too, deep down, if you only know it.
ESTRAGON: Happy about what?
VLADIMIR: To be back with me again.
ESTRAGON: Would you say so?
VLADIMIR: Say you are, even if it's not true.
ESTRAGON: What am I to say?
VLADIMIR: Say, I am happy.
ESTRAGON: I am happy.

VLADIMIR: So am I.
ESTRAGON: So am I.
VLADIMIR: We are happy.
ESTRAGON: We are happy. *(Silence.)* What do we do now, now we are happy?

And, here, emotions too are a façade concealing emptiness:

VLADIMIR: Moron!
ESTRAGON: That's an idea, let's abuse each other.
. . . .
ESTRAGON: Now let's make up.
VLADIMIR: Gogo!

In its way, this is a brilliantly witty play, and witty in a specifically modern manner. Its wit is not as conscious and elegant as Wilde's, and neither is it as nonsensical as Lewis Carroll's; Beckett's *non-sequiturs* and other absurdities ought to purvey play-wit, and sometimes do, but mostly his is tendency-wit. Note, for example, the acid suggestion that much pity and good works is self-indulgence, in the following:

POZZO: Wipe away his tears, he'll feel less forsaken.
(Estragon hesitates)
VLADIMIR: Here, give it to me, I'll do it.
(Estragon refuses to give the handkerchief. Childish gestures)
POZZO: Make haste, before he stops.

Or, more symbolically, the implication of futile effort and servility, as the overloaded Lucky is being whipped on:

VLADIMIR: What is there in the bag?
POZZO: Sand. *(He jerks the rope.)* On!

It is this element of sharpness in the texture, allied to the starkness of the structure and the poverty and ill-health of the protagonists which justifies the description *tragi*comedy. Yet its comedy is what makes the play a masterpiece; for the absurdities, the empty formalities are strikingly related to life. The 'tragedy' is not. It may seem to derive from the philosophy, and the philosophy may be true. But in fact the apparent derivation is a cheat. After all, we are not all the time poor, ill and filled with boredom; and many of our pursuits, in the short view, are in fact purposeful. In a very long view, perhaps, it may be just to see life as essentially a painful progress to the grave, disguised by play-acting. But nothing in a truly sceptical philosophy compels us to prefer the long view to the short. So the tragic (or near-depressive) element in the play seems less vital than the comic (or near-savage-farcical). Certainly it is much less striking; we refuse to be depressed because we perceive this not to be the whole truth that it purports to be. Yet paradoxically, it is the tragic element that makes the comedy possible. The lack of belief allows us to laugh at the absurdities, the weaknesses, the failings, without feeling for the suffering.

Even so, if we compare *Waiting for Godot* to the epic comedy of Joyce—to whom Beckett seems to owe so much—it appears a much lesser work, lacking not only the stylistic, but also the human range of *Ulysses*. Joyce's work may be less philosophical, but it is much more reasonable; in with the self-deception, the absurdity, the fundamental isolation and pointlessness of the human situation, it includes the achievement, the gusto, the variety and, when all admissions are made, the worthwhileness of life. Beckett's is a masterpiece of the modern theatre; but a minor masterpiece.

11

Author – Times – Audience Equals Distance

No esthetic problems are simple, but those of literature present special difficulties. That literary critics have tended to shy away from them is, however, probably due not solely to the intricate nature of the working but also to the unpalatable nature of the answers.

The most basic of these problems—and the key to their solution—seem to spring from the interanimation of material and immaterial worlds in the literary experience—a fact sufficient in itself to account for that sense of almost theological dilemma which has long haunted critical theory. It lurks behind the recurrent opposition of Platonic and Aristotelian criticism, and obliquely affects even the most pragmatic of critics:

> He that can take the stage at one time for the palace of the Ptolomies, may take it in half an hour for the promontory of Actium.

wrote Dr. Johnson with sturdy commonsense, sweeping the doctrine of the Unities into Criticism's out-tray. And, he went on:

> where is the absurdity of allowing that space to represent first Athens, and then Sicily, which was always known to be neither Sicily nor Athens, but a modern theatre?

Rather inconsistently, however—perhaps when his commonsense was losing the endless battle with his neurosis—he also recorded his unwillingness to bear the pity and terror of the last scenes of *Lear* for a second time, and thus left open the question of detachment or involvement.

Indeed the truth is that Johnson's invaluable critical service was performed under the aegis of an over-simple theory. Why not abandon costumes and scenery as well as the Unities if there's no illusion anyway? And if there *is* no illusion why should Brecht and, more subtly, Shakespeare feel the need for alienation devices? Moreover what do we receive from a play (a novel or a poem) if we don't participate in it? And how can we participate if no illusion is created? (But perhaps only naïve audiences become *fully* involved, and thereby lose the chance of esthetic appreciation?) In practice we seem to be sometimes much more involved than Johnson suggests (save when speaking of *Lear*); sometimes, on the other hand, much aware of the theatre and the fictionality of the performance; but mostly—at any rate with major plays—at once involved and contemplative. The achievement of this complex effect (one of the last refinements of art) appears to be largely dependent on a capacity to exploit certain characteristics of *Style* and *Time*.

Trying to find an adequate formula to summarize it reveals just how complex the effect is. Even a basic discussion of what happens at the performance of a literary work—whether dramatic, narrative or lyric, by others or by oneself in silent reading—is found to involve at least the author's fictional content and formal time-structure, the audience's experience of real time and fictional time, of the real and fictional situations, and the audience's (partly esthetic) appreciation.

'Author/Times/Audience = Distance' perhaps contains enough terms to summarize it—but only by exploiting an ambiguity, implied by the capital T. Since even basic discussion involves so many items, it would obviously not be inappropriate to interpret the equation as Author + Times + Audience = (Esthetic) Distance.' But as much that has to be spoken of successively occurs simultaneously, and as the simultaneous interaction of the elements creates a total experience greater than the sum of its parts, the idea of multiplication, (Author × Audience . . .) would also be appropriate.

Accepted, this equation entails some unpalatable conclusions: realism turns out to be an esthetic form of alienation technique; a coexistent awareness of the real world to be a necessary condition for appreciating worlds of fiction; and modern philistines to have been more justified that sophisticates. Rejected, however, it leaves unanswered a number of difficult questions in literary criticism and esthetics—in particular the questions of how we accept as lifelike novels, plays or films whose time-structure is clearly not synchronous with that of life, how we manage to combine—as we usually should and sometimes do—vital participation with critical detatchment, and how in the complexity of the literary experience esthetic pleasure may depend on artful form being combined with humdrum content.

In understanding this interanimation of disparates, esthetic and temporal concerns—much neglected in current criticism—turn out to be crucial. The accompanying diagram *(Theorem of Worlds, Appendix C[1])* shows graphically how they are related to each other and to everything else.

What takes places is necessarily interior, but a proper interior appreciation is grounded in the world of available experience. As the taking place is not separable from the appreciating, two worlds, fictional and real, are in simultaneous interaction. So in a right performance, by an audience of one, of the shortest lyric poem a complex situation results which is essentially the same as that operating in the theatre (Blake's *Sick Rose* would be eccentrically interpreted as either a poem about gardening or a poem about a girl called Rose, but a more central, symbolic interpretation—involving jealousy amongst other things—would require some acquaintance with roses and women). Criticism must balance the re-creative interiority of the literary work, as it comes into significant being in performance, against Johnson's undeveloped perception of the importance of the Outer Situation, the shared world. The diagram—which relates the resulting compound situation to esthetic effects and esthetic effects to time-structures—is more easily applied to drama and narratives, though in principle it applies equally to lyrics (where images and the writer's *persona* replace characters).

This scheme represents the critically desirable, but not invariable, state of affairs during a literary performance. The area of overlap between the world of the audience and the world of art may, of course, increase to the point of total eclipse. We are then entirely swallowed by the work of art, becoming, in effect, extras in the fictional cast, *en soi*, thinglike, and incapable of a *placing judgement* of content or of an *esthetic contemplation* of form, or, equally esthetic, a contemplation of form in relation to content. A more likely, and less undesirable, state of affairs in a farce than a comedy, a thriller than a tragedy. Indeed it is arguable that farces and thrillers fail unless they are at all events *nearly* all-engulfing (complete involvement, obviously, being nightmare). Fulfilling their nature, then, they inevitably fail as art, for works of art may be formally defined as those artefacts which give esthetic pleasure. And this seems sufficient reason for the lower ranking traditionally given to farces and thrillers in the hierarchy of literary kinds. They demand

[1] P. 171.

not responsive effort from the audience but rather that it should abandon itself—but only superficially—in order to be swept along.

That any possibility of judgement requires a certain 'distance' is self-evident, but that esthetic appreciation is akin to judgement perhaps warrants further comment. Kant's definition of esthetic as non-utilitarian pleasure, connected neither with morality nor with self-interest, and not springing direct from the nature of the content, seems adequately to pinpoint something important and distinguishable in artistic experience, whether acquired or innate. In literary art the esthetic, though the defining, is comparatively rarely the most important element, since meaning and emotion are primary in language. Nevertheless esthetic pleasure *may* sometimes result from the contemplation of pure form—the spiralling of a sestina's elaborate rhyme-scheme or the permutations of a Restoration plot—though such pleasure from 'composition' is the special province of painting and music. But esthetic pleasure from 'complementarity', the interrelationship of form and content, is particularly characteristic of literary art. Since any other literary esthetic effects will be found to be minimal examples of one of these two kinds, it is evident that all esthetic pleasure depends on formal perceptions—and the perception of form is impossible if we are engulfed in the content (rolling in the aisles, chilled to the marrow or naïvely writing advice to characters in TV serials such as *Coronation Street*). For esthetic appreciation, as for judgement, we need to keep our distance; esthetic pleasure, almost by definition, turns out to be the most judicial of the emotions. That is why a comedy can afford to offer it in compensation for being less funny than a farce, as it must be if its amusement is to be seen as purposive.

There are, then, two good reasons for the crude alienation techniques of Brecht (mainly to encourage the duty of judgement) and the subtler ones of Shakespeare (for esthetic effects allied with judgement)—techniques such as moving from prose to verse, referring to the stage during the play ('All the world's a stage——', 'and these our actors, as I foretold you——') or displaying disguise (most notably in the scene where the boy actor playing Rosalind in *As You Like It* is disguised as a youth playing at being Rosalind, so that the audience experiences the content while being aware of a boy playing a girl playing a boy playing a girl).

Alienation acknowledges the fact, pace Dr. Johnson, that an audience left to itself may well forget that it is in a theatre, a cinema, a library. On the other hand if alienation effects are too successful the audience is given only the empty glass of pure form or the dusty answer of didacticism. In each case certain literary possibilities have been neglected, potential riches lost. Better works, by various means, achieve a nice balance between *participation* in the Inner Situation, the world of the characters, and *awareness* of the Outer Situation, oneself and one's own world, judiciously varying the degree of overlap according to the degree of involvement required as the work progresses. Without participation we shall not only be conscious of *irrelevant* elements of the Outer Situation and bored by obtrusive techniques—as so often in 'experimental' works—but also be denied all that is most vital in the raw material for re-creative appreciation. The double idea in *re-creation*, in short, is wholly appropriate. On the other hand without awareness we shall not be superior to the characters, who of course don't know they are in a play or novel: that is to say, are unaware of themselves as Form. If, however, we can share their life while being just sufficiently de-tached to see them also as components and expressions, then we get the best of both worlds (dramatic ironies, perceived significances, and esthetic pleasures being the bonus added to interest deriving from the content). So both alienation and involvement are essential to good fiction. But during the modern period alienation seems to have been a good deal the more risky.

In a sense all modes, even realism—the most effectively engulfing —have built-in safeguards spring from the nature of style and of time-structure. Firstly, the mere fact of specialization, of using only words (or paint, or stone, or music) is itself somewhat alienating. Living an experience we are usually unable to consider it or to appreciate it esthetically, chiefly because too many sense-impres-sions are involved and possible consequences are too personal and material. Removed, however, from the realm of action to the realm of words, it becomes the focus of a different sort of attention. Admittedly if the words are pretty ordinary, the effect is minimal. This explains the paradox of mediocre works tending to be those with the greatest power of totally eclipsing the Outer Situation. But if the degree of verbal skill in attaining an illusion of reality is sufficiently high, we can get esthetic pleasure even from realism: not from the realities of the content, but from the superb handling of language—a medium of vital importance to us, after all. The apparent paradox here is not to be explained by the notion of the artist cunningly including a bit of clever falsity in his realism (or whatever) while the hack just acts as a human tape-recorder, but simply by the concept of specialization, of putting what is eminently more than verbal into nothing more than words—but doing it better than the reader could. A totally new world is thus opened, though not one independent of the old. This explains why certain pieces of writing please although they tell us nothing new or strange, whose effect indeed *depends* on our knowing perfectly well already what is now being put into words ('—the hither-and-thithering waters—' Marvellous! But we've seen such waters with our own eyes, *have* to have seen them to appreciate the phrase. This is the pleasure of recognition *in another form*; as much of words as waters).

Here we have the most basic of esthetic effects, since the choosing of one way of putting what starts as the same content rather than another way ('the maplike Frisian' rather than 'one of those piebald cows')—in a word, style—must be the most fundamental aspect of form; it begins with the first bit of texture, the first phrase, before any structural relations have been set up. It follows from this that all those critics, over the course of two thousand years, who have been so despised in the twentieth century for naïvely praising artists, and sometimes writers, for their wonderful skill in creating an illusion of reality may have been right, or not so wrong, after all. For note, they do praise the skill. It remains true, of course, that the esthetic effects of *non*-realistic literature are likely to be more easily created and more clearly apprehended; for if the realist's style draws more attention to itself than to the realities of the subject, the work must cease to seem lifelike, and therefore cease to count as realism. Nevertheless a master-illusionist, like the Joyce or *Ulysses*, may get the best of both worlds by superb control of style. In such cases the technique of realism can be claimed as the subtlest form of alienation.

Now if skilful realism, or more imaginative mimetic[1] writing, brings the Inner Situation to life as phantasmal 'proof on the pulses', and simultaneously distances it, as a perceptible verbal form (not a mere life-substitute), then it acts rather similarly to the usual form of time-structuring (the second built-in safeguard against the more

[1] The mimetic is here taken to be contrasted rather with the didactic than the unrealistic so while all realism will be mimetic, not all *mimesis* will be realistic. A fantasy-world to be imaginatively 'lived in' would be an example of *mimesis* though obviously not of realism. A fantasy-world to be read as allegory would be an example (in the main) of didacticism, not *mimesis*.

engulfing literary modes). Therefore a consequence of any work being a work of *art* as defined is that it must be characterized by a total irony: a formal irony analogous to the sporadic 'dramatic irony' which is connected with content. For in all irony, by definition, there is an interaction of disparate worlds similar to that of literary experience in general. In both cases what should happen may not happen (hence the need for critics). Witness the prim old lady praising Mr. Gibbon for his pious footnotes. So if only one world 'takes place', there can be no irony. But to see two worlds or two meanings is not enough, not enough even if both are seen together. We must see one while *seeing through* the other. In the case of dramatic irony we see through what the character believes caged in the Inner Situation, to the true facts, which are usually derived from the Outer Situation (the Greek audiences' knowledge of the Oedipus story, or our knowledge of the way certain fictional kinds always do turn out). Occasionally, of course, we know from within the action something the character doesn't know (in which case we usually share the dramatic irony with some other character). In each case we see more than the character, because we know what's coming next and he does not; for him his world is all content, whereas we also perceive it as form.

The perception of style as form puts us in a position similarly godlike to that of dramatic irony but more sustained. We don't merely see through what characters *say*, which is only sometimes less than we know, but through what they *are*, which is always less than we are, since we are living in two worlds not one. In relation to the phantom reality they constitute for us, we are *pour soi*; in relation to our reality, they are *en soi*. Such formal irony, being total and necessary, inherent in the nature of literary appreciation, has no name and is not normally apprehended so consciously as the contingent varieties, but its absence is a major cause of the darkness in cases of total eclipse. Yet where style proves inadequate to prevent this fate there is always the second of the safeguards, time-structuring—a feature which shares so many of the 'spatial' peculiarities of the situational complex that it may serve as the final clue to the delicate *ménage à trois* of author, art and audience.

No doubt it is obvious that putting into sequence, like putting into words, must have an alienating effect since the time of performance, even in the test-case of the most realistic works, never corresponds to the fictional period (and where it approximates to it, as in *The Alchemist* and *Ulysses*, it does not run evenly in every part). The more interesting question, then, seems to be how a fiction ever does come to strike us as lifelike. Associated with this problem are the questions whether more ingenious time-structuring increases alienation (thus making a structural parallel to the textural effect of brilliant style), and whether there is an interaction of fictional time and real time akin to that of inner and outer situations (as there ought to be, since time seems integral with them).

Carefully avoiding the logical trap of 'is'—the temptation to make time a sort of intangible existent, like an invisible conveyor belt—we can sensibly and minimally say: Time is a mode of measuring change, as metrics is a mode of measuring amounts. We invent clocks, as we invent *foot*-rules, when psychological and physiological estimates cease to be accurate enough. We have, then, two sorts of time:

1. OBJECTIVE (*geographical*, measured by alternation of light and darkness, the earth's position; *calendar*, by days, weeks, etc.; and *clock*, by hands, radiation, growth-rings, etc.).

2. SUBJECTIVE (*observational* or *interior*; at its least precise it may be reduced to a mere sense of beforeness, nowness, and afterness).

Subjective time, of course, may be fast or slow in relation to objective time, but there is usually an interaction between the two (comparable to the way we live spatially, in both outer and inner situations during a literary performance). This GENERAL TIME, as we may call it, is 'comparable' because of certain oddities that make it so—in particular being objective in so far as we *know* but subjective in so far as we *feel*.

Perhaps it is because we are used to living in a temporal medium composed of an intermingling of feelings of psychological sequence and partial awareness of mechanical chronology, that we are able to 'correct' after being engulfed in subjective time. Thus we readily accept, for instance, that our interior clocks have been fast or slow if exterior ones (or other events) tell us so; we don't go to lunch as soon as we feel it's been a long morning. On the other hand we do not so readily accept that 'today' is not to*day* in Australia but to-*night* (by geographical time) and also to*morrow* (by calendar time). Psychologically, our instinctive *feeling* that 'now' for us equals universal presentness carries greater weight than our *knowledge* of relativity. We feel that their 'tomorrow' is really 'now' without daylight. This mixed attitude seems not only to account for much of what enables us to mingle inner situation and outer—thus at once *feeling with* and *knowing about*—but also to be the source of that psychological permissiveness which allows many modern authors to use time as if it were space.

The traditional novelist uses linear time; the sequence of events is structured chronologically apart from trifling exceptions by way of flashback or retrospection. Experimental novelists (and some playwrights) have realized, however, that as the art-world is merely a phantom reality there's no law of nature to prevent them from using time artificially (and there's no esthetic objection to artificiality either, within reason; no one would claim that verse must be esthetically inferior to prose, for instance; but rather the contrary). So novels like *Ulysses, Point-Counter-Point*, or *The Alexandria Quartet* treat time as if it were a deck of cards which can be shuffled at will. The most obvious advantage of this procedure is facility in producing striking juxtapositions—but this is a thematic rather than an esthetic advantage. The most obvious disadvantage is the sacrifice of suspense; fugal novels depend more on theme than story, linear novels need not.

Even in the linear novel, however, time is not simple, but fortunately the complications are analogous to those of real time. First there is *Author-time*, or page-space, the proportion of reading-time the writer allows to each period of his narrative, giving let us say one chapter to the whole of the heroine's girlhood and ten to the brief months of her courtship. The relationship between reading-time and narrative-time, that is to say, is not a mechanically regular one, and therefore Author-time is the fictional equivalent of Subjective-time in life, and may be fast or slow in relation to Narrative-time (the fictional period covered in hours, days, seasons or years, and thus the phantom equivalent of objective-time). These correspondences are what allow the author to emphasize and diminish, manipulating his audience's response to content and theme, while still appearing lifelike if he wishes. Our knowledge that time goes evenly, moreover, is easily subordinated, owing to the habits of normal living in General-Time, to a participatory feeling for the living presentness of each part of the text. *Subordinated*, not necessarily *eliminated*; we need not be engulfed by the *temporal* Inner

Situation either. In time, as in space, we may be superior to the content, which cannot know it is being concertina'd. If we retain a vestigial sense of 'correction' by objective time (helped, perhaps, by slight stylistic alienation), we enjoy again the situation of godlike dominance, of being *pour soi*. And we again have the possibility of esthetic pleasure; of complementarity in so far as the time-structure seems artfully matched with content, of composition in so far as it matches other aspects of structure or texture.

Fugal works are more complex, since their overall time-structuring is contrapuntal, but *each separate episode*, of course, is linear. Within itself, therefore, every part may have the fullest realistic pull towards involvement (stylistic considerations apart). As wholes, however, fugal works are structurally much more alienating than linear ones. The risk they run is that of rendering form too obtrusive, and thus tipping over the complex situational balance needed for a rewarding performance. (The risk they never run is that of over-involvement, or total eclipse, the temporal safeguard in fugal works being strong enough to outweigh any other factors). The reward offered is an esthetic perception more complex—and therefore less vulnerable to boredom on re-readings—than linear works can hope to compass. Not only is normal chronology, within episodes, played against fugal reshuffling in the whole but also narrative-time is played against real, psychological time (our awareness of before and after). The normal narrative-time, A-B-C, of three sections of such a novel as, say *Point-Counter-Point* may have become in terms of structural author-time C-A-B; but of course we read C first, A next, and finally B—and only then, retrospectively, do we know the 'true' chronology. By that time, though, we have acquired an a-b-c chronology of our own, based on reading-order. We correct this, but not so as to correct it away, only so as to end with a more complex experience aC-bA-cB—an experience presumably rendered possible, against all apparent likelihood, because of our previous acclimatization in the duality of General-Time.

The circle can now be completed by briefly putting time-structuring back where it belongs, in that variable area where Inner and Outer situations overlap—the crucible where formal appreciation, contentual involvement and relevant aspects of reality are fused into one experience.

Characters, and other elements of content, exist only in the Inner Situation. For them, therefore, narrative-time is all. It may be formally fast or slow as mediated by the author, or even reshuffled, but they do not know it; for they cannot know themselves as Form. Being wholly *in* the world of art and moving there only from moment to moment, they cannot apprehend either style or time-structure. The audience in normal life is in the same case, but during the literary performance is given the godlike experience of being at once dominant over time, immanent and transcendent, and delighted and enlightened by creation. No wonder Arnold thought poetry would take over from religion—it certainly seems to offer the more uplifting illusion.

THEOREM OF WORLDS

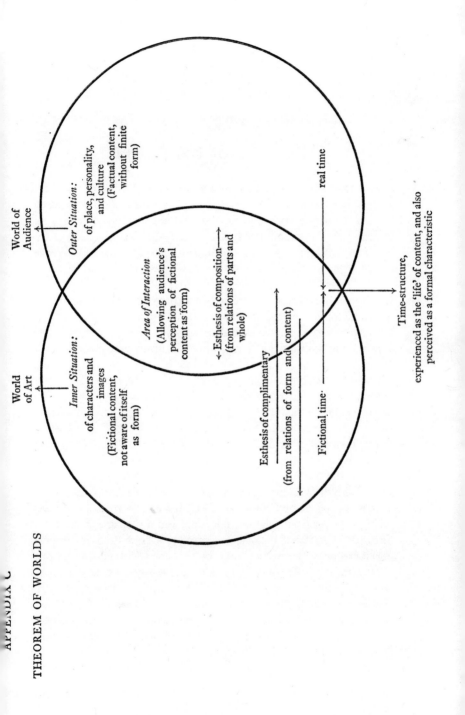

World of Audience

Outer Situation:
of place, personality, and culture
(Factual content, without finite form)

World of Art

Inner Situation:
of characters and images
(Fictional content, not aware of itself as form)

Area of Interaction
(Allowing audience's perception of fictional content as form)

← Esthesis of composition →
(from relations of parts and whole)

Esthesis of complimentary
(from relations of form and content)

Fictional time

real time

Time-structure,
experienced as the 'life' of content, and also perceived as a formal characteristic

12

Modernism and Form in the Esthetic of the Novel

FOR a broad topic like this only a summary version of what has already been said about 'form' is required. Organic or imposed, form is the way a work is presented, and has therefore two aspects: *textural*, the presentation of surface detail, and *structural*, the ordering of the material. Structural form, since it is a matter of sequence, involves *time*—whose presentation may be *linear* or *fugal*.

'Modernism' too may be briefly defined as whatever is anti-traditional. The inter-war period of experiment in the arts is responsible for this meaning; what was then modern or contemporary was experimental and anti-traditional. Nowadays, when so much new work is traditional in form, when the up-to-date cry is consolidation rather than experiment, it has become necessary to distinguish between the contemporary and the modern. The latter indeed is rather old-fashioned. In the case of the novel, there is the further paradox that the modern novel—perhaps one should say anti-novel—comes into being almost as early as the traditional novel. However, this definition of modernism is what we are stuck with today.

As for the 'novel'—well, it is not easy to define since it is an exceedingly broad kind. However, it can be sufficiently defined for present purposes by a process of elimination. Both in its *romance* form (deriving from religion, fairy-tale and myth) and in its *report* form (deriving from history, biography, letter-writing and reporting) it can be distinguished from the *chronicle (Moll Flanders)* or the *series (Gulliver's Travels)*. That is to say, it must not be a sequence of separate incidents or a number of short stories featuring the same character, even if the stories have a similar theme. To count as a novel, a work must have not only the requisite (though undetermined) length, but also unity; it must deal with one main situation or theme—though it may be given depth by subsidiary ones.

The apprehension of formal qualities, it has been argued, is crucial for esthetic pleasure, and such apprehension requires a certain distance—though not too much. Poetry gets such distance, psychologically, merely by being in verse, a more obviously artificial use of language than prose; drama gets it, physically, by the separation of auditorium and stage (or, in reading, by its radio-like world of voices alone). The novel, on the contrary, is not given distance automatically, and has traditionally striven to be as concrete and unalienating as possible. In so far as it has acquired formal elements that might give esthetic pleasure it has done so in pursuit of a realism that would tend to take it away. Both report-novels and romance-novels as they developed became in some sense more realistic, that is to say illusionistic. Their history is technical—the discovery of devices for gripping the reader—rather than theoretical. So any evolution of esthetic form is likely to be an accidental by-product.

The report-novelist, of course, wants to give an illusion of real life, the romance-novelist an illusion of real myth (once the reader has crossed the border, that is to say, he wants to make the suspension of disbelief easy thereafter, to hold him, as in the grip of a *convincing* nightmare, until he has made his point). Both extend a possibility of esthetic appreciation with one hand while taking it back with the other, for their form, in most cases, was developed to inveigle the reader, not to distance him.

Are things the same in the modernistic, experimental, or anti-, novel? (The last might be the best name, had it not become attached recently to one specific form of experimental novel, for in that such novels are consciously in opposition to the traditional forms they are *anti*.) Certainly one would expect deliberate contrast to result in different effects. And the modernistic novel *is* in deliberate contrast from the start. No sooner have Fielding and Richardson established ways of mediating more or less unitary phantom worlds enclosing one variegated action—worlds respectively *physical* in the main (existing primarily in fictional space) and *psychological* (in fictional time)—than along comes Sterne to disestablish them both. There is nothing to indicate that he did so because he recognized the esthetic cost of realism; nor even that he consciously realized that experiment could be something other than *improvement* (a progressive, successful effort to eliminate technical clumsinesses that stood in the way of unity and believable illusion). Rather, it seems to be a non-Romantic reaction against the prevailing

Augustan doctrine of commonsense Reason. Taking over Locke's associationism, he shows how fundamentally *in*consequential men's minds are. Two effects on structural form immediately follow. Firstly, he reverts from the newly discovered *plot* of Fielding to *story*.[1] Secondly he narrows the world of the novel, using alienating techniques rather than illusionist ones, in order to emphasize something that the commonsense view of reality has neglected. Essentially, that is what every wave of experimenters has done—often enlarging but never for long supplanting the traditional mode. Indeed much of the force of modernistic experiments comes from the base they push off from, a base that is apt to look less dated after a few decades than the modernist reaction.

Sterne uses both structural and textural methods of alienation. By temporal and stylistic devices he forces the reader to recognize that this is *not* a real world, not even a phantom real world, nor even an imaginary romance world bearing a symbolic relation to the real world, but a verbal artefact, a form of words and a structure of artifice; a man-made fiction. But on the other hand he uses many of Richardson's and Fielding's naturalistic techniques, and adds some of his own (providing, for example, the first stream-of-consciousness writing). This leads to a peculiar tension, which is handed to the *reader*, like a hot plate, to bear as best he may; whereas before it was in the *author*, trying to preserve a balance impossible to sustain. T. C. Livingstone, in his Introduction to the Collins edition of *Tristram Shandy*, London and Glasgow, 1955, puts it well:

> Odd the book certainly is. Published in pairs of volumes from 1760 until the single ninth was put out in 1767, a year before Sterne's death, *Tristram Shandy* is unfinished and without the possibility of any compassable finishing; its nine volumes contain over 300 chapters of the most capricious nature and length—chapter 24 of Volume IV is entirely omitted, and chapter 5 of the same volume consists of a shortish sentence, as does Volume VI, 15; chapters 18 and 19 of Volume IX are left blank, to be inserted after chapter 25, which itself consists of an explanation of this odd arrangement; chapter 28 of Volume VI is mostly a blank page on which the reader is invited to supply an ideal description of the Widow Wadman; chapter 33 of Volume VI finds

[1] Story is sequential, plot is consequential. As E. M. Forster said, 'The king died, and then the queen died', is story, 'The king died, and then the queen died of grief', is plot.

itself in inextricable difficulties, and has to be begun again as chapter 34; at the end of chapter 12 of the first volume the reader, having followed Parson Yorick to his tomb and read its Shakesperean epitaph, is confronted by a page whose recto and verso type-areas are each a rectangle of solid black—is this the monumental marble, or the dark night of death, nescience, nonentity?—Sterne does not tell us, but in Chapter 36 of Volume III he writes, '. . . without *much reading*, by which your reverence knows, I mean *much knowledge*, you will no more be able to penetrate the moral of the next marbled page (motley emblem of my work!) than the world with all its sagacity has been able to unravel the many opinions, transactions and truths which still lie mystically hid under the dark veil of the black one.' Does Sterne imply that for the impercipient reader all the text-pages of a book may as well be like the unidea'd endpapers? These are curious object-lessons, as curious as the diagrams or route plans of his conduct of the novel which he supplies us with in chapter 40 of Volume VI.

It is not only by his chapter divisions and his instructions to the printer and to the bookbinder that Sterne puts his novel out of the common way. The very punctuation is personal, especially in its translation of Sterne's peculiarly intimate and insinuating approach to the reader. The celebrated Shandean dash which (it is not too much to say) determines the appearance of the pages of *Tristram Shandy* and the associated *Sentimental Journey*, conveys in a typographical gesture the changes of tone, the confidences, the implicatory silences, the veerings of the narrative, the doublings of meaning, which characterise Sterne's method as a writer. Characteristic also are his impudent appeals to the reader's own bawdy imagination, and often for these, like a lascivious Jack-o-Lantern, he uses a star or asterisk—'the stars,' he says (VI, 33), 'which I hang up in some of the darkest passages, knowing that the world is apt to lose its way.'

These superficial [*textural*] oddities are but symptoms of the enormous idiosyncrasy of the narrative itself [*structural*]. Bettering the usual autobiography (for an autobiography is what it purports to be), *Tristram Shandy* begins not with the birth but with the begetting of the autobiographer. This excessive and pedantic regard for the order and origin of events seems to exhaust the author's sense of his duty to temporal succession, and the rest of the book is devoted to a defiance of ordinary procedures, a defiance based on a desperate loyalty on Tristram's part to the mysterious logic of association and a progressive recognition of the fact that the understanding of any single event depends on the knowledge and understanding of all antecedent and subsequent events. This leads to a series of fascinating and bewildering flashbacks and anticipations beside which the technique of the cinema is simple-minded and straightforward. Volume I begins in the year 1718, and Volume IX, the last to be published, ends in 1713, five years before Tristram's birth. In like manner, the unlucky descent of the sash-window, which belongs to the year 1723 or 1724, leads in the most natural Shandean manner to the account of Le Fever's death, which took place in 1706. Such are the vaultings and somersaults in which the reader of *Tristram Shandy* must exercise himself.

Nothing needs adding to this admirable account apart from the paradoxical fact that the very oddities and irregularities do produce an esthetic effect—naturally only of condensation—for the style matches the structure, each bit of texture is likely to be a model of the structure. In addition both happen to be psychologically naturalistic while also being esthetically distancing because they differ so much from what is expected of a novel.

Once you've tumbled to the fact that all the strategies evolved by the traditional novel for representing a unit of life (with whatever degree of implicit or explicit comment) are only *conventionally* not *necessarily* geared to reality as we live it—they're only *words*—then all sorts of possibilities become available. You can dissolve character in a haze of moods, as in Virginia Woolf—or you can try to outdo Sterne in alienation:

> The story-teller in this rumbustious, boozy novel is an Irish student who devotes his time to reading in bed, touring the local public houses and writing a novel about a man with the not-very-Irish name of Trellis who is himself writing a book about some people who are getting their own back by writing a book about Mr Trellis.
>
> (Blurb for Flann O'Brien's *At Swim Two Birds*,
> Four Square edition, London 1962)

Sterne in one way, O'Brien in another are juxtaposing fictional realism with fictional fictionalism. Dos Passos, in that monsterpiece, *U.S.A.*, juxtaposes two sorts of fictional realism, interspersing the narrative with bits of 'Newsreel' and 'Camera Eye'. B. S. Johnson, on the other hand, is highly experimental, or anti-novelistic, in *The Unfortunates* (London, 1969) because he is attempting to be utterly realistic. The book comes in a box of unbound sections the first and last of which are marked as such: the rest may be shuffled by the reader and read in any order. Since the work consists of random memories, and thus has a stream-of-consciousness texture, this randomness of structure is appropriate enough. However, *any* random structure, if it really is random, is as random as any other; so the book is no more realistic when shuffled or reshuffled than it would have been bound. There is no gain, and there is one loss: the desire for randomness necessarily obviates art (as defined earlier), requires the sacrifice of esthetic pleasure. This sort of experimental novel, then, is subject in an extreme degree to the same penalty incurred by the traditional novel—one might almost say in proportion to its pursuit of structural realism, for textural realism is less inimical to esthetic effect than structural realism (which must normally mean lack of structure, since life doesn't arrange itself in patterns often enough for a complete realist to risk them in his fiction).

The danger in all such novels—and also, as we've seen, in the fugal novel, and the French anti-novel that tries to eliminate our instinctive humanizing of the world of things—is that of tiring the reader, boring him with a too-austere rhetoric. The interest-devices of suspense and story-curiosity and heightened atmosphere have to be sacrificed for the sake of surprising juxtapositions, counterpointing, reality being given a symbolic significance, or the elimination of scales of convention from the reader's view. Sometimes it pays off, sometimes not. There seems no possibility of working out any general rule, nor any likelihood of being able to assert with reason that the traditional or the experimental is the better mode. It may be reasonable to ask, though, if one or the other is likely, in general, to be *esthetically* better (while bearing in mind that, in the novel particularly, esthetic effects may properly be regarded as much less important than other qualities).

Do the greater obtrusiveness of *form*, then, and the lesser compulsiveness of *content* combine in the experimental or modernistic novel to yield esthetic rewards greater than those of the traditional novel? The answer seems to be Yes, but not nearly to the extent that might have been expected.

The chief reason is implicit in what has already been said. No more than the traditional report- and romance-novel did the experimental novel (which can itself be divided into these two kinds) acquire form for Art's sake. With one or two exceptions, it acquired it for Reality's sake. The differences lay in the definitions of reality. Virginia Woolf's assertion that Bennett, Wells and Galsworthy had got it wrong could be matched, *mutatis mutandis*, by many:

> ... If a writer were a free man and not a slave, if he could write what he chose, not what he must, if he could base his work upon his own feeling and not upon convention, there would be no plot, no comedy, no tragedy, no love interest or catastrophe in the accepted style, and perhaps not a single button sewn on as the Bond St tailors would have it. Life is not a series of gig-lamps symmetrically arranged; life is a luminous halo, a semi-transparent envelope surrounding us from the beginning of consciousness to the end. Is it not the task of the novelist to convey this varying, this unknown and uncircumscribed spirit, whatever aberration or complexity it may display, with as little mixture of the alien and external as possible.
>
> (*The Common Reader*, London 1948, p. 189)

Life is ... But one of the main causes of experiment has been the disintegration of a generally accepted view of 'life' or 'reality'. So *is* it the task of the novelist 'to convey *this* ... spirit'? Certainly there is good reason, as we've argued, for having some sort of 'truth' to your fiction; it can claim little value without it; but 'truth', 'life', and 'reality' are words of multiple meaning, and the fact seems to be simply that you pay your money and take your choice. Virginia Woolf handles language marvellously (and most experimental writers are good in this department—they need to be) but Wells, Bennett and Galsworthy are stronger on story. The probable price, then, for experimentalism will not only be that already mentioned, the sacrifice of suspense, but will include an obtrusion of *form* at the expense of content. Verbal quality, the artificial, created character of the work will be underlined, if only because extraordinary stylistic devices have to be evolved to overcome the reader's habitual idea of reality (or extraordinary structural devices to overcome his habitual idea of chronology). In terms of what novelists, traditional or experimental, seem usually to have been aiming at—conveying reality—this is a fairly heavy price. On the other hand it might seem to offer an esthetic bonus as a by-product, for attention to verbal quality, when one is not spellbound by the story, gives opportunities for the esthetic of condensation to come into its own, and the obtrusiveness of form in general gives distance, and therefore more chance for the appreciation of any harmony of new style with new content (if it should exist) or of compositional merits in the structure. But in fact since form is emphasized by necessity, not choice, and since formal wholes and a balance of parts smack of tradition, this compensation tends not to be as large as one might imagine. It is symbolically significant that Sterne does not even finish his books—and in *The Sentimental Journey* makes a teasing, brilliant, but not esthetic, virtue out of it. The only experimental novel to give all three kinds of esthetic pleasure, and in such super-lative degree as to more than compensate for the drawbacks of the kind, seems to be Joyce's *Ulysses*—and whether that counts as a novel, or even an anti-novel may be a matter of dispute. Perhaps it is what Fielding thought he was producing when in fact he made the novel, a comic epic in prose.

13

The Need for Formal Criticism

KANT went to some pains to distinguish the esthetic from the gratifying, the practical, and the didactic. Beauty allied to the good, for instance, was not free beauty—and therefore esthetic—but dependent beauty. And modern psychological research has shown the existence of at least a rudimentary inborn esthetic sense; but estheticism has remained in disfavour. Kant's system, it has been recently pointed out, conceived Homer and Shakespeare as less esthetically pure than wallpaper—a just remark, and one apparently confirming the proper place of esthetic criticism as the lumber room. But is not Kant right? Homer and Shakespeare *are* less esthetically pure than wallpaper. The obvious retort, of course, is so much the worse for estheticism! And indeed it has to be conceded that the esthetic element in literature will rarely be the most important one, only the most essential; it could be (and is) what most aptly defines it as verbal art. It is where Homer's work differs from wallpaper that is more important, but it is what it shares with wallpaper that makes it a work of art. So if it would be wrongheaded to overestimate estheticism, it seems equally wrongheaded to neglect it entirely. And since esthetic pleasure depends on the appreciation of form (whether in relation to content or not) we may well extend our interest to formal criticism in general.

Modern criticism has persistently ignored specifically esthetic matters and, until very recently, much neglected the assessment of formal qualities in general. Has it then been wrongheaded? Hardly that, perhaps, for in some fields its advances have been almost as spectacular as those of science. As George Watson remarks in *The Literary Critics* (Penguin Books, 1962):

> The average schoolboy of today is probably capable of analysing more closely and more accurately than Dryden . . . and the ordinary reviewer often enjoys a similar unearned advantage over the greatest of English critics before the twentieth century. (p. 18)

Rather, criticism has become the victim of its own success and got too big for its boots. This is no doubt why certain alarmed academics wish to suppress criticism altogether and make students stick to literary history. Their most formidable exponent now is probably Professor Helen Gardner, who writes as follows, in *The Business of Literary Criticism* (Oxford, 1959):

> The notion that anybody with natural taste, some experience of life, a decent grounding in the classics, and the habit of wide reading can talk profitably on English Literature is highly unfashionable. The cynic might point to other more sinister signs of professionalism . . . (p. 3)

The advocate of the amateur approach, then goes on:

> The attempt to train young people in this kind of discrimination [*by comparatively objective standards*] seems to me a folly, if not a crime. (p. 13)

After these strong words, however, she goes on to demonstrate unwittingly the limitations of amateurism, and the need for close discrimination:

> Statements about relative values are either unnecessary, elaborate attempts to prove what cannot be proved and can only be accepted as established by the judgement of the ages or else they are rationalizations (p. 8)

If there is nothing between absolute proof and mere rationalization why should we accept the judgement of the ages? And if people in the past could make judgements worth treating with respect why cannot we—and why cannot we judge among their judgements?

> I feel little confidence in the judgement of any critic who does not make me feel, however minute his analysis, and however laborious his researches may have been, that his motive force has been enjoyment (p. 75)

Enjoyment of poor work, for instance?

> The primary critical act is a judgement, the decision that a certain piece of writing has significance and value (p. 6)

Primary? Surely one must read it first, with an open mind, in order, secondarily, to judge that it has significance and value? And does this mean that bad writing is never to be criticized, that the public is not to be alerted to the dangers of pretentiousness masquerading as profundity, propaganda as play of mind, prophecy as considered prediction?

The excuse for such alarmism and for the retreat to literary history and scholarship ('facts') on the one hand, and dilettantish amateurism on the other, is that the status of criticism has been inflated, it has been too speculative and subjective; and when it has tried to become objective it has become something other than literary criticism: usually an amalgam of sociology and history or of several of the less exact sciences. Sometimes, as Hyman has claimed, it has become so creative as to aspire to be an art in its own right (but that is as much as to say, no longer criticism in any sane sense of the word).

Related to this access of grandeur is the ambition of a scientific criticism. For various theoretical reasons this is not possible anyway; a much better model for full yet fairly objective criticism, as we shall argue in the last chapter, is law. There, each case, like each book, is unique, evidence may be largely circumstantial, yet the final judgement is not arbitrary, but 'beyond reasonable doubt'. What needs emphasizing at the moment, though, is the way in which the use of science has translated much recent criticism into metacritical spheres (usually sociological, psychological, anthropological, or marxist-economical). To quote Hyman again:

> What modern criticism is could be defined crudely and somewhat inaccurately as the organised use of non-literary techniques and bodies of knowledge to obtain insights into literature . . . Traditional criticism used most of these techniques and disciplines, but in spasmodic, haphazard fashion. The relevant sciences were not developed enough to be used methodically.
>
> (*The Armed Vision*, New York, 1955, p. 3)

The reference to traditional criticism is apposite. Criticism has always tended to sit on one of two stools instead of falling between them as it ought. The existence of a literary work is so intangible and so multifaceted that it has always been tempting to study, instead of the work itself, its causes in the writer or society (criticism then becoming a disguised form of psychology, biography or history) or else to study the work's effects on the audience (a kind of sociology, anthropology or mass-psychology), and to imagine that by doing so one was obtaining 'insights into literature'. Modern improvement has enabled this mistake to be made more methodically. The difficulty, as we have seen, is that literary works 'exist' only as an experience in the producer or the receiver. Yet there is a difference between examining *in the work* the cause of some effect in the audience and examining the cause of that cause in the writer; between examining *in the work* some effect of the writer and examining the effect of that effect in the audience. That these causes and effects in the work are the right ones, that what does take place when it is read is what should take place, depends on the type of reading the work is given. It is here that formal criticism may bring its modest rewards; and it is now that it is needed. For even the criticism that has neither tried to be a science nor a work of art in its own right, the criticism that has developed the laudable habit of close reference to the text, has tended to be speculative and subjective.

This criticism is chiefly represented by two species: symbolizers and moralists. Both have shed a good deal of light—though not much sweetness—in their time. But it is arguable that they need a rest; at their best they were invaluable in making literature a matter of serious concern; latterly that has passed into a near-religious fanaticism, and their excesses have begun to discredit criticism as a whole. No critical method can be proof against a practitioner without common sense, but their approaches are easier to abuse than most, since they have no safeguards against subjectivity and bias. Sane symbol-hunters may find something actually there, fanatics can always maintain they have found something when they have not, because it is impossible for the hapless author to protect himself from them. Suppose I definitely do not want my novel to be a profound allegory of Good and Evil, Sin and Redemption, or Lust and Love, can I avoid—for instance—having my hero enter his own house and switch on the light? (Symbol of redemption, the sinner returns home to God, and his darkness of soul is dispelled by Illumination. Or, if you prefer, symbol of transfiguration through sex: by entering this vaginal security—which, note, he 'possesses'—darkness and misery turn to joy and light). Symbol-fakers sometimes are as egregious as this. Moral critics have usually been less so—but they have been more bitter, easily tending to forget that once you leave the realm of the clearly-harmful-to-others questions of moral value become so shifting and complex, so near to matter of opinion, that vituperation is out of place.

More important, for critical purposes, the moralists have tended to ignore the fact that there are sensory values as well as moral ones —some sensory experiences are undeniably preferable to others, even if they do no demonstrable good. These values—at least in the phantom reality of art—seem to have something in common with Kant's esthetic qualities; they prompt disinterested appreciation. To be sure, literature is made of words, and words are chiefly purveyors of meaning. So sensory qualities are likely not only to be inseparable from meaning but subordinate to it. Nevertheless, if we *start* at the phantom sensory values we shall be starting with the quintessence of what we have called its essential (if not its most important) element. And it is apparent, then, that we shall have to start not with content but form.

We need a more objective criticism instead of a criticism which becomes rhapsody or sermon, but not one that gets objectivity by turning itself into literary history or science. The development of technical criticism has been hampered, however, not only by the lack of an agreed terminology and the tendency of modern critics to merge distinctions in one term (as metaphor, simile, metonomy and other figures have been absorbed into 'imagery'), but more importantly by the dogma of the indistinguishability of form and content. This is a way of speaking that does point to a truth. On the other hand, it is a way of speaking that makes it difficult to talk about certain aspects of literature at all.

Since Ben Jonson wrote his plays in prose first, and then put them into verse, it would be hard to maintain that you cannot have *roughly* the same content in two different forms; and if you want to talk about the difference of literary effect made by the change of form you must be allowed to distinguish form and (paraphrasable) content. By saying whatever he has to say in one way rather than another—in verse instead of prose, with much metaphor or little in complex or simple syntax—a writer creates the texture of his work. By organizing his material in one way rather than another—in terms of plot rather than story, with time-shifting or without—he creates his structure. Both structural and textural form may be either organic, fitting the content like a velvet glove, or imposed, an iron gauntlet that the content must fit itself to. (And, of course, one may have a sense of organic textural form within an imposed structural form.)

That imposed form is bad form has been another modern dogma.

Yet it must seem that where a writer is dealing with widely disparate groups of people or amorphous material—where, in short, there is not an inherent, organic relationship—imposed form is likely to be a good thing. Certainly, esthetic effects are easier to achieve and easier to perceive with imposed form.

14

The Technique of Formal Criticism

OTHER things being equal, it is better for a work of creative literature to make a formal impact than not; for without this, two qualities valuable for *any* worthwhile effect are apt to be missing: unity and intensification.

Intensification is valuable in helping to overwhelm the habitual world so that one is forced to respond freshly, forced to imagine instead of just dully living one's life of quiet desperation, with attention dispersed by action and sense-data of five varieties. A painting would not be better if it talked or took us by the hand to stroke it. Its *raison d'être* is precisely that it makes us look—and only look—sensing movement, mass, and even texture, only through the eye, by an effort of sensory imagination. This specialization of painting (and the same applies to music and literature) of itself gives a kind of unity, which may then be extended and varied by internal relationships of form and content. Unity aids significance, and variety-in-unity seems to be one of the chief sources of esthetic effect.

Intensification and unity (that is to say, concentrated attention and absence of internal contradiction or irrelevance) are obviously valuable assets, even to the propagandist—who neglects form, therefore, at his peril. Variation and contemplation, which also contribute to esthetic radiance, relieve the strain, enabling one to stand the pressure without a slackening of perception.

That these effects are easier to obtain with imposed form than with organic form seems clear. It is difficult to obtain an effect of variety-in-unity, for instance, if you have no obvious unifying basis, and the firmer it is the better. Freedom, so to speak, requires a framework of order. So, with metrical verse you can play off speech-rhythm against metre; with free verse you cannot (though you may establish some other sort of order; but it won't be so secure). Again, you cannot finely balance intense attention and detached contemplation if your entire technical effort is devoted to giving an illusion of life. Similarly, just as it is esthetically necessary to be aware of a canvas as a painting and not simply as a window on to life, so it is necessary to be aware of literature as a verbal form and not merely a form of communication. One should be aware, in varying degree, of the words as well as the meanings. However, all this goes counter to some central doctrines of modernism: literature should be lifegiving, it should work by image not precept, it should be natural not artificial, its form must always be organic not imposed. Undeniably, these doctrines have been useful both to creators and critics; but they are not the whole truth, and the fact that they have been taken to be so represents the soft underbelly of the Armed Vision.

The truth is that the techniques of modern criticism have served admirably for romantic, symbolist, or metaphysical literature, for work that was complex or obscure, mystical or intuitive. To put it crudely, they could make exciting sense (if not in strictly critical terms, then in metacritical ones) of works that would have seemed absurd if taken literally. They could show that the meaning might be more than the sense, that what seemed to be a bad case might be acceptable as a good experience or a mode of ritual activity. But what of literature which is neither obscure nor mystical, whose meaning *is* more or less contained in its statements, whose 'levels' are usually no more than one: that of the surface? What of augustan or classical works, the literature of Good Sense?

Romantic work is typically concerned with states, and prefers organic form (at risk of unesthetic formlessness). Augustan work is typically concerned with relationships, and goes for imposed form (at risk of remoteness). From this it seems likely that while semantic study is profitable for romantic work a study of syntax — small-scale relationships — could point a new way into the heartland of augustanism (large-scale study of structure might be equally useful, but since it has to presume knowledge of whole works is less practicable here). To take an example:

> Still round and round the Ghosts of Beauty glide,
> And haunt the places where their Honour died.
> See how the World its veterans rewards!
> A Youth of Frolics, an Old Age of Cards;
> Fair to no purpose, artful to no end,
> Young without Lovers, old without a Friend;
> A Fop their Passion, but their Prize a Sot,
> Alive ridiculous, and dead forgot!

The first untypical couplet of these famous lines from Pope's 'Characters of Women' can be profitably treated by modernistic methods, and was so treated at some length by one of the most brilliant of modern critics, William Empson, in *Seven Types of Ambiguity* (London, 1930). But on the remaining six lines—which are typically unambiguous—he found little to say, and was unconvincing in that:

> An impression of febrile and uncontrollable hatred is given to the terrible climax of this passage by the flat, indifferent little words *fop, sot* . . .

And again:

> Never was the couplet more of a rocking-horse if each line is considered separately; but all the inertia of this flatness is needed to give him strength . . .

Surely we have here a winged intelligence struggling in treacle. No words could be less appropriate than 'inertia' and 'flatness' for the balanced and mounting energy of these formal couplets. And how can we say the hatred is uncontrollable in view of the very evident control of the medium? Moreover, it is difficult to see how the power of the climax could be attributed solely to the words 'fop' and 'sot'. Would it not be more true to say that the extreme formality, the series of simple antitheses and plain emphatic rhymes, distances the hatred for contemplation?

It gives a sense of measure, almost of fairness. Even the biting line Empson takes his examples from, 'A Fop their Passion, but their Prize a Sot', sterilizes the bite by the esthetic device of introducing the first major syntactical variant; the simple antitheses (up to 'Young without Lovers, old without a Friend') give way to a mirror-antithesis in which the last half is turned inside-out ('A Fop their Passion, but their Prize a Sot'—instead of the expected 'A Sot their Prize'). Furthermore, the 'terrible climax' of the last line, in which every word (save 'and') hammers a nail into the coffin, seems to come as least at much from the omission of 'they were' and 'they are' as from the flatness of 'fop' and 'sot' in the preceding line. The words left out are as much part of the poem as those put in. The feeling of climax comes not so much from progression of sense as from increasing syntactical concentration. More merely grammatical words—'see', 'are', 'was', 'is'—are omitted; fewer, such as 'the', 'it', 'an', 'to', are retained, until we reach the concentration of the last line.

This, of course, is a structurally highlighted part of a long poem, and perhaps a point where the sense is so important that attention to textural form—however integral to the total effect—may seem of minor value, especially when limited to the syntax. It is worth noting, however, that this could be described as an example of organic textural form given extra effect by being contained within the imposed structural form of the heroic couplet.

Let us, though, take a few average verses from a poem of middling quality, Pope's 'Essay on Man', Epistle III, 191/4:

> In vain thy Reason finer webs shall draw,
> Entangle Justice in her net of Law,
> And right, too rigid, harden into wrong;
> Still for the strong too weak, the weak too strong.

Here there is a similar slight sacrifice of grammatical correctness for syntactical strength ('shall' must be carried on through all four lines but 'in vain' only as far as the second). However, there is nothing very striking about the form. Compare it, though, with a prose version:

> Trying to make the law more rational will merely diminish its justice. It will remain ineffective for the powerful and harsh for the poor, its inflexibility constantly leading to hard cases.

It is evident that if we appreciate Pope's version more, it must be for reasons of form, quite apart from one's agreement or disagreement with the statement. How does this effect come about, this example of the esthetic of condensation? There is grammatical economy again, leading to a sense of words being skilfully handled. Speech rhythm is played against metre. Again 'Justice' is neatly balanced against 'Law', in a way not easy to naturalize in prose. The prose version, however, is slightly more logical than Pope's, in placing the matter of ineffectiveness and harshness immediately after the advice not to attempt reform, yet it lacks the impression of climax that Pope gets—an impression resulting, then, not from progress of the sense but progress of the antithetical Augustan dance of syntax. The first line is not antithetical at all ('In vain thy

Reason finer webs shall draw'), the next is very simply so ('Entangling Justice in her net of Law'); the third line, however, *contrasts* 'right' and 'wrong' at each end of the line; and, in the middle, on each side of the caesura, *associates* 'rigid' and 'harden' ('And right, too rigid, harden into wrong'). Finally, the last line subtly manipulates an antithesis of four terms that look like two: 'Still for the strong too weak, the weak too strong.'

Although there is some degree of grammatical elision—since we do not have 'And right, *becoming* too rigid, *shall* harden into wrong' —this line obviously has not the concentration of 'Alive ridiculous, and dead forgot'. Yet it does manage to insist on its existence as a verbal form, by getting more into its syntax than meets the needs of sense or emphasis, but not more than can be apprehended subconsciously in an esthetic way—especially if we can be brought to attend as closely to the figures of the augustan dance of syntax as we now do to the emotive friction of connotation in romantic works.

Within the one apparently simple antithesis of the last line we have in fact four antitheses. Firstly, an antithesis of *sound* (and sight), strong-weak/weak-strong, the mirror-antithesis that first meets us. Secondly, an antithesis of *sense*, which is not a mirror antithesis, because the words that look and sound alike in fact have different meanings. If we were to symbolize the first antithesis as *ab/ba*, this next balance, of concrete-metaphorical/concrete-metaphorical references, should be symbolized as *a & not-alpha/not-a & alpha* (the second 'weak' being a genuine opposite of the first 'strong', whereas the first 'weak' only appears to be an opposite). Thirdly, an antithesis of *grammar*: noun-adjective/noun-adjective (*cd/cd*)—again, not a mirror antithesis, and therefore counterpointing the obvious surface antithesis of sound, while supporting the less obvious one of sense. Finally, an antithesis of *implication*, based on the fact that while the noun uses are fairly neutral in tone the adjectival ones, 'too weak' and 'too strong', are both pejorative, and thus alike in tone, though differing in sound and sense *(ef/ef)*.

Here, then, we have a verbal interplay that calls forth—at least if fully responded to, in terms of tone and movement as well as sense— sufficient disinterested appreciation to make a suspect statement esthetically pleasing.

Structural analysis, of course, could demonstrate similar effects on a larger scale in certain works (v. the quotations from Calderwood and Toliver in Chapter 1, for instance). Syntax could be seen as a part in relationship to the complex whole of a work, to give an esthesis of composition, or in relation to some aspect of general meaning (tone, theme, story) to give an esthetic of complementarity. However, the study of syntax and large-scale structure is of peripheral interest in formal analysis, and it might prove more central to turn briefly to other aspects of structure. What is probably overlooked is the fact that short works, even lyric poems, may be of structural interest.

Clearly ballads and other narrative poems share the structural characteristics of plot, story, and even point-of-view, that are to be found in prose narratives, and quite a lot has been written on this. There are other aspects of structure, however; some other sort of order may act as an equivalent of, say, plot—as in this tiny short story by Kafka:

A LITTLE FABLE

'Alas,' said the mouse, 'the world is growing smaller every day. At the beginning it was so big that I was afraid, I kept running and running, and I was glad when at last I saw walls far away to the right and left, but these long walls have narrowed so quickly that I am in the last chamber already, and there in the corner stands the trap that I must run into.' 'You only need to change your direction,' said the cat, and ate it up.

This has a formal structure that could have been different. The order in which the items are given could have been altered without any alteration of the facts; but no other order would have been as effective in vitalizing the content as this one. And that very aptness gives rise to a structural esthetic pleasure, of complementarity. A tonal, or emotional trap is set at the beginning by the use of similar signals, 'alas' and 'afraid' for what seem to be opposite cases. This prepares us emotionally for the denouement, and the conveyor-belt of the long middle sentence, running from agoraphobia to claustrophobia without the slightest meander turns the feeling into ordered action (vast emptiness—distant walls—narrowed walls—last chamber—corner—trap).

Similarly one may get in certain poems that have no kinship at all with narrative something like painterly composition. In imaginary space, that is to say, objects can be arranged randomly or significantly, so as to lead the inner eye, as it were, with the sense or the mood and thus clarify and support it, or haphazardly so as to confuse it. In Hopkins's 'Hurrahing in Harvest', for example, '. . . the stooks arise' in the first line; in the second, '. . . what wind-walks!'; and on to '. . . silk-sack clouds' in the third. And thus naturally to the result: '. . . I lift up heart, eyes, Down all that glory in the heavens to glean our Saviour.' Then (round the dome of heaven) to the distant 'azurous hung hills' and back to 'the beholder' whose 'heart rears wings bold and bolder' and (as his eyes have already done) '. . . half hurls earth for him off under his feet'. An esthetic sense of composition here; and a touch of the esthetic of complementarity may be felt too. Compare, though, this poem by George Woodcock (*Modern Welsh Poetry*, London 1944):

SOUTHERNDOWN BEACH

Fluid ebon masses, flow
sculptured waves to broken snow
and, speedwell-eyed, delphinium blue,
sky to sea cleaves. Gleaming, new,
of cosmic conjugation born
clouds from the faint horizon spawn,
rise on the landward wing, impart
misgivings to the tripper's heart
and, hundred-browed, attack the sun.
Dancer's feet of ripples spin
up the firm sand. The swimmers glide
beachward on the swelling tide.

This is not an especially bad poem, but if it has a general point to make, the ordering of its items does nothing to bring it out, and if it is merely scenic description it does nothing to aid visual composition. We look out to sea, into the breaking waves on the shore, leap out to the meeting of sea and sky, up to clouds—but then suddenly find we should have been looking sideways (presumably, since the clouds 'rise on the landward wing'), then up to the sun, and in the next line down and back to the sand, and finally a little out to sea where the swimmers 'glide beachward'. In short the composition is haphazard, and the poem must rely for any effect it may have entirely on little textural touches.

Formal analysis applies more obviously—though not so obviously as to augustan works—to certain novels, especially those with some element of the experimental in them. Joyce and Golding, for instance provide very different examples. Joyce's *Portrait of the Artist* is characterized by organic form, both textural and structural, since the style matures with the growth of the central character and the general structure tallies with the biographical sequences of the content and also with the central artistic doctrine enunciated. *Ulysses* is characterized by imposed form, both structural and textural. The general organization is an ironic replica of Homer's, and each section has its own special style—to enforce what appears to be the theme of the work: the relativity of experience. In both books, the changing style and remarkable structure claim appreciative attention, though *this* esthetic awareness is nicely balanced by awareness of their suitability to the subject; so that the esthetic of composition becomes assimilated to that of complementarity.

In Golding's brilliant *Lord of the Flies* (and even more in his later novel *Pincher Martin*) this is not so clearly the case, for there is a clash between intrinsic symbolism—that which is related organically to the content—and extrinsic symbolism—that which is arbitrarily imposed upon it. The texture is magnificently experiential: one lives the novel. Although most of the details are in fact symbolic one experiences them more as image than idea; yet slowly these perfectly lifelike boys and their physically rendered island grow to remind us of human types and the human condition in general: there is a broad intrinsic symbolism. However, there is also a detailed extrinsic one. For example, the realistic dead airman, according to Golding, symbolizes—of all things—History! Luckily, the writing is so naturalistic that one need not (could not) pick up this symbolism, of which any possible esthetic effect from its ingenuity would be far out weighed by its incongruity with the texture. That is why the end of *Pincher Martin* seems so gimmicky and journalistic. The texture has been far too physical to be appropriate for a structure suddenly revealed to be supposedly metaphysical. In *Lord of the Flies*, on the other hand, the increasing pace from beginning to end (which finely matches the theme of an accelerating Fall) and the inevitable movement from a miniature paradise to a miniature inferno are signs of a large-scale structure that unites the naturalistic and the symbolic—and is perhaps just sufficiently evident as form to give a slight esthetic distance to what could easily have been, despite the symbolism, a morbid eruption.

Both Joyce and Golding obviously call for a great deal more in the way of formal criticism. All we have been able to do here is to raise the question whether such an approach might provide a sound introduction, or a useful supplement, to a full critique.

15

Theory and Practice: Wilbur's *Beasts* and *In the Elegy Season*

BEASTS

Beasts in their major freedom
Slumber in peace tonight. The gull on his ledge
Dreams in the guts of himself the moon-plucked waves below,
    And the sunfish leans on a stone, slept
    By the lyric water,

    In which the spotless feet
Of deer make dulcet splashes, and to which
The ripped mouse, safe in the owl's talon, cries
    Concordance. Here there is no such harm
    And no such darkness

    As the selfsame moon observes
Where, warped in window-glass, it sponsors now
The werewolf's painful change. Turning his head away
    On the sweaty bolster, he tries to remember
    The mood of manhood,

    But lies at last, as always,
Letting it happen, the fierce fur soft to his face,
Hearing with sharper ears the wind's exciting minors,
    The leaves' panic, and the degradation
    Of the heavy streams.

    Meantime, at high windows
Far from thicket and pad-fall, suitors of excellence
Sigh and turn from their work to construe again the painful
    Beauty of heaven, the lucid moon
    And the risen hunter,

Making such dreams for men
As told will break their hearts as always, bringing
Monsters into the city, crows on the public statues,
Navies fed to the fish in the dark
Unbridled waters.

IN THE ELEGY SEASON

Haze, char, and the weather of All Souls':
A giant absence mopes upon the trees:
Leaves cast in casual potpourris
Whisper their scents from pits and cellar-holes.

Or brewed in gulleys, steeped in wells, they spend
In chilly steam their last aromas, yield
From shallow hells a revenance of field
And orchard air. And now the envious mind

Which could not hold the summer in my head
While bounded by that blazing circumstance
Parades these barrens in a golden trance,
Remembering the wealthy season dead,

And by an autumn inspiration makes
A summer all its own. Green boughs arise
Through all the boundless backward of the eyes,
And the soul bathes in warm conceptual lakes.

Less proud than this, my body leans an ear
Past cold and colder weather after wings'
Soft commotion, the sudden race of springs,
The goddess' tread heard on the dayward stair,

Longs for the brush of the freighted air, for smells
Of grass and cordial lilac, for the sight
Of green leaves building into the light
And azure water hoisting out of wells.

I FOREWORD

Beneath the procedural problems that beset literary critics, as we
have seen, lie two major problems of theory. The first is to do with
the literature's mode of existence, the second with the critic's mode
of apprehension.

Works of literature—unlike painting, sculpture, and even music—have no significant material existence at all: their significance is 'all in the mind'. True apprehension of that significance, in the work as a whole, clearly depends on a correct interpretation of its parts—but since these are non-material parts their nature is unfixed, and it is often impossible to decide what sort of parts they are without knowing what sort of wholes they are parts *of*.

So literary criticism is a vain attempt to do the impossible with the non-existent? Not quite; but it does have to steer a difficult way between the Charybdis of arrogant opinionation and the Scylla of slavish submission to authority. Critical methods, then, should allow for these problems of theory and the practical dangers associated with them.

If a work's significance is all in the mind, how are we to see that what does take place in the mind when it is read is what should, is a product neither of arrogance nor slavishness but of a controlled responsiveness? Well, firstly by cultivating knowledge of our own times, prejudices and predispositions of temperament, and knowledge of other people and other periods; secondly, by 'practical criticism': the criticism of works whose authorship is unrevealed, or works like those of Wilbur as yet unburdened by an established reputation—criticism, that is to say, which is forced to be independent. It could still, of course, turn out to be unsupported opinionation rather than *justifiable* assessment. To start with technical interpretation or description, rather than evaluation, is the best way of avoiding that. Self-knowledge, situation-knowledge, and (the thing that is relevant here) a technical method deal with the first problem, then. But what of the problem of parts and whole?

In the case of an obviously careful writer like Wilbur, clearly in control of his material, 'coherence' carries most weight as evidence of valid interpretation. In such cases the interpretation that has to strain probability in order to account for various features of the poem is unlikely to be right. However, it is not an infallible test even for carefully written short poems. Take parody, for instance. A good parody of, say, a poem of Wordsworth would be as coherent as the original. Proper appreciation, though, would depend on the reader's knowing what *sort* of coherent whole this was (namely, parodic). Only with that knowledge could the reader correctly interpret the quality of various parts as being praiseworthy comic caricature rather than the deplorable coarse exaggeration they appeared to be.

And it might well be that he could not reasonably be expected to recognize the whole as parody—let alone appreciate its merits as such—without external knowledge (namely, of the Wordsworth poem). Sometimes, too, it could happen that *only* peripheral, 'scholarly' knowledge would lead to that interdependent apprehension of parts-and-whole required for valid assessment. Take this poem:

> She dwelt among the untrodden ways
> Beside the springs of Dove,
> A maid whom there were none to praise
> And very few to love:
>
> A violet by a mossy stone
> Half hidden from the eye,
> Fair as a star, when only one
> Is shining in the sky.
>
> She lived unknown, and few could know
> When Lucy ceased to be;
> But she is in her grave, and oh
> The difference to me!

Now this can be read in two different ways, so as to give two coherent but contradictory significances. Is it as a whole mocking or elegiac? On the first assumption we read the parts ironically—especially the last line and a half of each stanza (or, to put it the other way round, if we take these parts to be ironical the whole becomes a lampoon on Lucy). On the second assumption we read them movingly. Nothing in the language compels us to one reading rather than the other. What items of circumstantial evidence there are more or less cancel out. Yet, of course, everyone knows that the right reading—that which would have been adopted by an intelligent contemporary reader of Wordsworth—is the serious one. But how do we 'know'? Surely only by knowing, perhaps subconsciously, that Wordsworth didn't have a macabre sense of humour, or indeed any sense of humour; by knowing the characteristic tone of the other Lucy poems; by knowing that the ironic was never a Wordsworthian mood. Of course he *might* here have written uncharacteristically. But this would not be a poem suitable for the pedagogical exercise of practical criticism.

For poems that demand little or no external knowledge, and are presented in a practical-criticism situation where it is not available (to give a lead, or to mislead), there seems to be only the way previously mentioned to resolve the chameleon-like relationship of parts and whole. It is the hard way: of working bit by bit in a constant alternation of experiment and hypothesis, and with frequent triangulation, say, by form, tone or theme—for literary wholes are complex—as a safeguard against going astray and then insensibly straining the evidence instead of altering the hypothesis. The evidence of each line as it comes tends to validate or invalidate that tentative hypothesis about the sort of whole which the title and previous lines have given rise to (especially in so far as the evidence from one aspect, say the thematic, is supported or not by evidence from the tonal or formal aspects). This procedure may and ought to be adopted, of course, even if we are not doing practical criticism, as a sort of general triangulation to check whatever appraisal seems to be indicated by the external information.

That all this leads only to the most valid *interpretation* that the nature of literature permits does not matter as much as it might seem to. If we have revealed what seems to be genuinely the public poem, not a private misreading, and have brought to light features that might have escaped notice, we have done all that is *literally* required: made a small new world available.

All critical evidence is necessarily circumstantial evidence. Whether we accumulate it in the way described, in order to escape the basic dilemmas, or more esthetically in order to define our perception of certain qualities, the two procedural problems that face us are these: where to start and when to stop. Here only good sense and sensibility can help. As everything is ultimately fused with everything else in a poem a start at any point will lead eventually to every other; it's simply that some starting places will be more convenient than others. As for when to stop—well, before dissection becomes murder; but there are no rules for deciding when that is. Happily, even poems that seem to have been murdered often come to life again, if they are laid aside till the overzealous analysis has settled at the bottom of the mind, and are then re-read for pleasure—but, presumably, with heightened awareness.

II BEASTS

Briefly, then, what sort of whole is this poem—mimetic? Does it try to make an imaginative solid world, that of beasts? The first stanza might tempt us to think so, but hardly the last. Anyway, what about the 'major' freedom of the first line? Major as compared with what? And what about the general structure? The first two stanzas are the only ones that deal exclusively with beasts; the next two are about a man-beast; the last two largely about man. Is it then a didactic poem? Does it purport to *say* something rather than *be* something? Has it a theme? To put it bluntly, does such a title for a poem clearly not only about beasts mean we are being told that men are beasts, and bad beasts at that? Certainly the movement is downward, from 'lyric' to 'unbridled' water, peaceful to night-marish dreams, and the word 'degradation' for the descending streams seems too striking not to be significant. Suppose we were to say: this is indeed a didactic poem, whose moral theme is that the nature of beasts is harmonious while man's is discordant. This certainly gets support from 'moon-plucked', 'lyric', 'dulcet', and 'concordance' in the first section, and 'painful' in both the other sections; moreover the musical implications of 'major' and 'minors' hint a change of key, a darkening of tone. But what of the 'ripped' mouse? And why does the moon feature, differently, in each section? Simply as a unifying agent? Or is it a symbolic property, acting as a kind of visual pun on *lunar* and *lunatic*? Surely, this is likely, for if this poem is didactic it is not so in either a narrative or an argumentative way; it tries to combine the intellectual benefits of didacticism with the concrete benefits of mimesis—and only sym-bolism combines the concrete and the abstract. Let us then re-phrase the theme as follows: *The harmonious, if ruthless, nature of beasts contrasts favourably with the doubly discordant nature of man, warped by physical and spiritual lunacy.*

The moon, of course, is *also* a unifying agent, helping to ensure that the three thematic (and tonal) sections are parts of a well-integrated whole, contributing to that sense of variety-in-unity which is so important a part of aesthetic effect. Another such factor is that of sleep. This, too, is a repeated but varying motif. The sleep of beasts is peaceful; their 'major freedom' is freedom from pain, degradation and terror. We are told, as a thematic assertion that they 'slumber in peace'. Tonally, this statement is reinforced by the musical words mentioned and by the pun on 'spotless' (free of sin as well as clean). And formally, it is both implied and accounted for by the kind of grammar used. Wilbur should have said the gull 'Dreams . . . *of* the moon-plucked waves below' because dreams, having no physical dimension, cannot accommodate real objects. He says the sunfish '(is) slept By the lyric water'. But 'to sleep' is an intransitive verb and cannot have a passive mood, since something you only do yourself cannot be done to you. He should have written 'sleeps', at any rate if he'd wanted to be grammatical. Clearly he did not want to be, but rather wanted the odd grammatical form to impress on us the unsayable difference of the beasts—so much a part of nature that the fish is not separable from the water, the dream from the guts, nor the guts from the waves that feed them. That is why the ripped mouse paradoxically 'cries Concordance', and is 'safe' in the owl's talon in two senses: held firm, and fulfilling its destined (but happily unanticipated) rôle in the natural order.

In the second section 'degradation' is the obvious pun. A formal device—choosing to fuse two meanings rather than separate them—a tonal device (since, taken in context, together with 'heavy', it suggests the *blood*stream), and a contribution to the thematic development. In so far as it is connected with water, it is part of another motif (again a changing one, and therefore part of form). A less obvious pun is that on 'panic' (to do with the lustful earth-god, Pan). The warping window-glass suggests those round bottle-glass windows associated with legendary castles or sinister old mansions; it symbolizes man's distortion of nature, accounts for the disturbed rest, and prepares for 'degradation'. Both the paradox of '*fierce* fur *soft* to his face' and the transferred epithet (from wolf to fur) formally mimic the larger statement of change in this section as a whole. Somewhere in the background there seems to be a suppressed image of masturbation—suppressed, one might guess, because the author merely wished to refine on the complex mood that would accompany *anything* in human experience that the werewolf might symbolize.

In the last section the moon is 'lucid', seen through 'high', not warping windows; but it is associated with 'the risen hunter'; Sagittarius: like Pan half beast and half man—and an archer, so not a natural hunter like the owl. Similarly, the dreams of the last stanza are not natural like those of the beasts. They are *made* by the 'suitors of excellence'; who are not in harmony with the heavens but trying to 'construe' the 'painful' beauty of the moon and stars. Presumably these are the idealists—poets, philosophers, theologians, political theorists—who move too far to the spiritual end of the human spectrum, as the werewolf-type moves too far to the animal end, with even more 'lunatic' results. The grammatical parallel, 'making . . ., bringing . . .', suggests that the disasters mentioned are not part of the 'dreams' (prophetic threats, so to speak) but actual results of idealistic speculation—the disasters of religious or ideological or romantic-nationalist wars.

Only the stanza-form is repeated *without* thematic variation; all other unifying motifs take some colouring from the different parts. They can afford to: for the stanza-form is strongly unifying, the development is unforced, and much of the supporting detail wonderfully delicate. Note, as a concluding example, that the last word of the last stanza could perfectly well have matched the last word of the first stanza exactly. That it doesn't is not merely elegant variation. 'Waters' is more disunified than 'water' (as 'lyric' suggests a single harmony and 'unbridled' a stormy herd of white-horses). Down to the very last words then, Wilbur controls and combines sense and form; thus having the poem itself act as an example of the integration that its total significance indicates to be desirable.

III In the Elegy Season

An elegy. So perhaps we should start with the tonal aspect of this poem. But what is its tone? If the first two stanzas are 'elegy' enough, are not the next two 'Elgar'—imbued with pomp and circumstance—and the last two positively celebratory? Have we indeed jumped to a wrong conclusion in supposing it an elegy at all? That noun acts as an adjective in the title. Is this a piece of wit (in one of the older senses: intellectual play)? Is it teasing us by holding out the idea of an elegy, only to snatch it back with the suggestion that the word merely describes a kind of season? And what kind? One that is itself sad (elegiac), or one suitable for writing elegies on the past year? In fact, it turns out, Wilbur gives us the elegiac *tone* of autumn in the first section (of what turns out to be again a work in three parts of two stanzas each), goes on to an elegy for summer, with a very unelegiac tone, and then switches to a tone of celebration for what has not yet happened! Clearly the title's teasing ambiguity was not accidental. Nevertheless, we can profitably pursue the matter of tone further—nothing, however, that the tonal blocks correspond with thematic blocks introduced by logical links: 'And now', 'Less proud than this', and these in turn with formal qualities appropriate to the 'envious mind' and less proud 'body'. But in the first section the tonal aspect is dominant. In formal quality it is neither predominantly physical nor mental; nor does it so clearly make a conceptual point as the other two sections. In them the thematic, formal and tonal are equal partners.

Bearing in mind, then, a rather negative idea of the whole—not simply elegiac or celebratory, not obviously either the more mimetic or didactic—let us examine the first part. 'Haze, char, and the weather of All Souls': clearly sets up an autumnal feeling, a sense of the tonal quality of the day. But once again it is impossible to separate tone and form and referential meaning (which can come under the other umbrella-term, theme). The fact that the first two words and the last two are both stressed and long-vowelled slows down the line, so that, in combination with the implications of 'Haze' and 'char' (presumably charred wood), there is a sense of looking round, taking in the scene. 'All Souls' gives just a hint of ghostliness in the air—the hazy weather being apt enough in more than one sense. That hint, of course, is brilliantly and wittily picked up—after the phantasmal 'chilly steam' has been added to 'Haze', and 'brewed' and 'steeped', have brought in faint aromas of witch's potions—by the word 'revenance'. As striking and un-expected as 'degradation' in *Beasts*, it insists on its literal meaning (cp. *revenir*), a 'coming back', and carries along with that the idea of a revenant or apparition from the 'shallow hells'. All these words, then, add tonal touches to an impressionistic picture. However, they are not only elegiac but also, paradoxically, witty; the tonal colour of this section, ambiguous as the title, changes like shot silk according to the way you look at it. The tone, in fact, expresses the paradoxical quality of autumn, the ghostliness of presences that are made of absences—beautifully hit off in the second line's metaphor of the striking absence of leaves as a giant, invisible, forlorn bird. The same subtlety of wit is evident in the synesthesia of 'Whisper their scents' (where the sound is a sonic reference to the rustling leaves while the sense speaks of their more ghostly emanation, as scent). And, of course, 'potpourris' (mixtures of dead leaves, flower petals and herbs kept in bowls, in past times) is perfect both visually and nostalgically. Negative emotion and ghostly being, spiced by a wit aware of the dangers of delicious nostalgia, are what this section evokes. Since the other sections are less dominantly tonal it might be as well to approach them via matters of general structure.

Clearly there is a temporal movement from present (late autumn) to past (summer) to future (through winter to spring); these sections are concerned, respectively with emotional, mental and bodily reactions to the season; the narrative, moving from impersonal and intangible to personal and tangible, is enabled by the logical links mentioned to retain the immediacy that comes from using the present-tense, despite the time-shifts; and in the first section the most ethereal of the senses, smell, predominates, in the second, sight (and paradoxically, sight of much more tangible things than in the first, although it is only in memory), in the third, probably touch (the closest of the senses). But one has to say 'probably' because smell, sight and sound are also insisted on. In fact, this poem does not so much develop as *accumulate*. Its stages are less of argument than of mounting vitality. If *Beasts* was, finally, didactic in kind despite some appearance of mimesis, *In the Elegy Season* is finally mimetic in kind despite some appearance of a didactic theme (to do with the human tendency to live more vitally in memory and anticipation than in present reality). There is not only a progressive increase in tangibility, but also a progressive increase in *movement* (and a consequent sense of vitality), and then in the last stanza 'smells' in the first line, 'sight' in the second, 'building' (a muscular image) in the third recapitulate in order the predominant sense impressions of the three sections.

It is as well to recall, however, that poems may well have items of local texture that are esthetically pleasing, though they may not be *essential* to the theme. Indeed a poem without any textural superfluity, any esthetic sense of delight in language almost for its own sake might appear too starkly functional. In this poem, the clearest example is the word 'conceptual'. It is, of course, *appropriate* to the theme. But 'imaginary' would have been equally so, indeed rather more so—in fact so obviously so that one gets a sense of verbal pleasure from Wilbur's avoiding it. Similarly, the latent image of the summer as a wealthy relative, and the 'envious mind' as a young heir glorying in his inheritance rather than mourning the dead gives a witty twist to the second 'elegiac' section, and supports it formally by a parading rhythm emphasized by the 'b' alliteration, and tonally by the overtones of 'Parades' and (in this context) the absurdly romantic 'inspiration'.

In the third section we might note such points of delicate, thematically 'superfluous' detail as the metrical pause arranged so that 'the sudden race of springs' can come with a rush (and the tactful use of thawed *springs* as a sign of *spring*), or the effect of stepping in 'tread', 'heard', '-ward' as the goddess climbs the stair from darkness to light, winter to spring.

The goddess is, of course, Proserpine; and that oblique reference to the underworld recalls the 'shallow hells' and 'pits' of the first section—the places spring and summer have been sadly banished to—, just as the 'azure water hoisting' (as if by its own energy, like the plants' 'building', though it is in fact hoist*ed*) reminds us of the slightly sinister stagnant wells of the first section. So, too, the differing trees in each section help to unify a variety that is witty and sensuous, elegiac and celebratory, mocking and affirmative, progressive and accumulative.

16

Logicless Grammar in Audenland

> Beware. All those who follow me are led
> Onto that Glassy Mountain where are no
> Footholds for logic. . . .
> *(For the Time Being.* Faber 1945, p. 84)

A FAIR warning. The reader of the later Auden is to be led into dangerous territory where landmarks may be mirages, signposts meant to mislead. To act as surefooted guide in that sort of non-land is a praiseworthy technical feat, though some might have reservations about the propriety of guiding followers astray in order to reveal to them their 'condition of estrangement from the truth' (op. cit., p. 55).

Since the most interesting developments of the poetry from the first post-war volume in 1945 to the last—namely, strange landscaping and grammar—seem to have been developed in the service of this new end, it is obviously impossible to ignore Auden's preoccupations during that period. Nevertheless, a primarily technical approach is likely to do more justice than any other to the surprisingly uncelebrated late work.

Doubtless, Auden was blamable for the way his *Collected Shorter Poems* was compiled, shortly after his conversion from socialistic humanism to existentialist episcopalianism—blamable not so much for omitting or altering every poem tainted with his former views as for the silence with which it was done, indeed the pains taken to cover his tracks.[1] Doubtless, too, *something* was lacking in work of a texture so rarefied that merely capitalizing words like 'love' and 'father' could turn a Freudian-marxist poem into a Christian one. Furthermore, this sleight-of-hand was followed by several long poems with more preaching, less structure and more patchy a texture than their intermittent brilliancies of comment and style could compensate for. Add the weight of modern critical opinion

---

[1] Full details are to be found in J. Warren Beach's book, *The Making of the Auden Canon* (1958). See also 'An Altered Auden' by A. E. Rodway and F. W. Cook, *Essays in Criticism* (July 1958).

against the idea of abstract poetry, poetry of ideas, and it is easy to see why the books of the last decade or so should have received less praise than is due to their range of subject, their play of intelligence and humour, and the effortless mastery of their technical accomplishment. For their textural density is even more rarefied than that of the earlier work, despite a constant use of metaphorical landscape and the extension of image-making into the realm of grammar, which is the main concern of this study.

Auden's imagery always was more conceptual than emotive, his geography indicative rather than evocative. Yet if the opening lines of 'Memorial for a City' *(Nones)* are compared with the well-known pre-war injunction, 'Consider this and in our time', it immediately becomes apparent that a considerable change has taken place:

> Consider this and in our time
> As the hawk sees it or the helmeted airman:
> The clouds rift suddenly—look there
> At cigarette-end smouldering on a border
> At the first garden party of the year.
> Pass on, admire the view of the massif
> Through plate-glass windows of the Sport Hotel;
> Join there the insufficient units
> Dangerous, easy, in furs, in uniform
> And constellated at reserved tables
> Supplied with feelings by an efficient band. . . .
>
> The eyes of the crow and the eye of the camera open
> Onto Homer's world, not ours. First and last
> They magnify earth, the abiding
> Mother of gods and men: if they notice either
> It is only in passing: gods behave, men die.
> Both feel in their own small way, but She
> Does nothing and does not care,
> She alone is seriously there . . .
> . . . .
> The steady eyes of the crow and the camera's candid eye
> See as honestly as they know how, but they lie.

The panoramic view and the invitation to consider rather than emote remain, but not 'in our time', just in Time (the crow and camera lie because they 'Record a space where time has no place').

Moreover, in the first case, it is implied that an objective, contemporary view ought to be taken (and, later in the poem, acted upon); in the second, that it ought not, for it is too limited (and belief, not action, is required). In his pre-war, English, socialist period any metaphorical indications were derived from and related to a particular time and place (the Thirties in England) and particular groups of people (affected, whether they knew it or not, by the Slump and Hitler). In his postwar, American, religious period, it is *all* time, places and people— the human situation *sub specie aeternitatis*—that he is interested in; and his geography, once economic, political and psychological, becomes philosophical, moral and metaphysical. At any rate, such new growths appear alongside the old and gradually come to dominate them. The more relaxed movement of the second passage, too, is not uncharacteristic; nor is the change from satirical wit ('Supplied with feelings. . . .') to wit of metaphysical paradox ('See as honestly . . .').

Even Auden's use of sudden alterations of perspective is affected by the general change. In 'The Fall of Rome' (note, not the modern West, though careful anachronism suggests analogies) an accumulation of significant details is given wider significance by a concluding cut to an alien, indifferent, indestructible nature:

> Altogether elsewhere, vast
> Herds of reindeer move across
> Miles and miles of golden moss,
> Silently and very fast.

This is effective, but its effect is of a different order from that in 'Consider this'. Here, the calm use of a zoom lens, so to speak, gives an impression of disinvolvement; the fall of a civilization seems ultimately not so important. Before, the darting close-up of a cigarette-end 'smouldering' like a fuse on a border which for the airman could only be political, and the constant imperatives, 'Consider', 'Pass on', 'Join', by their urgency strongly discourage any such philosophical long view.

Often, to be sure, Auden's later non-lands are felt to be sadly menaced, but in a more general way: sometimes by nature (whose alienating otherness, however, is also seen as an assurance of man's potentiality—nature's essence being given, and therefore fixed, man's constantly to be created—), more often by surrounding badlands; arcadias threatened by utopias:

Both simultaneously recognise his Anti-type: that I am an Arcadian, that he is a Utopian . . . between my Eden and his New Jerusalem, no treaty is negotiable.

('Vespers' *Shield of Achilles*)

Sometimes the setting is historical, as in 'The Fall of Rome', sometimes contemporary, as in 'Hunting Season' *(Shield of Achilles)*, where the malicious violence in man is set beside the unintentional cruelty of nature. Or it may be geological, as 'In Praise of Limestone' *(Nones)*, where the moderate land whose rivals are 'sometimes arm in arm, but never, thank God, in step' calls in question 'All the Great Powers assume'. Or it may be metaphysical, like 'Numbers and Faces' *(Nones)* and 'Old Man's Road' *(Homage to Clio)*. Often, the setting is legendary, as in 'The Shield of Achilles', where pastoral ideal is contrasted with a paradigm of modern lands run by such military heroes:

> She looked over his shoulder
>> For vines and olive trees,
>> Marble well-governed cities
>>> And ships upon untamed seas. . . .

> Out of the air a voice without a face
>> Proved by statistics that some cause was just
> In tones as dry and level as the place:
>> No one was cheered and nothing was discussed;
>> Column by column in a cloud of dust
> They marched away enduring a belief
> Whose logic brought them, somewhere else, to grief.

What is always made clear is that the setting springs more from an idea or set of ideas than from any particular place and time, that permanent types are in question, not merely contemporary groups, and that the evils are in some sense necessary, inherent in the nature of fallen man in a fallen world, and therefore call for contemplation rather than action.

The last line quoted indicates that Auden is far from urging escape from an imperfect empirical world to a logical one. As an existentialist, he knows himself committed to existence as it is. What he *is* advocating, however, is more subjectivity in belief. These two poles, of being and believing, between which his most interesting later work subsists, are respectively illustrated by the first and last lines of what is probably his most difficult and distinctive poem to date, 'The History of Truth' *(Homage to Clio)*:

> In that ago, when being was believing
> . . . .
> A nothing no one need believe in.

The opening phrase, in which an adverb is used as a noun, points to the end of the process of landscaping ideas. In this poem, despite the emphasis on 'being', time and place as we know them have disappeared. 'They' who 'strove to build a world of lasting objects to believe in' cannot be placed as any particular people, nor their world as any particular place. The reader is led into an intangible metaphysical limbo, where abstract existents are given spectral solidity by the reification of minor parts of speech (a process which at the same time deprives him of normal landmarks).

No doubt Auden will be much censured for this development. But should he be? In a sense, all verse is a torturing of language to make it yield its secrets, and he is simply extending the process to a new area. His language has to confess what it has never known. Altering its elements, then, is reasonable enough (once empirical and logical bases for belief have been abandoned), for the language we have is largely formed by the need to deal with the world we have, in the way we usually meet it (in small parcels). Auden's shift away from that world is well illustrated in a late poem 'Objects' *(Homage to Clio)* which is concerned, metaphysically, with relating extreme generality to extreme abstraction (*all* objects to '*One* Person who is not'):

> All that which lies outside our sort of why
> Those wordless creatures who are there as well,
> Remote from mourning yet in sight and cry,
> Make time more golden than we care to tell
>
> . . . .
> . . . . though of course we care
> Each time a shadow falls across
>
> One Person who is not: somewhere a soul,
> Light in her bestial substance, well aware,
> Extols the silence of how soon a loss.

Here, dislocations of language help to give an illusion of logic—a fourth-dimensional logic, so to speak, concerned with problems of existence and essence seen from a Christian-existentialist stand-point. That the dislocations are comparatively small, beside those of 'The History of Truth' indicates that it might be profitable to follow the growth of this linguistic experiment in other poems before concluding with a detailed botanizing of its late flowering in that distinctive work.

* * * *

> To find those clearings where the shy humiliations
> Gambol on sunny afternoons, the waterholes to which
> The scarred rogue sorrow comes quietly in the small hours
> . . . .
> Pure scholarship in Where and When . . . .
> ('The Sea and the Mirror', *For the Time Being*, p. 11)

Here, the personified abstractions resemble those of the early Auden, though they are rather more bodiless—somewhat like characters in a Morality play. In the use of 'Where' and 'When', however, we have something different: still reification, but reification that is not metaphorical but grammatical—done not by imagining an abstraction as a living thing in a material setting, but by making an adverb a noun and cutting away all setting so that the word refers not to the known world but to a non-land. The two effects in this case are similar, though the techniques are opposite. Eventually, however, we shall reach a stage where the effect is

> as if
> We had left the house for five minutes to mail a letter
> And during that time the living room had changed places
> With the room behind the mirror over the fireplace
> ('For the Time Being', p. 65)

The following lines from *The Age of Anxiety* may serve to illustrate an intermediate stage:

> His sacred soul obscenely tickled
> And bellowed at by a blatant Without (p. 35)

'By a Without' could mean 'by something outside' (the adverbial use of 'without'). 'Blatantly without' could mean 'obviously in need of something' (the prepositional use). Turning 'without' into a sort of proper noun (a personified but indefinite want) tends to merge these possibilities, with the effect not so much of making the need concrete as of making it external—metaphysically separating body and soul, or sexual desire from the person feeling it, as if it were a sort of dangerous animal.

Similar uses of incorrect grammar are to be found whose nature is neutral: a shorthand-technique accepting loss of logic for the sake of saving time:

> (the sailors) are not here because
> But only just in case
> > ('Fleet Visit', *Shield of Achilles*)

> . . . the dead remains too nothing
> > ('Nones', *Shield of Achilles*)

> (Is there a once that is not already)
> > ('Not in Baedeker', *Nones*)

> . . . . faces
> That wore expressions of alas on them,
> And plains without a blade of grass on them
> > ('T the Great', *Homage to Clio*)

Such exploitations are never merely playful as many of those in E. E. Cummings are; they do a job of work—giving the poem extra density and animation rather by packing more *meaning* than (in the usual imagistic way) more *sense-data* into a given space. Nevertheless, they are not central and important. That others are—and are associated with the use of imaginary lands—is sufficiently shown by a stanza from 'The History of Science', printed as a companion-piece to 'The History of Truth' in *Homage to Clio*:

> Trusting some map in his own head,
> So never reached the goal intended
> (His map, of course, was out) but blundered
> On a wonderful instead.

At first, the habit seems merely an extension of the poet's normal tendency to reify, since Auden usually appears to be using various other parts of speech as substantives—and since substantives so often do refer to substances (are names, in fact) there's a psychological tendency to feel them always as referring somehow to entities; a feeling not attaching to adverbs, adjectives, conjunctions and prepositions. But why should a poet who obviously makes a great effort to be as clear, interesting and entertaining as his material allows surrender so much in the way of comprehensibility for so small a gain in solidity? A glance at the predicament Auden's Christian existentialism lands him in makes it plain that, in fact, quite a different gain is what he is after: a way of unifying disparates, of putting over a difficult case; and the queerness of practice is allied to a queerness of principle. He must contemplate and apprehend, and if possible present as one experience, the objectivity of the given world and the subjectivity of the chosen self in it. The task is complicated by uncertainty as to the right nature of the self, and a belief that no particular is ultimately better or worse, more or less interesting than any other: going to the bad is as much a way to God as being good. Examples related to the first part of the predicament are multifarious:

Remember as bells and cannon boom [*the common verb subjectively unites opposite signals*]
The cold deep that does not envy you. . . .
('The Sea and the Mirror', For the Time Being, p. 23)

The world is present, about,
And I know that I am, here, not alone
  But with a world and rejoice
Unvexed, for the will has still to claim
  This adjacent arm as my own,
The memory to name me. . . .
('Prime', Shield of Achilles)

No one of them was capable of lying,   [i.e. birds and vegetables]
There was not one which knew that it was dying
Or could have with a rhythm or a rhyme
Assumed responsibility for time
('Their Lonely Betters', Nones)

Thousands have lived without love, not one without water
('First things First', Homage to Clio)

So large a morning so itself to lean
Over so many and such little hills
All at rest in roundness and rigs of green
. . . .
(the song)   ends
Denying what it started up to say

('The Song', *Homage to Clio*)

To this dual concern with the thing-in-itself and the self in things
the second part of the predicament adds a viewpoint which tends
to remove the writer from much of the human material, many of the
discriminations, normally dealt with:

> Again, other selves undoubtedly exist, but though everyone's pocket is
> bulging with birth certificates, insurance policies, passports and letters
> of credit, there is no way of proving whether they are genuine or
> planted or forged
>
> ('The Sea and the Mirror', p. 54)

> . . . the lover's nip and the grip of the torturer's tongs are all—ask
> Ariel—variants of one common type . . . to be distinguished solely by
> the plus or minus sign which stands before them, signs which He is
> able at any time and in either direction to switch (ibid., p. 45)

> . . . for since of themselves all men are without merit, all are ironically
> assisted to their comic bewilderment by the Grace of God. . . . Nor is
> there any situation which is essentially more or less interesting than
> any other.
>
> ('For the Time Being', p. 110)

Now such a standpoint can, and sometimes does, unexpectedly
lead to frivolity. The result of existentialist despair is gaiety, for it
allows the poet to satirize without responsibility, since a reformed
world—were fundamental reform possible—would still be a fallen
one:

> In my Eden each observes his compulsive rituals and superstitious
> tabus but we have no morals; in his New Jerusalem the temples will be
> empty but all will practise the rational virtues.
>
> ('Vespers', *Shield of Achilles*)

So in such poems as *Pleasure Island* and *The Managers (Nones)* the
satire is mellowed with humour and enlivened with a constant

sparkle of bright ideas. In each case a playful—and original—rhyming technique, managed with consummate ease, links line to line with sophisticated casualness. One line is a foot longer than the other, and one of the rhyming words uses an extra, unstressed syllable further to avoid assertive chiming:

> What there is as a surround to our figures
>   Is very old, very big. . . .

> In the bad old days it was not so bad:
>   The top of the ladder
> Was an amusing place to sit; success
>   Meant quite a lot—leisure. . . .

Further, he can be religious—and commentatory—without preaching. Indeed, he can now take not only himself but St. Augustine lightly:

> Who is Jenny lying to
> By long-distance telephone?
> The Love that made her out of nothing
> Tells me to go home.
> But that Miss Number in the corner
> Playing hard to get. . . .
> I am sorry I'm not sorry. . . .
> Make me chaste, Lord, but not yet.
>
> ('The Love Feast', *Nones*)

In a way, too, his later beliefs lead him to be less unworldly rather than more. Useless

> To face the sky and roar
> In anger and despair
> At what is going on,
> Demanding that it name
> Whoever is to blame:
> The sky would only wait
> Till all my breath was gone
> And then reiterate
> As if I wasn't there
> That singular command
> I do not understand,
> *Bless what there is for being*
>
> ('Precious Five', *Nones*)

On the other hand, the same views can give rise to quite contrary results. For when he is concerned not with the world but with his ideas of it a different situation arises. 'Bless what there is for being'—but what *is* 'being' when people, not things, are involved? If 'compulsive rituals and superstitious tabus' are to be balanced against 'morals' and logic, the one attitude may sometimes need to be justified, the other undermined. It is at this point, committed to a version of the Two Truths theory, that Auden's logicless grammar and unempirical models come into their own. After all, one of the two truths is a good deal more obviously true, by normal standards, than the other, and exceptional weapons are needed to defend the less obvious. 'The History of Truth'—with one or two other poems in lesser degree—marks the culmination of an original, technical development devoted to revealing one's common truth as an estrangement from what Auden considers the Truth.

> In that ago, when being was believing,
> Truth was the most of many credibles,
> More first, more always, than a bat-winged lion,
> A fish-tailed dog or eagle-headed fish,
> The least like mortals, doubted by their deaths.
>
> Truth was their model as they strove to build
> A world of lasting objects to believe in,
> Without believing earthenware and legend,
> Archway and song were truthful or untruthful:
> The truth was there already to be true.
>
> This while when, practical like paper-dishes,
> Truth is convertible to kilowatts,
> Our last to do by is an anti-model,
> Some untruth anyone can give the lie to,
> A nothing no one need believe is there.

Generally speaking, we can say that the poem moves from an emphasis on being to an emphasis on non-being, from positive to negative, and each stanza repeats that movement, starting in the physical, and turning itself inside out to end in the metaphysical. The first stanza deals with the nature of 'truth' *then*, the second with its application, and the third with its nature and application *now*. The detached tone—didacticism relieved by humour and cleverness—is appropriate for the form, and both are in keeping with the apparent intention, to promote a persuasive definition. If then the texture should turn out to be strange, it must seem probable that this is not accidental, an outburst of poetic *élan*, but carefully contrived.

In the first phrase, 'ago', an adverb, is not used substantively for brevity's sake. 'In that era' or even 'once upon a time' would have done equally well. Its effect is to generate a slight feeling of queerness (this is *not* a time in history; it's a metaphysical space-time with hints of Greece, the Near East and medieval Europe). That queerness is developed by the existentialist pun on seeing and being, which leads to the near-paradox of an equation of 'being' and 'believing'— though, of course, the idea of a lived truth as opposed to an understood truth is not startling. The syntax of the second line at first leads us to take the adjective 'most' as a noun ('Truth was the tops'), especially as 'credible' is used in this way ('credibles' suggests things, existents, though all it can really mean is 'logically—not empirically—credible *stories*'). However, when we come to the last line of the stanza, we realize that we could paraphrase 'the most' as 'the most credible' (contrasted with 'the least credible'). The apparently impossible 'more first' and 'more always', make sense if we take an evolutionary view of religious truths: the fittest to survive are the truest. All religions were once 'first' and 'always'; the Christian God, having outlived the others mentioned, is therefore 'more first, more always'. The least credible are so, precisely because by dying they have shown themselves dubious. The statement, then, makes sense, but odd linguistic usages keep the reader in a world with its own laws—usages sustained to the end of the stanza. 'Doubted by their deaths' is a strange way of expressing the idea intended. Moreover the first part of the line is ambiguous. The most obvious paraphrase, 'The least credible, like mortals . . .' implies that mortals who don't doubt don't die (and this sufficiently accounts for the active construction of the last part of the line; it slips in the idea of mortals doubting, while speaking of credibles becoming dubious), but this reading really requires a comma after 'least'. The lack of a comma allows one to make out also the idea that those gods least like mortals (the animal gods) were the ones that died, whereas the one most human. . . . And this is what causes one to suggest that it is in fact the Christian God who is 'More first . . .' With all this going on, we may not have consciously noticed that the primary idea of mortals of undoubting belief attaining immortality, though good Christian doctrine, is a reversal of the notion that *being* is believing; believing, in this case, is deathless being. The secondary idea, however, of the most human religion lasting best, fits in well enough with the subjective, existentialist notion of truth; its kind of being makes it believable. This is not quite the same notion, though, as that of a lived truth which we swallowed so innocently to begin with.

The first four lines of the next stanza are in normal language and make clear enough sense—provided one doesn't think too hard. Carefully considered, the idea of 'believing in' something without believing it to be truthful (or untruthful) becomes more and more difficult (and what sort of a 'model' is that truth—or Truth?). The last line of the stanza, however, tends to prevent any such philosophical considering, for it seems to give an easy and adequate explanation. But the explanation turns out to depend on more logicless grammar, which seems natural now that we have allowed ourselves to be led into a non-land. 'The Truth' (not just 'truth') was 'there already'—that makes sense; it existed as a model, in some other realm, and the model could be imitated without the believers mistaking the imitation for the original. The capital 'T' helps us to take truth as a sort of thing, an existent. 'The truth was all ready to be true'—that too makes sense: potentiality becomes fact, a truth, when embodied in lasting objects. So 'The Truth was there already to be true' unites objective fact and subjective truth, and explains the inexplicable, by fusing two ideas in one poetic statement: (a) existing before the symbols, (b) needing them in order to exist. The fusion, however, is neither logical (a matter of good argument) nor experiential (of good imagery) but linguistic: spelling supports (a), grammar (b). Thus we start with a 'model' and end with a potentiality without noticing the gap.

The last stanza begins by contrasting 'that ago' with the equally abnormal 'This while when'. Again, it is done not for brevity's sake, but in order at one and the same time to reify (by turning a conjunction into a noun) and to abstract (by removing the reader from the normal world, of 'Today' or 'These days when'). The resulting queerness allows him to accept new ideas of truth and belief, as people abroad may do things they wouldn't at home. 'Practical like paper-dishes' brings us into the present and insinuates a sneer at practicality (paper dishes being so much cheaper and nastier than the 'earthenware' of an 'impractical' past). The next line obviously refers mainly to scientific truth, though '*convertible*' in this context inevitably carries a reminder of the religious Truth that has been made to seem *more* solid and factual ('being . . .', 'model', 'there already' as contrasted with a mere measure of energy). 'Anti-model' in the third line relies on this insinuation of the intangibility of scientific truth—really belief according to testable evidence—in order to equate it plausibly with negative scepticism. 'To do by' picks up the idea of a lived truth which the first line of the poem implied amongst other things (the phrase is used in this sense in 'One Circumlocution', *Nones*).

The paradoxes of the last two lines can now be accepted as plain facts. Scientific truth, being a matter of converting reality into abstractions ('kilowatts'), is mere negation, therefore (since Truth is 'being' and objectivity) it is by definition 'An untruth'—and anyone can give the 'lie' to it by positively living his unprovable but 'credible' belief instead of sceptically denying all that can't be measured. Since this scientific 'untruth'-truth is not a fact or model, it is 'A nothing'. And naturally you not only don't need to believe nothings are there, you *can't*, because they are not; only existents can be 'there already'.

In its perverse way, this is beautifully logical, like n-dimensional geometry, and it is very difficult to resist such manipulations of language in the weightless realm one has been translated to. If we do resist, however, it is hard not to find Auden unfair to empiricists. 'Untruth' suggests lying (and 'lie' follows), but all it really refers to is any belief based on a sceptical weighing of evidence, or any attitude opposed to that behind the acceptance of 'compulsive rituals and superstitious tabus'! Auden's Truth, coldly considered, seems to be non-material but a model, potential but actual, without public evidence but to be believed in (which is taken to be the same as committed to). And the last phrase of the poem, 'no one need believe is there' implies the virtue of *willed* belief, a Kierkegaardian leap in the dark, from trivial nothing-truth to a 'model' Truth it is important to believe in.

It is to create suitable conditions for this conversion that the poem behaves as it does. Whether its logicless grammar is considered sophistical misleading, or subtle guidance into new existential territory where subjectivity and objectivity are one, will depend on whether the creative maltreatment of the poet's material is considered to be as fair a warning of 'no footholds for logic' as the plain 'Beware' uttered fifteen years earlier.

17

Elements of a Working Procedure

In a sense, all worthwhile creative works are crimes—breaking and entering into closed minds being their chief offence. Modern criticism has aspired to be scientific, but law provides a better analogy. Like the law, literature deals with unique human cases—lying, truthful, passionate, pleading, complex—and like the law it cannot avail itself of prediction and control-experiments. Courts, like critics, cannot completely *prove* a case since much of the evidence must be circumstantial and empirical; yet no one would maintain their judgements to be therefore merely subjective and arbitrary.

If criticism, then, cannot be scientific, it can be objective.[1] However, it has not usually been so. For one thing, it has not been a detached activity, but rather an activity in a world of changing challenges and responses, some of them concerning the critic's bread and butter. Nevertheless there has been a slowly accumulating deposit of theory independent of literature's, and the critic's, struggles for survival and influence—an accumulation that has speeded up somewhat since the introduction of literature as a University study. Another factor militating against objectivity has been the lack of a neutral terminology; most terms used about literature have had persuasive overtones, and no *agreed* technical terms have been found to replace them, though plenty of jargon has come into being. Then again, critics naturally tend to feel with their contemporaries that certain *values* are *facts* and so take what later turns out to have been only for an age to be for all time. And, of course, there are the fallacies, the result of an inveterate human desire—especially in conditions of contention, about things that matter—to have one truth, one touchstone, one right answer. No wonder some modern critics have ambitioned a scientific status!

The effort has not been entirely vain. As we have seen, science has indirectly promoted metacritical studies—some of them more fascinating than the works they sprang from. It has given rise to

[1] See Chapter 1 for supporting argument and definition.

interesting results in some borderline cases; and sometimes flashes of genuine critical light have been thrown on a work itself as by-products. Moreover, science has impelled attempts in literary theory to avoid the multiplication of hypotheses and to attain what objectivity the nature of the material (so different from the material of science) will allow. The question is: can anything more be done now to mitigate the hindrances to objectivity?

That they will never be eliminated seems obvious; that they can be mitigated has been the implicit assertion of most of this book. A worthwhile terminology, for instance, must have some built-in flexibility, as works of literature are not static, but dynamic structures; and most descriptive terms, much though we may regret it, do in fact carry evaluative suggestions; these can hardly be eliminated because they are determined by the audience's reaction to context, and would therefore become attached to any jargon-word that might be substituted. Speak of a risibility-quotient if you like; it will soon come to imply degrees of praise for comedies, disparise for tragedies, just as references to amusement or humour do. In any case, scientists are commonly writing for other scientists; critics are normally writing for people less expert than themselves: that is the basic point of their activity. So, though a certain amount of jargon may be unavoidable in the interests of precision, the less there is the better. Yet, when these qualifications have been made, it remains true that an agreed terminology of the right sort would help enormously; so many wrangles are in fact purely verbal. In lieu of such an agreed terminology, it helps to define one's terms and to make appropriate disclaimers (a critic who doesn't want to be thought to approve frivolity in a farce, but only to note its presence, can and should make a disclaimer). The smaller and more homogeneous the group addressed, of course, the smaller the need for definitions, disclaimers and reminders, to avoid unwitting deception.

Assigning to a mode, type or kind, standing back to philosophize, moving in at selected places for intensive stylistic analysis, preferably of a formal kind to begin with, triangulating by form, theme and tone (or anything else that seems appropriate to the particular case), cultivating self-knowledge and situation-knowledge, operating dialectically—all these piecemeal procedures, and others, already dealt with, will clearly help the critic to become more independent of fashionable or personal biases and value-systems than he would otherwise be. Probably the greatest benefit produced by all these activities—and thinking about terms too—is simply that they discourage rashness, jumping to conclusions, stock response, and encourage a perception of 'the multivalence of magisterial views and the multifacetedness of masterpieces'. When that state of mind has been achieved it is probably both possible and desirable to proceed to the summit less mechanically, by one's own route.

Is there, though, any more general procedure that might be adopted without rendering the critical process unimaginatively mechanical, without causing the critic to lose sight of the ultimate individuality of each work, each reader? If we say that the primary business of a literary critics is to point out to some potential public what might otherwise be missed, to assess what might well be undervalued or overvalued, to explain what might well be mis-understood or misinterpreted, we start with a clear if modest function, and we allow for as much objectivity as the case permits.

The first task, then, of a general procedure would seem to be that of *analysis* (not judgement, scholarship, or the reduction of litera-ture to an offshoot of some science). However, a mere list of charac-teristics is not likely to satisfy even the blindest potential reader. Some indication of their quality will be looked for, their degree of intensity, their weight, subtlety and so on. What this amounts to, is what our discussion of the Tree of Fallacies implied: the possi-bility, often the desirability, of setting up various standards and measuring the work against them. Provided the criteria are made explicit, *any* could be invoked without disaster, though it is ob-viously preferable that they should be centrally relevant to the nature of the work, or, failing that, to the special interests of the intended audience.

Secondarily, then, the critic's job must be *evaluation*—but in purely literary terms. His method, comparison with similar works. The value-judgements inherent in this, and the previous stage, it is to be noted, are those of *significance* (choosing what to analyse, to avoid the impossible task of complete description, what criteria are relevant and what works are most suitable for comparison, to bring out their degree or quality). These are different in kind from those of *preference* (deciding what is right or wrong, better or worse, morally condemnable or approvable), though there is a shading off, owing to the preferential overtones of many descriptive terms. However, in principle the first two stages need be only minimally subjective.

Suppose, though, the work is passionately putting a case. Is the critic doing a satisfactory job by coldly restricting himself to comparatively objective *technical* analysis and evaluation? Is it just either to public or author to consider, say, Huxley's *Eyeless in Gaza* as if it were an experimental novel about potatoes instead of pacifism? Where the work insists on it, the critic evidently has, thirdly, the duty of *debate*. His method, that of *argument*, must ultimately involve value-judgements of the preferential sort—but the degree of subjectivity can be considerably reduced if he has knowledge of subjects other than imaginative literature. It is at this stage, paradoxically, that scientific (or semi-scientific) subjects may be of most use to criticism, helping to make tertiary discussion more than mere opinionation.

This distinction between primary, secondary and tertiary criticism is, of course, overschematic. Works of pure persuasion or propaganda might need only the third treatment; works of pure shared experience (some short lyric poems, perhaps) only the first and second—indeed only the first if the critic's assignment can be measured fairly enough against the common experience of his assumed audience. Most works, however, like most criminals, are thoroughly mixed up; so a good critique of them will also need to be mixed, in proportions dictated by the nature of the work. This, surely, is a requisite of any critical procedure: that it should be flexible enough to be geared to the complexities of the literary work instead of enmeshing the work in an arbitrary 'scientific' (usually metacritical) system. Not that the whole tripartite process should be solemnly plodded through in measured steps. Most of the procedure can generally take place in the head, and stay there. The ideal would be a readable essay that had *previously taken into account* the nature of literature, the analogy of much critical evidence with that of the lawcourt, and the procedural stages available.

In principle, then, the critic's most general procedure—which can encompass all the piecemeal methods—involves analysis, comparison and (as he moves away from strictly technical concerns) argument.

For *analysis* he needs a refined and trained sensibility (to see more than his readers), a combination of common sense and imagination (to convey the precise flavour of what is there, and to refrain from finding what really isn't—a common habit of symbolizing critics whether mystical or anthropological), and he needs a terminology to convey with as little ambiguity as possible what he has seen and sensed.

For *comparison* he needs a sense of *genre* (mode, type, kind), so that only comparable works are compared. This involves some judgement, for generic categories cannot be known by rule as a given pattern can (sonnet, rondeau, etc.). He also needs wide reading well remembered in order to choose the most fruitful of comparable works.

So far, there is no bar to as much objectivity as a reasonable, readable criticism can aspire to.

If even a moderate degree of objectivity is to be retained in tertiary criticism, however, a good deal of restraint is likely to be required. For *argument*, the critic needs a grasp of logic, a habit of detachment, and a knowledge of various fields from which he may derive basic judgements and supporting evidence more objective than his own opinions would provide. If he feels unable to restrict himself to evidence from such publicly available, *comparatively* objective fields as anthropology, sociology, psychology, philosophy, history, and writes from a Catholic, Communist, or Flat-Earther standpoint, the best thing he can do is to admit it, to himself and his readers. But such bias will nevertheless diminish the value of his tertiary criticism, no matter how intelligent he is, since it will bring into his argument a bigger proportion of belief to evidence than is critically necessary.

In all this, purport must be taken account of. Does the work *purport* to be moral, philosophical, propagandist (is it, looked at from the other end, in the didactic mode)? Then it demands argumentative consideration. And its failure to be what it purports is clearly *one* defect, its success in being so, *one* merit. Further we cannot decide what to compare any work with unless we know what kind it is, and therefore at least one aspect of its purport (e.g. is it satirical, and thus to be compared only with other satires?). We cannot assess the organization of a work unless we know to what end it has been organized (i.e. its purport), since the same organization might be suitable for one end and ludicrous for another.

Suppose a work turns out to have no very clear purport, no consistent image-structure, coherent internal organization or theme? These will be very grave defects, but there seems no good purpose served by applying any one test or attitude. This is not the way a mature man deals with life, and literature whether directly or obliquely reflects life (if it is worth critical attention at all). As in living, we should in criticizing take fullest advantage of our human potentiality by *keeping all aspects 'in play'*, as it were, though *in everchanging proportions* according to the demands of each, always unique, situation. One unambiguous judgement will rarely be possible, and should never be required by one's theory or procedure. Criticism is not a form of Last Judgement, but of controlled discussion. The experiments enabling us to recognize qualities pointed to (wit, passion, subtlety, crudity and so on) and to frame progressive hypotheses about purport are mostly those of a lifetime's living in a common culture. At all three levels, the resources of scholarship, historical, biographical or scientific, may provide support (largely psychological) for what seems likely on critical grounds, but at no level do we attain to absolute Truth, or even Truths. The critical evidence is mostly circumstantial, the truths of fiction always contingent.

Index

INDEX

INDEX

INDEX

INDEX

123–26, 184, 221; for comedy, Chap. 9
passim
Texture, 114–16, 119, 153, 172, 174, 184,
193
Their Lonely Betters (Auden), 213
Theory of criticism (or literature), see
under 'Criticism'
Theory of genres, 19–20
Theory of Literature (Wellek and Warren),
19, 61, 120
Time, 7, 117–18, 161, 166–70, 171, 174;
author-, 168–9; fugal, 168–9, 172, 177;
general, 167; linear, 168, 172; narrative-,
168–9; objective, 167; reading-, 168–9;
subjective, 167
To A Steamroller (Moore), 147
Tone, 98, 100
Tragedy, 130–1, 136, 152
Triangulation, 31, 35, 39, 221
Tristram Shandy (Livingstone ed.), 174
Truth, Chap 7 *passim*, 216–19, 225; and
appraisal-statements, 99, 105; and
falsehood, 97–9; and knowledge, 101;
and religion, 101, 216–19; and usefulness, 24; and value, 99, 102, 103, 105;
as accuracy, 101; as constancy, 96; as
correctness, 101; as fact, 90, 101, 216–
219; as logic,90; as loyalty, 96; as reality,
90, 96; as recognition, 99, 101; as
sanity, 96; as sincerity, 96, 97, 99, 100;
as verisimilitude, 90, 101; propositional,
90, 101; as unity, 101
T The Great (Auden), 212
Twelth Night (Shakespeare), 30, 138
Type, 114; critical example, 26–7; definition of, 24; see also under 'Criticism'
'Types' Approach to Literature, The
(Ehrenpreis), 18

Ulysses (Joyce), 70, 138, 150, 156, 159,
165, 179, 193
Unfortunates, The (Johnson), 176
Unities, The, 68
Unity, 101, 172, 186
U.S.A. (Dos Passos), 176
Uses of Literacy, The (Hoggart), 81, 88

Validity, 16, 32, 35, 47
Validity in Interpretation (Hirsch), 4, 8, 9,
87, 91, 92
Value, and truth, 47, 99, 101, 102, 103,
105; literary, 12, 66, 83, 184, 222
Variety, 27, 39, 114
Vaughan, H , 104–6
Vespers (Auden), 209, 214
Vocabulary of Politics (Weldon), 99

Waiting for Godot (Beckett), Chap. 10
passim
War Cry, The, 65
Waugh, A., 73
Weldon, T. O., 105
Wellek, R., 58, 59, 70, 71, 78, 83
Wheel of Fire, The (Knight), 80
Whitman, W., 67
Wilbur, R., 195–6
Wilde, O., 158
Williams, R., 81
Wit, 133, 145–50
Wit and its Relation to the Unconscious
(Freud), 145
Wodehouse, P. G., 147
Women in Love (Lawrence), 29
Woodcock, G., 192
Woolf, V., 178
Wordsworth, W., 46, 52, 67, 68, 198
World, The (Vaughan), 104–6